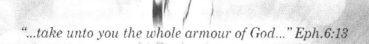

"...take unto you the whole armour of God..." Eph.6:13

POWER
INFUSION

*Spiritual Warfare that Changes Everything and
the Joys in Battle through the God of Victory*

SANDA ALLYSON

Power Infusion

Spiritual Warfare That Changes Everything and
the Joys in Battle through the God of Victory

Published by Myrtle Ministries 2019

Power Infusion – Spiritual Warfare That Changes Everything and the Joys in Battle through the God of Victory

© 2019 by Sanda Allyson
All rights reserved
Cover design by Jeffrey W. Mardis
Interior design by King's Custom Covers: kingscustomcovers.com
Visit the author's website: myrtleministries.com
MM Myrtle Ministries

Library of Congress Cataloging in Publication Data
Allyson, Sanda
Power Infusion by Sanda Allyson
1. RELIGION / Christian Living / Spiritual Warfare | 2. RELIGION / Christian Living / Spiritual Growth |
3. RELIGION / Christian Living / Personal Growth
Library of Congress Control Number: 2019912019
ISBN 978-1-64438-133-5

Printed on acid-free paper.

All scripture quotations, unless otherwise indicated, are taken from the *New American Standard Bible – Reference Edition*. NASB. Copyright © 1960, 1962, 1963, 1968, 1971, 1972, 1973 by The Lockman Foundation.

While the author has made every effort to provide accurate Internet addresses at the time of publication, neither the publisher nor the author assumes any responsibility for errors or for changes that occur after publication.

First edition

Printed in the United States of America.

To my goel, my kinsman redeemer, Yeshua Jesus, Who loved me with an everlasting love and drew me with lovingkindness. He has answered my prayer, taking the rubble of my life and making something beautiful, taking the devastating pain and giving it meaning by calling me to minister to others...
in a way I could never have imagined.

Praise For Myrtle Ministries

Here are thank you notes from real clients who have been on the *Power Infusion* journey:

> "I've been to counseling all my life and have never had as much breakthrough, spiritual discipleship, or inner healing EVER. The more I learn and grow the deeper my relationship with God gets, and I praise Him for this ministry!"
>
> -Female, 30s, August, 2019

> "This is an amazing ministry!"
>
> -Female, 60s, April, 2019

> "Myrtle Ministries has made a major difference for my family and me. We now feel equipped to do the work that God has called us to do."
>
> -Male, 30s, March, 2019

> "It's not just the prayer that has been so valuable. Your counsel and insight has been right on and life changing."
>
> -Male, 50s, May, 2019

> "I'm very familiar with spiritual warfare but this is the most balanced approach I've ever seen."
>
> -Male, 30s, March, 2019

> "You teach me whole pieces of information, not bits. This deliverance process has made my prayers more effective."
>
> -Female, 60s, February, 2019

"When I saw the other counselor last week she asked if I wanted to keep seeing her; I said no. I've made more progress with Myrtle Ministries in four visits than I made with her in three months."

-Female, 60s, October, 2018

"This ministry has dramatically touched our lives. It has opened our eyes to the spiritual realm and the demonic forces that have twisted, deceived and robbed us from every spiritual blessing in Christ. It has not only opened our eyes, it has changed our hearts. It has opened new doors for ministry and given us more power in prayer."

-Couple, 50s, 2019

"The inner healing process not only opened my eyes TO the battle but how to fight IN the battle. I learned that there was territory that had been stolen and must be reclaimed. I never knew what it felt like to have a quiet mind. For as long as I could remember, my mind had always been so noisy, filled with thoughts I knew were not my own, and racing many different directions often times even contradicting itself. I could now actually think for myself, hear God much more clearly, and experience true Shalom!"

-Male, 20s, 2016

Contents

For this reason also, since the day we heard of it, we have not ceased to pray for you and to ask that you may be filled with the knowledge of His will in all spiritual wisdom and understanding, so that you will walk in a manner worthy of the Lord, to please Him in all respects, bearing fruit in every good work and increasing in the knowledge of God; strengthened with all power, according to His glorious might, for the attaining of all steadfastness and patience; joyously giving thanks to the Father, who has qualified us to share in the inheritance of the saints in Light.

Colossians 1:9-12

"God never works in ones."
Sanda Allyson

Preface

For the weapons of our warfare are not of the flesh,
but divinely powerful for the destruction of fortresses.
2 Corinthians 10:4

There are mainly three types of people who are reading this right now: those who have been suffering supernatural attack or demonic bondage, those who are curious about supernatural power, or those in ministry.

A word to those experiencing attack by supernatural forces

If you are already suffocating with demonic bondage, you just want to be free. Maybe nothing you've tried has worked. Your church probably has nothing that would help, or you can't even speak of such things to your pastor and church friends without being ostracized.

You may be exhausted: from searching for years for the answers; by the questions that constantly run through your mind; by the heavy burden of silent uncertainty about God, His Word, and your place in this life; by the secrets you keep locked away from your closest friends and pastor; by the often meaningless, misused, or at times illogical "Christian" platitudes that are so often regurgitated in your direction.

These are things that erode the very foundations of faith. After all, either God is real or He is not. And, if He is real, you wonder, why haven't you been able to break the demonic bondage and recurring attacks?

A word to those curious about supernatural power

Maybe you're intrigued by ghost-hunting television programs, books about the paranormal, movies about vampires, and spell-casting that actually works. You wonder if supernatural power is real. You may know someone who is into witchcraft and you are thinking about attending a coven meeting with them but you still have some mixed feelings about it.

You ponder, if the power they use is real, what does that mean in spiritual reality? If it is real and you can access it any time you want, why shouldn't you learn more about it? Doesn't that prove that Christianity is just too narrow? Doesn't it support the idea that all paths lead to God; you just have to pick one?

A word to those in ministry

Do you wonder if there is more? Is this Christian life really just about ticking the box of attendance, getting together in a mid-week bible study or fellowship group, and saying a sixty-second prayer at the end of Sunday service? Do you long to see evidence of God's power, the fingerprints of a God at work on, in, and through His people, and wonder why it's not happening through you?

Your spiritual life with God may be dry, rote, stuck on a plateau, centered on trying to be a better person and doing the right things, laying up your treasures in heaven.

Yet, you have questions that run through your mind, if you let them, about the Acts church, seeing people healed and delivered, reading about the relationship God had with Paul, Abraham, and with John. You just have a feeling that something is missing, that there's more.

Well, signs and wonders are not just things of the past, they are part of our present and foretold of our future. The workers of dark magic prove that; supernatural power does indeed exist. That's just one of the reasons why so many people are interested in the occult right now.

God is not afraid of your questions. He has the answers you need.

Here is a truth you may not have heard. Ready?

You were created to have a supernatural relationship. But you were made to have that supernatural relationship with the Living God, the Creator of the universe, not with the Lord of Darkness.

Here is a major key:

There are only two sources of supernatural power, God Himself or the Lord of Darkness.

Without the well that exists in your heart being filled by the Holy Spirit's power the way it was meant to be, you can be drawn to 'another' supernatural power, become intrigued by it, or fantasize about having power and casting spells. In itself, this is a vulnerability to attack from the dark side. Remember these two words, they will come up over and over again: intent and longing.

I do what I do to show others that God is real, that He is alive, that His power is not only very real, but that it dwarfs all other powers just like the Bible says it does. He is truly the God of all gods. He is the Alpha and the Omega, the Aleph and the Tav, the beginning and the end, the first and the last, and the Hebrew concept of this statement is that there is no one else even in the line!

If you want to get answers to the questions you have about supernatural power, the demonic bondage you've suffered, or whether there is deeper water to be found in your relationship with God, this book is for you.

It is not just a book to read, it is a journey you embark upon to learn, to do, to experience, to leave the former behind and find what your soul longs for. Toward that end, I included a detailed table of contents so that you can easily find a section or reference when needed.

As I write this book, I pray for every person reading this, that your relationship with God will be transformed.

He is truly the Lover of our souls.

He is your goel, your Kinsman Redeemer.

He can be the love of your life if you will let Him.

He's waiting for you.

There are quite a few books on spiritual warfare. Why did I write another one, you ask? Because spiritual warfare is not just about demons and how to break bondage. Because, ultimately, spiritual warfare is about relationship; your relationship with God.

There is more; so much more.

Introduction: Critical Foundations

Infuse – to fill or cause to be filled.

I smiled as I took my position at the front of the platform and greeted the spiritual warfare conference attendees who, with only a few exceptions, wore very serious expressions. Some seemed somewhat nervous or uncomfortable, as is often the case with the subject matter.

After the pleasantries, I got started.

"I love teaching spiritual warfare," I beamed.

A quizzical look washed across their faces as I spoke.

"People often ask me why. I love it because it's a front row seat to watching God break bondage and deliver people. And God wins every time!"

Does that surprise you, as it did many of the conference attendees?

Is that a foreign concept to you, that God supernaturally breaks bondage for people? And, that this kind of work fills you with joy?

Have you assumed that spiritual warfare is dark because, you think to yourself, it's all about darkness?

Since you're reading this book, you have probably had experience with some things that have been difficult to talk about, that may have frightened you, that others have recognized in you, or that you have not been able to overcome no matter how hard you try.

Many people who need help have searched for years to find it and have experienced things that cause feelings of doubt and defeat.

This is especially true if you have been taught the idea that those saved by the blood of Yeshua cannot have oppression or any level of demonization.

> **A Side Note:** Yeshua is Jesus' Hebrew name, the name chosen by God for His Son. I choose to honor that. That is the name I use in my life and in my writing. However, that is not meant in any way to imply there is something wrong if you use the name Jesus. I will speak more about this later.

For those believers experiencing oppression or demonization, this contradiction leads to only two options: either, 1) "The Word of God is unreliable because I seem to be the exception to the rules in the Word of God as taught to me by my pastor." or 2) "God is not Who I believe Him to be."

In the first case that would mean, at minimum, if there are exceptions to the Word of God, the Bible can't be reliable, true, and inerrant.

In the second case, that would make scripture at best unreliable and at worst utter nonsense because God's very description of Himself is either partly or completely unreliable.

Obviously, these are the types of unanswered questions and doubts that erode the very foundations of faith and trust, in both the Word of God and in the person of God Himself.

I have experienced that and learned first-hand that what I had been taught as a child, that a Christian cannot experience oppression or demonization, was not correct. I have also experienced deliverance from bondage and understand not only the process but also the experience of feeling freedom for the first time!

You cannot walk in the power of the Holy Spirit with the thought and feeling swirling around deep inside your heart and mind that there are exceptions to God's Word, or that He is someone other than Who His Word tells us He is.

Teaching on spiritual warfare has been completely sanitized from most pulpits in the United States. In most cases it is mentioned only in passing, ignored, or completely suppressed altogether.

In "The Great Gambler", nineteenth century French poet, Charles Baudelaire, said, "The loveliest trick of the Devil is to persuade you that he does not exist." I absolutely agree on the importance of this both absurd and pivotal accomplishment. But there is more to this dastardly, in my opinion, second greatest achievement.

I believe the devil's third greatest achievement was when he convinced pastors to stop teaching spiritual warfare, the very instructions and tools to defeat his efforts and plans!

> *In order to achieve both of those victories, however, his first and greatest achievement was to lure Christianity away from the Hebrew roots of our faith, leading many to loudly delete the Old Testament and any connections to the New.*

The ravaging effects of this cannot be overstated. This deletes the very bedrock on which our faith and walking out the faith are built, the repeated patterns that God uses as object lessons to tell His story and to explain what we are to do and how, and all of the repeating patterns that foretell what is coming, leading up to and including Christ's return!

And, in addition, it is in direct opposition to commands within the biblical texts, from God's own mouth, do not change a jot or a tittle. He meant it! There is a principle here.

Let's look at what Yeshua said in Matthew 5:17-18.

> *Do not think that I came to abolish the Law or the Prophets; I did not come to abolish but to fulfill. For truly I say to you, until heaven and earth pass away, not the smallest letter or stroke shall pass from the Law until all is accomplished.*

And earlier in Deuteronomy 4:2:

> *You shall not add to the word which I am commanding*
> *you, nor take away from it.*

In addition see Psalm 119:160, Proverbs 30:5-6, Revelation 22:18-19.

In Hebrew, this concept of jot and tittle refers to a particle, the very smallest thing. I think changing and removing entire books and instructions from our teaching is a much larger issue than the very smallest thing.

This should be a wake-up call to anyone reading this. Humans are taking it upon themselves to remove parts of scripture, and to preach and teach to scores of others around the globe that these parts are to be removed, and in some cases, they claim you are out of line with scripture if you maintain their importance!

That caution made by Yeshua Jesus was ignored and we are reaping the results. Once those foundations were removed, the enemy forces began the next phase of their operation as the dark commanders shouted the instruction, "Twist away!"

These are tactics of the dark side to pull us away from Jesus and the power we are to have as we walk with Him. And, they have been utterly devastating to Christendom.

But there is hope! You can repair this breach and finally have the freedom and victory of Yeshua flowing in your life the way it was meant to be!

As believers in Yeshua, we do not have to stay under bondage to the forces of darkness! We are actually commanded to "pull down strongholds" (2 Corinthians 10:4) and to "walk in the light, as He Himself is in the Light" (1 John 1:7).

Let's look at some scripture.

> *For God has not given us a spirit of fear, but of power, love*
> *and sound mind.*
> *II Timothy 1:7, KJV*

*And from the days of John the Baptist until now the kingdom
of heaven suffers violence, and the violent take it by force.*
Matthew 11:12, AKJV

*I am the Light of the world; he who follows Me will not
walk in the darkness, but will have the Light of Life.*
John 8:12

*The thief comes only to steal, kill and destroy; I came
that they may have life, and have it abundantly.*
John 10:10

*For the weapons of our warfare are not carnal [of the
flesh], but mighty through God to the pulling down of
strong holds.*
II Corinthians 10:4, KJV

*For you were formerly darkness, but now you are Light
in the Lord; walk as children of Light.*
Ephesians 5:8

The joy of the Lord is your strength.
Nehemiah 8:10

*Finally, be strong in the Lord and in the strength of his
might. Put on the whole armor of God, that you may be
able to stand against the schemes of the devil. For we do
not wrestle against flesh and blood, but against the rulers,
against the authorities, against the cosmic powers over
this present darkness, against the spiritual forces of evil in
the heavenly places. Therefore take up the whole armor
of God, that you may be able to withstand in the evil
day, and having done all, to stand firm. Stand therefore,
having fastened on the belt of truth, and having put on the
breastplate of righteousness, and, as shoes for your feet,
having put on the readiness given by the gospel of peace. In
all circumstances take up the shield of faith, with which you
can extinguish all the flaming darts of the evil one; and take
the helmet of salvation, and the sword of the Spirit, which
is the word of God, praying at all times in the Spirit, with
all prayer and supplication. To that end, keep alert with all
perseverance, making supplication for all the saints.*
Ephesians 6:10-18, ESV

Scripture has a lot to say about the supernatural. And there is good news found within these ancient and miraculous texts that comprise the Bible: God did not leave us defenseless! Our Lord loves us so much He gave us weapons of protection, defense, and offense, instructions for them, and the intel regarding the battle plans of the enemy forces, all so we will become adept warriors for the Kingdom!

Is every adversity the result of demonic attack? No.

Is every illness or disease caused by demonic attack? No.

But in both cases, we know that a lot of it is.

We must learn to use the tools our loving Father gave us and to become skillful with them. Then we must take our position on the field and get in the game that is already underway.

In order to effectively do this, we need to have a proper view of scripture. What I mean by that is that we must take the whole Word of God, not just the New Testament or just the four gospels, but the whole Word of God.

The Word of God is life!

The laws of God are not burdensome but are life to the wise.

The wise in heart will receive commandments.
Proverbs 10:8, KJV

For this is the love of God, that we keep His
commandments; and His commandments are
not burdensome.
1 John 5:3

Know therefore that the LORD your God, He is God,
the faithful God, who keeps His covenant and His loving
kindness to a thousandth generation with those who
love Him and keep His commandments.
Deuteronomy 7:9

15 If you love Me, you will keep My commandments. 21
He who has My commandments and keeps them is the

*one who loves Me; and he who loves Me will be loved by
My Father, and I will love him and will disclose Myself to
him. 23 If anyone loves Me, he will keep My word; and My
Father will love him, and We will come to him and make
Our abode with him. 24 He who does not love Me does not
keep My words; and the word which you hear is not Mine,
but the Father's who sent Me.*
John 14:15, 21, 23, 24

*The one who despises the word will be in debt to it, but the
one who fears the commandment will be rewarded.*
Proverbs 13:13

Walking out the instructions given to us in the Bible is a really big deal to God. Yeshua Jesus IS the Word. We can't love Him and not keep His Word; you cannot separate them.

According to the Bible, how many Gods are there in Christianity? One. Who wrote the Old Testament? God. Who is God? Yeshua is God, He is one with the Father. The whole Word was written by Him because there is only one God of the Bible! He was there at the beginning and all things were made by Him and through Him.

There were supernatural things that I observed in my life starting at a very young age. This book is born from my own journey of discovery and deliverance, and the revelations I received along the way, which eventually led to the establishment of Myrtle Ministries.

The ministry God led me to develop is dedicated to providing assistance to mature believers struggling with bondage and to equip the remnant in these last days.

But this journey of freedom is foundational for all believers and should be taught through discipleship from the moment of salvation. Sadly, that is not the case.

Bondage can come from many sources, and we will address that in this book, but ultimately all of it traces back to dark forces.

We have instructions in the Word of God on how to deal with the demonic. First and foremost, I rely on scripture. I also sought significant training over many years from multiple ministries that specialize in spiritual warfare and deliverance so that I would not fall into the trap of receiving only one point of view. My training also included biblical counseling with an emphasis in trauma. Then, after years of experience, the ministry framework the Lord intended to establish took shape.

What I share in this book is in no way meant to disparage anyone else's ministry or the way they perform their ministry. I am only responsible for what I believe God has led me to do. I have put in a whole lot of prayer, countless hours of study with mentors, and even more hours as I studied and researched on my own.

I was led to use a unique, three pillar approach, by combining *inner healing* counseling to address wounding and negative life patterns, with *spiritual warfare* to address bondage, together with a strong *discipleship* component. We will unpack this concept in detail later.

Many churches and congregations don't offer support services. If they do, they usually offer standard biblical counseling which can indeed be helpful when conducted appropriately. But there are two problems with that.

Here's the first problem. In general, pastors receive very little training in counseling, if any at all. Therefore, pastoral counseling is, unfortunately, too often conducted in an inappropriate manner and/ or the counsel given to clients is so off base and hurtful that they leave in a worse condition than when they went in. I have experienced this myself multiple times and so had many of my clients before they came to me.

The second problem is that it stops short; standard biblical counseling is not meant to address demonic bondage. In most cases the demonic is not even mentioned or referred to in any way, and the counselors are not trained to deal with it. All of my clients so far have had biblical counseling before coming to me, in some cases for many years.

Other congregations offer only deliverance, which, again, can be very helpful when done skillfully by teams who have been properly trained. But, if the ministry team doesn't take the time to learn where the open doors are, how they were opened in the first place, and then soundly shut them, there is a risk that the bondage and attack may return. Scripture warns us of this danger.

> *When the unclean spirit goes out of a man, it passes*
> *through waterless places seeking rest, and not finding any,*
> *it says, 'I will return to my house from which I came.' And*
> *when it comes, it finds it swept and put in order. Then it*
> *goes and takes along seven other spirits more evil than*
> *itself, and they go in and live there; and the last state of*
> *that man becomes worse than the first.*
> Luke 11:24-26

In addition, if there is no discipleship process included at the same time in the ministry clients receive, they don't learn how to break bondage for themselves, how to address future attacks, how to walk in freedom every day for the rest of their life, or how to minister bondage-breaking healing to others.

Why, as care givers, would we ignore in our support models the fact that what we battle and overcome will be used by our Lord to minister to others? Our clients should come out of the healing process ready and equipped to do so.

We must train the future trainers at every opportunity. This is, in my opinion, how we will turn the church around from weak to strong.

Even though it might be shocking or difficult to believe for someone who has endured long-term supernatural attack, breaking the bondage of the demonic and casting them out is actually the easy part. Addressing the negative life patterns and wounds of bondage is the more difficult part that takes some time.

It's not just about getting free: it is about staying free for the rest of your life and being able to minister to others. This is what we are all called to do.

Let's look at this a little more closely.

Trauma can create an open door for bondage

If you work through some of the trauma on an emotional and psychological level but never address the supernatural bondage that was created when it occurred, you only heal part of the damage and do not evict the dark forces that created the bondage in the first place.

Here's an example of that scenario. If the trauma was received by a child who is now my adult client, we can address the trauma with counseling but when trauma is experienced, especially by a child, there is usually a degree of spiritual bondage that was created at that moment in time. If we successfully achieve a level of healing emotionally and psychologically, but never address the dark supernatural bondage that was created at the moment of trauma, the bondage can continue unbroken or it can return. I hear this from my clients all the time. They don't understand why they still have supernatural bondage when they've been through Christian counseling. The answer is simple: standard counseling does not address demonic bondage at all.

Bondage can create trauma

On the converse, if you receive deliverance from significant spiritual bondage and do not address the emotional and psychological issues that either were the invitation to or the results of the long-term bondage, you can continue to have an open door that keeps you vulnerable to supernatural attack.

Here is an example of that scenario. Let's say you are a college student and a friend convinces you to attend a party where they perform occult rituals, and while there you experience a horrifying demonic attack. We can break the bondage of the demonic attack by the power of the blood of the Lamb without a problem. But if we do not address why you were drawn to attend an occult ritual in the first place, plus why you were even friends with people who would attend an occult ritual, and then also get you on a solid spiritual foundation, you could find yourself again drawn to dark powers, sometimes without realizing it due to a lack of discernment and maturity, or you could be the target of another demonic attack because you never learned spiritual warfare and you don't know how to defend against it.

So, in this case, the bondage from the attack must be addressed through spiritual warfare, but through counseling and inner-healing we must also deal with the trauma and related emotions created at the time of the demonic attack.

Spiritual warfare is not just for an emergency! It is a way of life. It is not like calling an exterminator to remove a pest, doing that work for you. It is the responsibility of every believer. We have to learn how to WALK in the freedom of Christ...every day, 24/7!

We can't move forward in life or in ministry if we are bound by the past. Counseling enables us to address wounds and discover veiled origins of pain, trauma, and ungodly life patterns.

As we prayerfully address past trauma and uncover the root sources of pain and negative life patterns, with the power and direction of the Holy Spirit, we break any bondage as it is revealed.

This ministry approach is based on a strong discipleship model where the counselor walks alongside you as you learn to break bondage and walk in power, love, and a sound mind: for life. It also equips you to be used in ministry to others.

Renowned spiritual warrior and deliverance minister, Russ

Dizdar, recently said in an interview, "I get to see people saved, real healing, people who had demons get delivered, stand up, yield to Jesus, their whole countenance, everything's changed. I get to see the power of God operate."

Then, he pointed out, "Only we can do this. The demons know this. Believers. Only we've been commissioned to do this, only we have the authority; nobody else does. No possessed person has ever gotten free on their own."

"What?" you say. "I'm supposed to minister this to others?" You bet!

Our biggest struggles in life often become our ministry. I know people who lost a child and ended up starting a ministry to support others who lost a child. Not every believer is called to this ministry in a formal way, but we are all called to minister in this way to one another within the body of Yeshua.

This can be so powerful. It is something that the soul is so hungry for that it comes up often outside church walls and can be the impetus for salvation just as it was in Jesus' ministry. The bondage is broken, the recipients see and experience the power of the one true God, and if given the opportunity will yield their heart to Him forever in that very moment. If this had been taking place in every church, there would never have been such an increase of interest in the occult and the profound moral decline in our culture.

This type of deep inner healing that I'm talking about is not fluffy and comfortable. Rather, it is messy, uncomfortable, and can at times be a bit scary as you confront your deepest issues that have held you back. It is warfare in the true sense of the word!

The process reveals the things that you often aren't able to or are not willing to see in yourself. It will ferret out the hiding places of darkness and break the chains of bondage. It is a conduit to minister the healing of Yeshua Jesus by the power of the Ruach HaKodesh

(Holy Spirit) and to provide via the process, the training necessary to walk in the "power, love and a sound mind", as described in II Timothy 1:7, every day for the rest of your life.

Using this approach, with the complete picture made by having all of the pieces of the puzzle in place, you are much less likely to ever fall into bondage again…and it utterly transforms your relationship with Jesus.

This is how we learn to walk in freedom, in power, love and a sound mind; for life.

This process is not a passive one where you rely on someone else to fix things for you. I have a client who recently said, "You can't just take the Fasting check-out lane or go through the drive-through window for your Mc-Healing."

This is a process that is more like a ministry boot-camp that trains you, using your own real life experience as the example, on how to recognize the powers of darkness in your life, understand how they got there, to break the chains, to walk in the Light of Yeshua, and to never again become victim to the deception, torment and oppression.

The process involves a commitment of time, a lot of prayer, seeking the Lord through deep repentance with fasting, and lots of homework – homework that no one else can do for you.

Unfortunately, there are very few ministries in the U.S. that deal with this issue of inner healing or deliverance, and as a result, because of the ever increasing need as darkness grows in the end times, many ministries that are anointed and good at what they do have a backlog; some have a one-year waiting list. There is a lot of time and prayer invested by these dedicated ministry teams.

This model that I use with my clients takes, on average, four months to complete. Obviously, I can't work with everyone who needs help one-on-one or in seminars. That's another reason I'm writing this book. The need is so great and it is increasing.

Just in the past few years there have been numerous articles revealing the fact that the Catholic Church is training exorcists as fast as they can, due to the explosion in demonic attack, possession, and influence. Look at just a few of those headlines:

Vatican rolls out exorcism training course to counter rise in 'demonic possessions, New York Post, Feb. 26, 2018

Top Psychiatrist: Demonic Possession Is Very Real and On the Rise, CBN News, July 6, 2016

As believers, we've been told the end of the story before it unfolds, so we should know that the end-times prophecies foretell a great rise in supernatural power. It will continue to increase.

God designed each of us to be born in this time. It is not a mistake. You have the ability to become a fierce warrior for the Kingdom! This book will show you how to get there and I pray it will be one of the most amazing journeys of your life.

Is this intense, no-stone-unturned healing journey worth it?

What is gained by going through spiritual boot camp to learn how to be effective at spiritual warfare and get free from bondage?

I feel called to equip and empower the Remnant to be effective in the last days. We can't be effective for Kingdom work, nor can we experience the fullness of the relationship with Jesus that is available to us, if we are bound by destructive patterns, trauma, and spiritual oppression. I work to minister the mercy and power of Yeshua Jesus to bring freedom from bondage and to move into deeper relationship with the Savior of our souls, so that we can boldly take back the territory the enemy has stolen.

I also work to educate believers in effective and powerful spiritual warfare according to the biblical model (which has largely been flushed from or diluted in many congregations), for both greater individual freedom and in order to be equipped for powerful ministry.

Does that sound intriguing?

Do you desire a deeper relationship with Yeshua?

Are you in ministry and feel restrained in a spiritual sense, as if something is holding you back from accomplishing what you are called to do?

Recall that I've been through this process myself over the years, in addition to ministering this type of healing to others. What is my suggestion?

DIVE IN!

You know, when I was younger, I heard a few older women say that Jesus was the love of their lives. Honestly, I thought that was just something they said to sound super-spiritual. I have learned I was completely wrong!

It is true that you can have a much deeper relationship with our Savior.

It is true that you can see the spirit of the Living God defeat the strongest forces of the demonic.

It is true that you can reach a point where He truly is the love of your life.

You can discover how to hear His voice more clearly.

And, if all this is true, what do you think the effect will be on your own faith and actual relationship with Yeshua?

It changes everything!

If I had to make one statement everyone could hear before they tuned out this critical subject, it would be this:

As goes your proficiency with spiritual warfare, so goes your relationship with Yeshua Jesus!

That's why I can say that this is not just about breaking demonic bondage.

Ultimately, spiritual warfare is about your relationship with Jesus.

Is this the first time you heard that?

Years after my own journey, I do not regret a single moment. I only wish I'd known sooner.

I invite you to come on a journey with me. Let's unpack this subject and find out what the church and the world are truly dying for.

INFUSION – to fill or cause to be filled.

With the revelation of the information, and aligning ourselves in obedience, we are infused with our King's supernatural power...and that changes everything in us.

In a message on July 13th, 2019, Pastor Mark Biltz went over the Torah portion for the Sabbath: Judges 10:11-16.

In verse 13, God is responding to Israel's disobedience after God had done so much for them. It says God's soul was grieved at their betrayal.

"Wherefore I will deliver you (יָשַׁע, *yasha*, Strong's 3467) no more," he said.

Then just a verse later, the children of Israel admitted they betrayed Him in sin.

And the children of Israel said unto the LORD, We have sinned: do thou unto us whatsoever seemeth good unto thee; deliver us (לְצַל, *natsal*, Strong's 5337) only, we pray thee, this day. Judges 10:15, KJV

Pastor Biltz was pointing out that a different word was used for what is translated into English in both places as 'deliver'.

The word God used was *yasha*, which means to deliver, to be set free, wide open, like a bird let out of a cage. It is also the root of Yeshua, Who is our salvation, foretelling our Messiah.

The word Israel used was *natsal*, which does mean deliverance but in a different way. Biltz described it, "It's not set free like a bird, it's more like, can you just get us out of this corner and put us in another corner, like another side of the bird cage."

This can only be seen in the original Hebrew.

The Old Testament is constantly revealing Yeshua and how to recognize Him.

God had complete deliverance in mind, Israel just wanted to move to a different spot in the same cage.

Yasha! Yeshua! Deliver us, Lord, as we give You the praise and the glory for Your mercy and power!

God has good plans for us and His instructions are enough. He will infuse us with His power if we will follow instructions. That filling can only come from Him and as it is filling empty places you didn't even know you had, you then realize: it changes everything.

Are You Ready?

The What & The Who

Those who seek inner healing ministry have often had a long struggle trying to figure out what they've been dealing with and how to become free.

Have you noticed an odd pattern with sickness through your family line?

Have you encountered odd or unusual adversity that seems to never end?

Maybe when you researched your family tree you noticed a pattern of infidelity that goes back generations.

When we read in Ephesians 6 about the armor of God, do you assume it is something someone else does on your behalf? Or that it was automatically done for you when you got saved?

Do you at times feel as though thoughts come to your mind from somewhere else or someone else, other than yourself?

A Calling On Every Believer

Spiritual warfare skills were the norm in the Acts church and throughout the New Testament. Let's look at Luke 10:19.

> *I have given you authority to trample on snakes and scorpions*
> *and to overcome all the power of the enemy; nothing will*
> *harm you. NIV*

Jesus gave all authority to the believers. When Jesus said, "I have given", because the Greek word *dedoka*, a primary form of the verb *to give*, is used in the perfect tense, it implies it is a permanent possession. He gave us that authority to do what? Trample and overcome! That is *not* passive.

Russ Dizdar explains, "The mission: tread, trample, crush the demonic world. Overcome all the power of the enemy and nothing will harm you! He sent [them] out to do it and they did it."[1]

In the beginning of the chapter, Jesus had equipped and sent out 70. They returned with joy:

> *The seventy returned with joy, saying, "Lord, even the*
> *demons are subject to us in Your name"*
> *Luke 10:17*

In 1 John 4:1 we are commanded to test the spirits.

Do you know how to test the spirits? I rarely meet someone who knows how to do this. Here is the scripture:

> *Beloved, do not believe every spirit, but test the spirits*
> *to see whether they are from God, because many false*
> *prophets have gone out into the world. By this you know*
> *the Spirit of God: every spirit that confesses that Jesus*
> *Christ has come in the flesh is from God; and every spirit*
> *that does not confess Jesus is not from God; this is the spirit*
> *of the antichrist, of which you have heard that it is coming,*
> *and now it is already in the world.*
> *1 John 4:1-3*

Obviously, this is a proof text that 1) spirits, both good and bad, exist and 2) we have interaction with them. If we had no interaction with them, there would not be a warning telling us we need to test them!

Since spiritual warfare is the call upon every mature believer according to scripture but the teaching has been removed from most pulpits, most believers no longer have the tools to battle effectively against the dark forces that never tire from plotting torment for all of the human race, including you.

You can't defeat an enemy you can't recognize.

You can't win a battle you don't even know you're engaged in.

What Am I Dealing With Here?

> *For our struggle is not against flesh and blood, but against
> the rulers, against the powers, against the world forces of
> this darkness, against the spiritual forces of wickedness in
> the heavenly places.*
> *Ephesians 6:12*

This is a good place to start.

We are struggling with spiritual forces and entities that scripture says are *not* human.

Though most congregations today do not teach anything about spiritual warfare, it is one of the paramount instructions and warnings we have in scripture. As believers we are hated because of Christ (Mark 13:13), because "the world knew Him not," (John 1:10), and we are told the forces of darkness are at work in the world (Ephesians 6:12).

> *From the days of John the Baptist until now the kingdom of
> heaven suffers violence, and the violent take it by force.*
> *Matthew 11:12, ESV*

> *The thief comes only to steal and kill and destroy; I have
> come that they may have life and have it more abundantly.*
> *John 10:10*

We are dealing with dark powers, fallen angels, and demons.

These forces of darkness are in some ways like very badly behaved children. More on this later.

They are fallen angelic beings or demonic spirits, and sometimes demonic spirits influencing humans to cause destruction. They are VERY legalistic. And, yes, they are very powerful. But, when confronted with the power of Jesus that indwells every believer, they must obey.

We have to be very intentional and specific in our language and commands. They know scripture better than most of us and they will twist it endlessly if we let them. They want to find a way around what you say to them and they are very skilled at it.

They will also pull every trick in the book to intimidate you. I heard a story from a pastor many years ago that illustrates this perfectly.

A ten-year-old boy has just been granted his deepest desire: a trip to the shelter to pick out a dog. He can hardly contain himself in the car and his parents delight in his joy. At the shelter the boy wants a big dog, not some little yappy dog. He wants a dog that's big and strong and will impress the other boys in the neighborhood. He picks a very large, beautiful German Shepherd that is stately and sure to impress his friends.

When they get home, he can hardly wait to walk down the sidewalk with his new, strong dog by his side. His beautiful, well-behaved dog is happy and impressive as they strut toward the boy's friends just down the block.

Just before the boy reaches his friends, a neighbor's Chihuahua comes running out of the yard barking furiously to meet the pair on the sidewalk. The boy thinks, huh, my dog is ferocious and strong, not some little yappy thing. With his loud bark, it will teach that little insect of a dog a thing or two!

As the Chihuahua runs up to the strong Shepherd yipping and snarling, the Shepherd plops down on the sidewalk and sticks his legs up in the air. The boy is stunned and brokenhearted as his friends laugh.

In the context of power, this is a great picture of the spiritual enemy we face. We have supreme power through Yeshua Jesus, power that no demon from hell can withstand (Matthew 16:18). The devil and his cohorts are loud with their yapping but they are just little minions compared to our King. If we lack the knowledge of who we are in Yeshua and the skills we've been given to defeat them, they will intimidate us. But God has given us access to His power! He is the Lion of the Tribe of Judah (Revelation 5:5)! No demonic force has power that can come close to the power we have in Yeshua!

> *Suddenly a man with an unclean spirit cried out in the synagogue: "What do You want with us, Jesus of Nazareth? Have You come to destroy us? I know who You are – the Holy One of God!" But Jesus rebuked the spirit and said, "Be silent! Come out of him!" At this, the unclean spirit threw the man into convulsions and came out with a loud shriek.*
> *Mark 1:23-26*

The Void In The Church

It is ironic that churches no longer teach this set of skills since the Christian faith has its foundations on ancient texts that describe extraordinary, supernatural occurrences, including the resurrection of Jesus from the dead, multiplication of small food resources to feed thousands of people, commanding nature in the form of the stormy winds and seas to come to a state of calm, healing all kinds of diseases and disabilities (some instant and some where a second prayer was necessary), translocation of Phillip, and an ascension transfer from this dimension to another.

Author and researcher L.A. Marzulli refers to the Bible as The Guide Book to the Supernatural, and he is quite correct in that description.

You will most certainly struggle with spiritual warfare if you deny the existence of the supernatural.

Author Cris Putnam in his book, *The Supernatural Worldview*, defines the supernatural in this way:

"The term 'supernatural' originates in the sixteenth century, medieval Latin: *supra*, which means 'above,' plus *naturalis*, meaning 'nature.' Thus, it describes transcendence of the natural realm."

The God of the Bible by very definition is supernatural.

He further explains, "A common mistake made by skeptics is to assume science has disproven supernatural phenomena. It is formally called a 'category error.' Science, by definition, deals with the natural; thus the supernatural is outside of its purview. When a scientist says the supernatural does not exist, he is making a category error along the lines of trying to weigh a chicken with a yardstick.

"The twentieth century marked a paradigm shift from the belief in an eternal universe to the mathematical certitude of a temporal one. This strongly implies the existence of God," he contends. "The cosmological argument states: 1) Everything that begins to exist has a cause; 2) The universe began to exist; 3) Therefore, the universe has a cause."[2]

A common phrase is, if there was a bang (as in Big Bang), then there must be a banger!

Whoever created the universe must have unimaginable power and, due to the "chance-defying precision" of the finely turned universe, that being must also be extraordinarily intelligent.[3]

Are you already beginning to see that this discussion is not just about spiritual warfare, it is about a relationship with a supernatural being in the Person of the biblical God and the way He tells us life exists?

If we deny spiritual warfare and the supernatural, we deny the very biblical model and description of this life and the next! No wonder so many people are abandoning Christianity! There is little of it left to recognize and it is too often reduced to what looks like a country club social event. You put clean clothes on, show up at a certain time, socialize with people in your inner circle, have lunch at a restaurant near the church and go home utterly unchanged.

For believers, the Bible is where we are to get our worldview, our understanding of life. The pastors who deny this, I humbly suggest, need to rethink the seven questions of worldview and make sure they're still building their beliefs and views on the biblical model and not the prevailing model in modern Western culture, which is naturalism. Naturalists deny the existence of angels and demons.[4]

Dr. James Sire, author of the classic text on worldviews, *The Universe Next Door: A Basic Worldview Catalogue*, defines worldview in this way: "A committed spiritual orientation that is expressed as a set of presuppositions concerning the basic makeup of the world."[5] He reasons that all worldviews basically address the following seven questions:

- What is really real?
- What is the nature of external reality?
- What is a human being?
- What happens to a person after death?
- Why is it possible to know anything at all?
- How do we know what is right and wrong?
- What is the meaning of human history?

Sire also points out that *Christianity makes the most sense of reality as we know it.* You'd never know that by attending the average American church in 2019!

Putnam refers to a 2009 Barna Group[6] survey that defined a basic Christian worldview in this way:

> "Believing that absolute moral truth exists; the Bible is totally accurate in all of the principles it teaches; Satan is considered to be a real being or force, not merely symbolic; a person cannot earn their way into Heaven by trying to be good or do good works; Jesus Christ lived a sinless life on earth; and God is the all-knowing, all-powerful creator of the world who still rules the universe today."[7]

The resulting survey data shocked the Christian world when it showed that *less than nine percent of professed Christians in America have a biblical worldview*[8]. The impact of this on our culture cannot be overstated.

And, that was 2009. It is worse today.

"If most self-proclaimed Christians do not have a Supernatural Worldview," Putnam observes, "our evangelism faces a serious challenge."[9]

No wonder people experiencing spiritual warfare and supernatural events can't find help, and no wonder so many people are leaving Christian churches.

See how Putnam sums up the problem, keeping in mind that approximately one-fourth of all the healings recorded in the Gospel of Mark were actually deliverances.

> "Would it even occur to you that an ill person might need deliverance rather than medicine? Does your church engage in deliverance? If Jesus thought it was important, shouldn't we?
>
> "As His followers, Christians should adopt and defend the worldview of Jesus. Unfortunately, many in the church have adopted a form of naturalism that relegates all supernatural activity to the biblical era. It is commonly called cessationism, based on the idea that spiritual sign gifts and miraculous forms of intervention ceased after the biblical canon closed. As a result, many times, the secular paranormal enthusiast's beliefs are more consistent with revealed REALITY replete with angels and demons interacting with humans than some of those who claim to believe in the Bible. This is unacceptable."[10]

I wholeheartedly agree!

> *See to it that no one takes you captive through philosophy*
> *and empty deception, according to the tradition of men,*
> *according to the elementary principles of the world, rather*
> *than according to Christ.*
> *Colossians 2:8*

In our time, as the wheels of history grind toward the one world government and increasing levels of control, perversion, deception, and supernatural power displays, we must get back to the scriptural view and method clearly laid out for us not only for our own protection as believers, but also so we can be ready for a mind-blowing move of God before Christ's return.

But, far too many pastors are not even preaching the gospel in today's church culture.

August 1st, 2019, Dr. Michael Lake[11] recounted a conversation he'd had with a leading Bishop. The Bishop shared a recent encounter he had had with a local megachurch pastor. During the course of that conversation, the Bishop had confronted the pastor about some things going on in the church that the Bishop believed were questionable in regard to scripture. The megachurch pastor replied, "We have to tolerate certain things to have enough people coming in to keep the lights on."

What a toxic environment. The model for centuries, to preach the gospel unapologetically and let the chips fall where they may, has long ago been replaced with never confront, always appease, and present a church service-entertainment experience that uplifts, encourages, and allows people to feel better about their lives and choices. That same church experience often includes encouraging or tolerating counterfeit supernatural encounters.

We Are Made Lower Than The Angels

These forces have been around a very long time, and have been at work trying to derail any good in your life since the day you were born and, in many cases, even before that.

Read this verse carefully:

> *What is mankind that you are mindful of them, human beings that you care for them?* ***You have made them a little lower than the angels*** *and crowned them with glory and honor. You made them rulers over the works of your hands; you put everything under their feet.*
> *Psalm 8:4-6, NIV [emphasis added]*

Never forget that. It is a part of why they hate us so much. Why?

We were created lower than the angelic beings, yet God sacrificed His Son to restore us to relationship with Him. There is no mention in the Bible of God doing that for fallen angels.

Can't you just imagine the pride-filled fallen angels complaining to each other around the Netherworld water cooler?

"Those stupid humans. They're pathetic creatures. Why does He love them? Why does He continue to work with them? He never did that for us!"

In espionage, when a spy is caught who will not yield to the torture, what is a next-level tactic that is used? If they can't get you to spill the state secrets, they will try threatening what you love.

In my opinion, based on what I read in scripture and what I see of the way the dark side operates, they fiercely and desperately want to do two things: 1) They want to torment you for all of eternity, not just in this life. And, 2) they want to stab God in the heart as deeply as they can because of their pride, jealousy, and hatred. By achieving number one, they achieve number two.

Speaking of the prophets who foretold the coming salvation through the Messiah, 1 Peter tells us:

> *It was revealed to them that they were not serving themselves, but you, in these things which now have been announced to you through those who preached the gospel to you by the Holy Spirit sent from heaven—**things into which angels long to look**."*
> *1 Peter 1:12 [emphasis added]*

Angels long to look into the things God has given us!

We do not have enough respect and joy for what God has done for us. The greatest mystery in the universe is: why does God love us so much? I say this often because it is one of the bases for everything else in this battle.

As we ponder how viciously the dark side hates humans and most especially believers, I wonder if there might be another layer of understanding in a familiar parable.

In Matthew 20:1-16 Jesus gives us the parable of the laborers in the vineyard. In verse one Jesus begins, "The kingdom of heaven is like a landowner..." This sets the foundation for the story; the heavenly realm is compared to an earthly vineyard.

The landowner hired some workers early in the morning for the wages of one denarius. He went out again at the 3rd, 6th, 9th, and 11th hours and hired others. The landowner went out and hired workers five times; five is the biblical number of grace.[12]

At the end of the day when it was time to pay his workers, he paid those who came to work at the end of the day first, and those who had been hired early in the morning, last. But the real trouble came when the early workers saw that the landowner did not pay them more than he paid the end-of-day workers. The landowner responded to their complaints.

> But he answered and said to one of them, "Friend, I am doing you no wrong; did you not agree with me for a denarius? Take what is yours and go, but I wish to give to this last man the same as to you. 'Is it not lawful for me to do what I wish with what is my own? **Or is your eye envious because I am generous?**" So the last shall be first, and the first last.
> Matthew 20:1-16 [emphasis added]

The landowner clearly represents the Lord and the vineyard represents His Kingdom.

Footnoted here is a great study on this parable[13]. Read through it and see if you can spot hints that it could represent something more, something that applies to our discussion.

The landowner went to another place to hire workers. Since we're talking about a heavenly realm represented by a vineyard, and the landowner represents God, I wonder if the marketplace could represent a different dimension.

I wonder if the early workers could represent the fallen angelic beings who were created and in kingdom service before humans, and if the late workers could represent humans. They were created to work in His Kingdom as were we. But we arrive later in the day and we have less to bring to the table. They are stronger, smarter, have abilities we don't have, and we know they have feelings because they can experience anger and jealousy. Yet, God raised us up with Him and seated us with Him in the heavenly places in Christ Jesus (Ephesians 2:6).

He asks the angry workers, "Are you envious because I am generous?"

I find this an interesting way of looking at the passage.

Whether theologians would agree or not, the parable highlights the envy that surfaced because of God's generosity, and that clearly applies to our discussion of the hatred the fallen beings have for us. We are the undeserving recipients of our Lord's unfathomable grace, mercy, and generosity.

We must never stop trying to understand the unearned, unreasonable love our heavenly Father has for us, and to praise Him for this gift every day for eternity. But, if we don't understand what He has given to us, we don't have a proper response.

Allow me to offer an illustration.

It's your birthday and your co-workers are celebrating with you in the lunchroom. A complete stranger gives you a present. You are glad to receive it, and no matter what's inside, the kindness fills you with a warmth. You remove the decorative paper and the ribbon. You lift the lid of the small box and look inside to see a coffee-stained ticket stub.

You think, what is this? Is this some sort of joke? Your co-workers are puzzled also.

The stranger sees your reaction and says, "I'm sure you're wondering why I gave you a coffee-stained ticket stub."

You're trying to be polite and you say, "Well, yes, I am wondering..."

He then says, "I own a company. God has greatly blessed me financially. I overheard a conversation involving a friend of yours, that you work in ministry and you have been praying for God to provide for a financial need. I bought this ticket last week; I don't even know why because I never do that. I felt the Lord wanted me to give it to you. It's a Lottery Ticket...and it's a winner. It won yesterday. You are now the winner of one hundred thousand dollars."

Your hesitation and confusion quickly melt away and that feeling is instantly replaced with an overwhelming sense of gratitude, amazement, shock and joy.

It was the same seemingly worthless, coffee-stained ticket. That didn't change.

The gift didn't mean much until you discovered what it represented.

In an instant, something you would have thrown away was revealed to be the most life-changing present you've ever received. And you will be able to use that gift to help others.

To summarize, in my opinion the greatest mystery in the universe is why God loves us so much.

> *There is joy in the presence of the angels of God over one*
> *sinner who repents.*
> *Luke 15:10*

> *Who will separate us from the love of Christ? Will*
> *tribulation, or distress, or persecution, or famine, or*
> *nakedness, or peril, or sword? For I am convinced that*
> *neither death, nor life, **nor angels**, **nor principalities,** nor*
> *things present, nor things to come, **nor powers**, nor height,*
> *nor depth, nor any other created thing, will be able to*
> *separate us from the love of God, which is in Christ*
> *Jesus our Lord.*
> *Romans 8:35-39 [emphasis added]*

I hope you can see, perhaps in a new way, that the forces of darkness are furious witnesses to the abundant river of God's love and mercy ever flowing in our direction...and they hate it.

Evil in the world spread around by these hate-filled beings causes so much suffering and my clients have dealt with more than they should have had to bear. Yet, when we realize what's really going on, who these forces working against us actually are, and how our Lord gave us weapons to defend ourselves, it's a game changer.

As one of my client's recently said, "If I'd known how to do this, I wouldn't have had to be on anxiety meds for years."

To be clear, these issues are not solved with positive thinking. Believe me, I tried. These supernatural encounters and issues may be deeply puzzling and often disturbing, whether you have been trained or not, because you have discovered that you cannot control them, and because you are tormented or severely oppressed by them.

The enemy is the Prince of Darkness and his minions. Their entire M.O. is to torture you mentally and physically. They lie, they twist, they distort, they condemn, they obsessively plot your destruction.

> *The thief comes only to steal and kill and destroy; I have come that they may have life and have it more abundantly.*
> *John 10:10*

> *He was a murderer from the beginning, not holding to the truth, for there is no truth in him. When he lies, he speaks his native language, for he is a liar and the father of lies.*
> *John 8:44, NIV*

The demonic can perform terrifying signs and wonders.

> *for they are the spirits of devils, working miracles...*
> *Revelation 16:14, KJV*

We are to address the demonic with skill, authority and anointing, the way the Bible tells us to.

Years ago, I got a call from a new friend. She was taught, as I had once been, that spiritual warfare did not exist for Christians.

"A friend of mine is encountering demonic attack," she said. "Would you get together with us to pray about the attacks?"

I'd had this conversation many times with others and was familiar with how it typically plays out.

I had explained to her on more than one occasion that spiritual warfare is real and that believers must learn the way God told us to deal with it. But she was not yet prepared to abandon what she'd been taught and did not receive my exhortation that the Bible instructs us to cast them out. She chose instead to hold to idea that Christians cannot be demonized, in spite of the fact that she was watching her friend struggle with a very powerful demonic force, AND that the two of them had already agreed that it was, in fact, demonic. So when they asked me to get together with them to pray about the demonic forces, as politely as possible, I declined and they were shocked.

I told them, "We are not to pray over or about demons: You cast them out. The Lord already gave us the instructions on how to deal with them. You find trained ministry personnel to assist you and cast them out."

At the time, they did not want to take that route and just went about their business. But, years later, that same person became a client and is now fully trained and adept in spiritual warfare.

> *Is this not the fast that I have chosen? To loose the bonds*
> *of wickedness, to undo the heavy burdens, and to let the*
> *oppressed go free, and that you break every yoke.*
> *Isaiah 58:6, KJV 2000*

We have identified what is going on, who is behind it, and why. Now we will look at one of the weapons used against us.

What are the flaming arrows?

What Are The Flaming Arrows?

In this discussion of what we are dealing with, we must address one of the most used weapons of the enemy: unwanted thoughts.

> *In addition to all, taking up the shield of faith with which you will be able to extinguish all the flaming arrows of the evil one.*
> *Ephesians 6:16*

The flaming arrows are unwanted thoughts from the dark ones.

Every client I've worked with comes face-to-face with this issue of unwanted thoughts.

These burning arrows can come in the form of a sexual thought screaming in your mind. They may melt weak defenses with an assault of doubt and confusion, whispering in your ear things such as, "You aren't really a Christian. If you were really a Christian, you wouldn't be having this problem."

Have you heard that one? A lot of my clients have.

Once you begin this process of spiritual warfare training you may hear, "What a waste of time. It won't work; they're way too powerful for you."

Or that mocking voice, "C'mon, there's no such thing as the supernatural."

They often say these things the very moment we start pressing into the Lord with our devotions. Sometimes they try to prevent us from speaking prayers against them!

That type of attack is one of the proofs of the origin of the thoughts, precisely because they attack when you reach for your Bible, or when you start to pray, or when you begin singing heartfelt worship to the Lord.

We are to immediately take every one of these thoughts captive.

> *We are destroying speculations and every lofty thing raised up against the knowledge of God, and we are taking every thought captive to the obedience of Christ.*
> *2 Corinthians 10:5*

Just today a client needed prayer. She had been doing great in the first few weeks of healing, already seeing the enemy losing territory. But when she left the house, and for the first time in a long time didn't have her Bible with her, a major spiritual attack showed up. Hmmm. What a *coincidence*! Prowling, watching, waiting for the smallest of opportunities.

I have a client who has been viciously attacked with thoughts she knows *are not* her own. One of the things the enemy does with her, on top of the assault itself, is to then try to convince her that the thoughts really *are* her own. But, she knows the difference.

Have you had that experience?

It reminds me of this common childhood scene.

When I was about five or six years old, there was a male family friend that would play with me like this. He would take my small hand in his, and he would bang my hand against my own head as he said, "Why are you hitting yourself in the head?" As I giggled he would continue, "Why are you hitting yourself in the head? Stop hitting yourself! I said, stop hitting yourself!" We would laugh and that would be it.

These wicked minions act like that but in very sinister ways.

They are the ones conducting the brutal thought assault, then as you try to defend yourself they attempt to invert reality in your head by saying, "These thoughts are yours, got it?? If they weren't yours, you wouldn't be having them!" They attempt to convince you that you are assaulting yourself and that the flaming arrows being shot at you from the wicked ones behind a rock, are your own fault.

Interestingly, this is the same kind of pattern we see in domestic violence. A man may beat his wife, then scream out in frustration, shouting at her that if she would just stop [fill in the blank here; e.g. breathing] he wouldn't have had to beat her.

Abusers beat spouses or their children not because of the behavior of the victim but because of the issues within themselves. The devil, our spiritual abuser, is the same. He is wicked, a liar, and there is no good in him. He never tires of inflicting pain, and he prowls around like a lion watching, waiting for opportunity, twisting and deceiving.

This mind game is part of the inversion that is both a major strategy and doctrine of the dark side. It is also a prominent symptom of the End of Days.

Recall this scripture.

> *Woe to those who call evil good, and good evil; Who substitute darkness for light and light for darkness; Who substitute bitter for sweet and sweet for bitter.*
> *Isaiah 5:20*

This verse hints at this same concept.

> *Know this first of all, that in the last days mockers will come with their mocking, following after their own lusts, and saying, "Where is the promise of His coming?"*
> *2 Peter 3:3-4*

Now, that sounds like a demonic voice engaged in a mind game if I've ever heard one-- mockers saying, "Jesus is not coming! Let it go! Just give in to the thoughts; they're yours anyway. Heehee."

The dark side has a doctrine of *as above, so below*. They imitate God's plan, structure, and Kingdom. But theirs is twisted, perverted, dark.

Where God wants you to serve Him in the beautiful light with free will and purpose filling us with His spirit, the enemy wants you bound in complete and ravenous darkness, serving him without free will as he takes over and consumes all you are until there's nothing left of you but a shell.

Praise the Name of the Lord, He gave us weapons against this! As you do this work and the truth of it moves from your head into your heart, the territory is won and the enemy is defeated.

Where Does Bondage Come From?

There are several ways bondage occurs in the life of the believer.

For our strategy of proofs, we always take scripture first, the fruit born of the concept, then evidence in the natural world around us that gives direction to a particular view. We will also deal with this in another chapter.

Bondage can come from many sources such as generational curses, poor choices, unconfessed sin, occult or demonic ties or practices, and various levels of brokenness.

First, let's look at sin.

Sin

It should be obvious (but it too often is not, for those who hold a worldview that there is no such thing as the supernatural, which means you can't possibly believe in the God of the Bible, therefore, logically there is no such thing as sin) that if we are engaging in sinful behavior it opens doors to the dark side and can invite a weighty bondage from which it may be very difficult to escape.

We are told to take every thought captive (2 Corinthians 10:5) binding them in the blood of the Lamb, so when we allow the thoughts that should have been immediately rebuked to linger and then choose to act on them, they have crossed over from a flaming arrow of the wicked ones (Ephesians 6:16) into sin.

When we are saved and cleansed by the blood of Yeshua, we are changed in a supernatural event called salvation. We are commanded in scripture to repent, to turn around from behavior and patterns that do not please the Lord or that are classified as sin, and to walk in holiness. We receive the righteousness of Christ as a gift. But, walking in holiness is a commandment and is our job. We can't do that if we don't understand what pleases God, what He doesn't like, what brings Him joy, what breaks His heart.

When a man is intent on getting into the heart of a woman, he wants to know what she likes, what makes her happy, what she likes spending time doing. He joins in those things with her, presents activities and items that mean something to her. That is the way we need to know the Lover of our Souls.

It's NOT about being under law, it is understanding what the laws of God do for us and desiring to do the things that please Him. The laws of God are life to those who will do them.

As an example, let's say that you got saved at age thirteen and you had a measurable change in your life that could have only occurred by the power of God in your life making you new. But a few years later at the tender age of 16, you were at a party where someone passed drugs around. You were so excited that you had been invited to a party with some of the cool kids that you did something you said you'd never do, and you smoked a joint of weed and cocaine. Your body went into emergency mode and chemical substances took control of some things you are supposed to be in control of. You willingly gave control to something else. Demonic experiences can happen in these situations and can often be an open door to ongoing attack and bondage, even if, later, you said you were sorry.

Sin can bring devastating consequences on us and on our loved ones. For example, everyone I know knows someone who is dealing with drug addiction. The ripples in the pond set off by addiction touch many people.

According to the 2018 annual survey of *Monitoring the Future*[14], 8th, 10th and 12th graders are vaping in record numbers. The vaping statistics jumped in all grades and from 2017 to 2018, 10th and 12th grade numbers exploded to nearly double.

6% of 12th graders are using marijuana daily.

Drugs continue to enslave more and more people, and the Christian community is not immune.

A 2013 article by CBS News said that 70% of Americans are taking at least one prescription drug,[15] while over half are taking at least two. According to a study by the MAYO Clinic[16], 20% of patients are on five or more prescription medications. While antibiotics account for most prescriptions, the second most common is antidepressants; the third is opioids.

When we open a door we shouldn't open, we can't always close it.

US drug overdose deaths have skyrocketed from 16,849 in 1999 to 70,237 in 2017. 47,600 died from opioids in 2017 alone.[17]

A study by Consumer Reports found that their test group also took over-the-counter meds in addition to prescription medications and that:

> "the total number of prescriptions filled by all
> Americans, including adults and children, **has increased
> by 85 percent over two decades,** while the total US
> population has increased by only 21 percent."

Natural News reported July 8, 2019, that Americans are now more likely to die of an accidental opioid overdose than get in a car accident.[18] The article, *Addiction and OD: Another side of being an American*, quoted a study done at the University of South Carolina. Study author Jessica Ho, assistant professor at USC Leonard Davis School of Gerontology stated, "For over a decade now, the United States has had the highest drug overdose mortality among its peer countries."

I have a dear friend who had a medical injury that caused great pain. The prescription from the doctor was not unusual at all for the type of pain he was dealing with. But, this strong man of God had no idea that it would lead him into addiction.

Once it reached the point he had to acknowledge it had become an addiction, which was not an easy thing to have to admit, he gathered a few of his closest friends, shared the struggle, and shared the battle plan that included spiritual warfare and accountability, to defeat this new enemy.

He went to his doctor who sent him to a clinic that specializes in helping people get off the drug that caused the addiction, only to find that, as he obeyed instructions to the letter, the new drug to help him get off the original drug was even more addictive!

He struggled for many months and endured multiple trips to the emergency room with dangerous blood pressure numbers and heart palpitations before he finally had the victory. The stress touched his whole family as he went through this battle.

Praise God he was resolute and the victory was won!

And he wasn't even trying to mess around with drugs! Drugs like these are being prescribed too easily and too often, and Americans have been programmed to expect to receive medications when they have an issue.

This is not healthy for our bodies or our communities.

And what about the numbers for porn addiction? Porn is all over social media. BuzzFeed normalizes it with viral videos and Twitter has an estimated 10+ million porn accounts.[19]

The website, *Fight The New Drug*[20] publishes shocking statistics on porn's presence and influence in our society:

> A 2015 meta-analysis of 22 studies from seven countries found that internationally the consumption of pornography was significantly associated with increases in verbal and physical aggression, among males and females alike.
>
> Porn sites receive more regular traffic than Netflix, Amazon, & Twitter combined **each month.**
>
> Recorded child sexual exploitation (known as "child porn") is one of the fastest-growing online businesses.
>
> A recent UK survey found that 44% of males aged 11–16 who consumed pornography reported that online pornography gave them ideas about the type of sex they wanted to try.

"Lesbian" was the most-searched-for porn term on the
world's largest free porn site in 2018.

Any wonder why our kids are confused? They are being force-
fed a toxic cultural brew that teaches them sex is not only okay but
should be embraced, and confusion about genders and age limits,
which ends in the complete perversion of God's beautiful design.
They have been sold the idea that, it's just sex, do whatever feels
good. But the *reality* is, sex has a supernatural component and has
profound impact on individuals, communities, and the world.

The *Fight The New Drug* site also publishes information on the
"proven harms of porn" including profound effects on the brain.[21] It
documents how porn: is an escalating behavior, affects sexual tastes,
can become addictive, actually changes the brain, and affects the
brain like a drug. It affects the heart, leaves consumers lonely, hurts
their partners, damages their sex lives, kills love, and is full of lies. It
fuels sex trafficking, warps ideas about sex, and can lead to violence.

And if that isn't bad enough, according to *The Conquer Series*[22],
68% of Christian men watch porn on a regular basis.

(Insert stunned silence here.)

Now what do you think about the dangerous lie that it's just
sex and doesn't hurt anyone? The families in our congregations
are hurting and addicted to drugs, food, technology, relationships,
and sex. They are suffering increasing domestic violence and deep
loneliness connected to the isolation and relationship destruction
effects of both drug and porn addictions, and sin that separates us
from our loving Abba (*abba*: Hebrew; daddy).

None of this would have happened if our congregations were
regularly infused with Holy Spirit power and consistently built up
in the supernatural relationship with Yeshua Jesus that we were
designed to have.

Sin may offer a temporary escape or a type of short-lived freedom from physical or emotional pain but in reality it only enslaves.

Promising them freedom while they themselves are slaves of corruption; for by what a man is overcome, by this he is enslaved. 2 Peter 2:19

Clearly there is something wrong in our country when we see this kind of rapid decline and exploding numbers of varying types of addiction. Americans are looking for ways to numb out or to artificially enhance what should be God-given feelings. An automatic by-product of this is that strength of character dissolves, along with patience. Everyone wants instant this and that and it's not healthy physically, emotionally, or spiritually.

Your body is not a group of inanimate parts, completely interchangeable at will. You have a body, mind, soul, spirit, and energy fields. We will discuss this later.

And, Jesus said everyone who commits sin is a slave to sin (John 8:34). None of us is sinless so we've all been a slave to sin until we are set free by the gift of salvation.

In fact, for many years there has been unconfirmed evidence that cycles of drug addiction, neuropsychiatric illness and other problems often seem to recur in parents and their children. More on this later.

There is so much we have learned to ignore, and because of changing church culture, we don't even recognize that it is sin, therefore it stays with us until we repent for it.

When we have sin that we have not repented of, the toxic, cancerous effects erode the progress we try to make and keeps us in bondage to events in the past.

A common example is something you did in childhood. Did you steal a classmate's lunch and pretend you knew nothing about it? Did you write it off as just kids' stuff?

Sin was the penalty that our Lord took upon Himself, the penalty we could not pay. But, we don't receive that gift of forgiveness unless we repent of our sin.

> *If we confess our sins, He is faithful and righteous to forgive*
> *us our sins and to cleanse us from all unrighteousness.*
> *1 John 1:9*

Yes, forgiveness is there! Praise God! But there is a big "if" at the beginning of that verse. We must take our sins, all of them, whenever they occur, to Him in confession and repentance, turning away from sinful behavior, taking responsibility for whatever consequences were birthed, and asking those we've hurt to forgive us.

Forgiveness is extremely powerful. It is essential to the process of breaking bondage. In fact, forgiveness and repentance are like kryptonite to the forces of darkness. When you forgive and repent, the minions loose what they had been holding onto.

When talking about where bondage comes from, this question eventually comes up: what about when it's not your own sin?

Generational Bondage & Generational Curses

In the Exodus story God delivered the children of Israel out of Egyptian slavery. Let's take a look at this.

In scripture, Egypt and slavery represent sin, bondage, and the sinful state from which we were delivered through the salvation made possible by God's Son, Yeshua Jesus.

We all were born in a state of bondage.

> *You are slaves of the one whom you obey, either of sin*
> *resulting in death, or of obedience resulting in righteousness.*
> *Romans 6:16*

We all have a throne in our hearts that was created to be occupied by our merciful Creator. But, because we are conceived in iniquity (Psalm 51:5), are full of sin (Romans 6:6-7), we've all sinned (Romans 3:23), are born into a toxic pool infected by sin (Ephesians 6:12 mentions the world forces of this darkness), and even our righteousness is like filthy rags (Isaiah 64:6), by default the Lord of Darkness is on that throne.

It is only through salvation made possible by Jesus that we can evict the Lord of Darkness from that throne in our hearts and invite the King of Glory to reign there. Once salvation takes place, we are bonded to Him and scripture says He places His mark on us. In Exodus 13:9, 16 we see this and we also see it during the Passover event where the blood is applied to the door posts and the lintel, forming the sign of the cross that would later become a universal symbol of the work done on Calvary.

Slave mentality is a very powerful thing. Hundreds of years of torture, trauma programming, breaking of the will, and a carefully implanted inability to think for themselves had firmly established slave mentality in the cellular memory of the children of Israel. Those who have a history of this may have hidden anger, fear, chronic victimhood, or aversion to trust certain types of people or situations.

Let's look at this from a counseling point of view for a moment.

Imagine the mud brick makers. Even if one of your neighbors was beaten to death right beside you as you were working, you were carefully trained to keep your eyes and attention on your job and not get involved. It may cost your life if you try to interfere. So, you may think, "I can't look at that. I just make mud bricks. I stay focused on my bricks so I don't end up dead."

We see this type of mentality from traumatized individuals especially when the trauma occurred in childhood. The view of the master, the view of self in the construct, the automatic burial of successive traumatic experiences while in survival mode. And when it is that way for a long time, it is not easy to break through.

These experiences and views also draw the boundaries in our

life, or the lack thereof. These views get transferred to God and are not usually immediately changed when we get saved. We often have to work through that prior programming to come to a revelation that *God is not like the earthly people in our life* who tortured us, or lied to us, or waited for irrational and often non-existent errors to inflict pain to keep us in the mentality of helpless slave.

It's one thing to read that statement but an entirely different thing to have it written on your heart.

I can't tell you how many clients I've worked with who discover they are struggling with negative views of God that came from negative earthly experiences many years before. They never even realized those views were there until they were uncovered in counseling. Nevertheless, those hidden views had been guiding their behavior and choices until they were discovered and removed. And, these views had dramatic impact on their relationship with the Lord.

You can take the Israelite out of Egypt but it's difficult to get the Egypt out of the Israelite. You can't remove a slave mentality from people just by walking them out of the physical prison.

God never does anything arbitrarily. He doesn't laugh and taunt His children, saying, "Ha, I've decided to make you wander around just to exert My control over you!"

God used the time in the wilderness to reveal Himself to them: His holiness, His ways, what makes Him happy, sad, or angry, His nature, character, faithfulness, and that He truly loved them. My clients, too, often have to wrestle for some time with the idea that God truly loves them. In healing encounters in the counseling room, many clients find themselves arguing with me in anger as the pain and trauma are released, some weeping and hardly able to bear hearing me say how much God loves them.

So the journey to the Promised Land took time. God didn't take them the short way but the long way (Exodus 13:17). They had to learn that God was merciful, His correction firm but always with a goal to restore relationship. They had to get to know Who God is.

And the putrid darkness of Egypt had to be slowly drained from their identity.

Some couldn't take the switch and wanted to go back to Egypt, to the slavery, to what was familiar and what was firmly implanted in their cellular memory. (Some people find it easier to keep doing what they've been trained to do even when it's killing them, rather than have to break through that mental prison wall.)

God said never go back to Egypt (Jeremiah 42:13-19) but some did (Jeremiah 43:7-12).

I encourage you to read this Exodus story again. As a kid, I often heard this preached in a way that was demeaning to the children of Israel, as if they were stupid and just plain "stubborn". Even though they are at times described as stubborn in scripture, I hope you can see it in a different way now, and that the new view inspires more compassion in your heart. That would be a very good thing because...

We need to understand: We are all the children of Israel in the story, wandering in the desert, rebelling against the very God Who saved us from torment.

There are things that aren't even good for you that you just don't want to give up. An addiction, a behavior, a person, a viewpoint...

We have looked at the Exodus story, we have seen the example of drug addiction being passed to the next generation, we have read some scripture, and we must note that God is faithful to keep His promises to save us.

> "God is not man, that he should lie, or a son of man, that
> he should change his mind. Has he said, and will he not do
> it? Or has he spoken, and will he not fulfill it"
> Numbers 23:19, ESV

As you come face-to-face with the lies about God that you didn't even realize you had believed, walls start to come down.

God's Word is true; we can count on it, and we can count on Him.

Next, let's look at what evidence we can see in the world around us for how behavior and sin are passed on in families.

Curses and legal agreements through your ancestors are a major factor in determining the source of bondage, spiritual oppression, and attack.

Though this has been rejected by many mainstream denominations in recent decades, I can assure you that it is true: generational curses are real. I see it all the time in clients and I saw it in my own life. It does not matter what we think or feel about it, it only matters what is true, what scripture says about it, what God thinks of it, and what He tells us to do about it.

> "There are a lot of anecdotes to suggest that there's intergenerational transfer of risk, and that it's hard to break the cycle[23]," said Kerry Ressler, neurobiologist and psychiatrist at Emory University.

Did that get your attention?

There is a startling study that was published in 2013 on epigenetic inheritance. The study[24],[25], conducted by authors Kerry J. Ressler, and Brian G. Dias, strongly suggests that "genetic imprint from traumatic experiences carries through at least two generations."

An article on the study in *Nature* magazine begins, "Certain fears can be inherited through the generations," and describes how the study showed this to be the case *even when in vitro fertilization was used.*

Some scholars were astonished at the findings, describing it as "the most rigorous and convincing set of studies published to date demonstrating acquired transgenerational epigenetic effects in a laboratory model."

Where else do we see this concept? Scripture. Did you already think of it?

There are four places in scripture[26] where God tells us that the consequences of iniquity can go to the third and fourth generations. The scientific study confirmed that the induced fear response reached to the children and the children's children just like we see described in Exodus 34:7. They plan to do more research to see if it goes beyond that.

So here we have significant support for generational bondage being passed down, first from scripture, then in seeing the fruit of this concept in the people around us, and finally in professional studies at universities.

I believe that DNA is not a static packet of information or instructions, such as lifeless text on a printed page, but more like an interactive computer that both records and reacts to what we think and do and experience in our lives.

With my clients, we discover patterns of bondage through their generations that they hadn't seen before. They don't know they are there until we take the time to look. By the time we are done, the chains are dissolved in the blood of the Lamb.

The Throne Of Your Heart

When we are born, we are born into an infected pool. This universe and the world that floats along in it are all affected by sin. I've had several people argue that children are born perfect, which is absolutely not a Christian tenant. In fact, we are even conceived in sin.

> Behold, I was brought forth in iniquity, And in sin my
> mother conceived me.
> Psalm 51:5

It is a new age concept, along with other religions, that children are both conceived and born in perfection. Scripture makes it clear that is not true.

When you were born, you had the Lord of Darkness on the throne of your heart by default. The only way to remove him from that position is to choose to invite Yeshua to sit on that throne for the rest of your life, by giving your heart and your life to Him.

> *He who believes in Him is not judged; he who does not*
> *believe **has been judged already**, because he has not*
> *believed in the name of the only begotten Son of God.*
> *John 3:18 [emphasis added]*

If you have not done that, you have no protection from the demonic forces that want to destroy you. And, just one of many ways they do that is to seduce you into a relationship with them, a relationship that you can't get out of, or that will hold you until you die, keeping you forever parted from the loving Creator Who gave His Son for you.

Sometimes the best way for the devil to keep you away from Jesus is to pretend to be your friend. In the end, the Devil has no friends. He is only out to cause you torment and pain, whether in this life or the next.

When Jesus sits on the throne of your heart, you have certain authority and protection, *if* you learn what they are and how to use them.

Unforgiveness

Unforgiveness is a very important open door. Therefore, we must reach a point where we are able to forgive even those who have harmed us, even those who have harmed us in unspeakable ways.

I do not say this lightly. My clients have experienced significant trauma in childhood. It takes time and it is a journey to reach the point where we are able to forgive abusers with a level of honesty. We must work with the body the way the body is created by God to function, which means we must deal with all of the emotions and trauma in order to reach the point where forgiveness is even possible.

But when we are obedient, honoring the body the way our Creator intended it to work, being faithful to do what we as believers are instructed to do, and allowing our Savior to lead us on the journey, the miracle of forgiveness begins to spring forth. We will address this topic more fully later.

Even when we think we've forgiven everyone and repented for everything we can think of, there are often layers that the Lord takes us through over time, and we find with counseling that we need to forgive people again, not because forgiveness through our Savior isn't complete, but because revelation and healing are taking place on deeper and deeper levels with increased understanding and awareness from multiple vantage points.

> For if you forgive others for their transgressions, your
> heavenly Father will also forgive you.
> Matthew 6:14

We must forgive all those who have hurt us, in order for us to be forgiven by the Father.

On the psychological and emotional level, unforgiveness hurts no one but ourselves. The offenders go on their way in life and the wounded are left to deal with the mess that was created. Holding on to unforgiveness actually creates a breeding ground for sickness and disease, prevents the fullness of peace and joy in our lives, and makes daily life far less enjoyable. *It also maintains a bond with the offender that must be broken in order to be truly free.*

There is no logical reason for us to hold onto unforgiveness. It is a bondage that the enemy uses to keep the Holy Spirit's power in our lives set on Low.

Unbroken Soul Ties

There are many types of soul ties. I've never worked with a client who didn't need to break soul ties of relationships that were sexual in some form. But these bonds can also occur in ways you might not have thought of, from relationships that were inappropriate in a variety of ways.

I've had multiple female clients who had a childhood friend who was also female, where they held that friend in too high esteem. It was almost as if they worshiped the friend, looked to them for all the answers, kept them on a pedestal, thought the sun rose and set around them. There are multiple ways this can occur, but it is rather common.

Did you have a friend that you idolized? Or was it an older person, such as when a young boy is allowed by his parents to idolize a professional athlete? Maybe you ran around with the wrong crowd in high school and participated in activities that were not godly and made oaths to keep the events secret.

These can be open doors to all kinds of bondage.

When it comes to sex, our biblical instructions say we are not allowed to have that kind of activity with anyone but our spouse.

In fact, I have become increasingly convinced that there is something very supernatural about sex that we don't understand. It is only supposed to happen with someone we marry before the Lord in a solemn commitment. This may be why everything the dark side does involves perversion of sex. When you engage in sexual activity, not just intercourse, with someone who is not your spouse, you can open the door to all kinds of demonic attachment and oppression.

Rituals performed by covens involve sex, Satanists use sex in ritual magik, and religions of the east use sex ceremonially or encourage an unleashing of every sexual thought or desire.

Interestingly, there have been studies that seem to support the theory that women may carry the DNA from every sexual partner they've been with[27],[28], [29], and may even have this DNA present in their children.

All kinds of bondage begin to break when we go through the list of possible soul ties and dissolve all of those connections in the blood of the Lamb.

Disobedience

Here is an interesting interpretation of James 2:26.

> *For just as a human body without a spirit is lifeless, so also faith is lifeless if it is unaccompanied by obedience. WNT*

When God has given us the instructions and we will not utilize them, we walk in disobedience in a refusal to completely yield to the Holy Spirit, the Word of God, and His perfect work in us.

> *Behold, to obey is better than sacrifice.*
> *1 Samuel 15:22*

If we are walking in disobedience, that can be a huge open door to demonic bondage, oppression, or attack.

> *And this is love: that we walk in obedience to His commands.*
> *2 John 1:6, NIV*

Occult Activities

If you willingly participated in any of the following, you have opened yourself up to the dark side in a big way:

- Occult activity
- Tarot cards
- Ouija boards
- Wiccan coven meetings, rituals, or ceremonies
- Charlie Charlie
- Mirror chanting
- Voodoo dolls
- Spell casting
- Drinking of blood
- Blood covenants and oaths (very commonly done by children with their best friends)
- Re-enacting scenes from occult ceremonies, horror movies, or music videos
- Glorifying death and horror (e.g. people who enjoy dressing up in bloody, zombie costumes and acting like a possessed corpse)

This is just a very short list of some familiar things and activities that glorify the work of the dark side, align with their methods and models, call upon them, and can open a door that may be difficult to shut. All occult activity is very dangerous but the more you have done, the more open doors there may be.

Music & Music Videos

Music videos and live performances over the past decade have become blatant propaganda for the dark side. They are now completely saturated, very openly, with occult symbols, rituals, and lyrics. Some of the songs that have reached the top of the charts contained lyrics that *literally asked for possession*, such as Katie Perry's 2011 *Futuristic Lover / E.T.* song.

That was 2011.

L.A. Marzulli has used this song as a demonstration in conference presentations. Kids in church sang this song and knew every word by heart. It is an invitation to the forces of darkness and the demonic deceivers don't care whether those church kids meant it that way or not: if that's what they said, they gave them permission. And worse, they chanted it over and over again every time they sang it. Chanting is used in many occult rituals and New Age practice to alter consciousness or summon demons.

And, even with basic psychology we understand that when you continue to repeat something over and over it drives it deeper and deeper into your core self.

Our Lord tells us to stay in worship of Him. It is more than just ticking the box of obedience. When we engage in true worship we stay connected to Him, and we are thinking, experiencing, and speaking out through singing, godly truths. Worship as God has planned for us is more than musical entertainment: it is a very powerful supernatural tool in our toolbelts that repels any forces of darkness that may be around you!

Do you see why the dark side would want to use the music industry? They get you to invite them in: repeatedly.

Does this fact make you uncomfortable?

In 2013, Kanye West released his 6th album, *Yeezus*, with the obvious play on the name Jesus. One track on that project is *I Am A God*. Lil'Wayne had a hit song titled, *Demon*. There are myriad examples.

We have been exposed to full-blown occult ritual on Super Bowl half-time shows and on the Grammy Awards by many artists such as Katie Perry and Madonna. Taylor Swift didn't want to be left behind so she played her part at the 2018 AMAs in an occult ritual singing her song, *They say I did something bad, then why's it feel so good?*

It is clear that the U.S. is now well into a Post-Christian culture. As never before, U.S. culture is literally sinking under occult influence and recruitment. Children are now exposed to these things in early elementary school and since the church has stopped teaching spiritual warfare, the church is both largely ignorant of the danger signs or how to protect against it, and they no longer even have a discerning sense of when intervention is necessary. We passed the danger zone a long time ago; the church is still silent.

Electronic Media

Television, computers, cell phones, tablets. Though many people try to dispute this (often the same people in the church who don't believe the demonic can touch a Christian and don't believe in spiritual warfare), dark forces are very active in electronic delivery systems. They love having a system that spreads their extensive menu of abomination at the touch of a button, or in some cases, it plays against our will when ads pop up on our computers while doing research on the internet, it's on the speaker systems in department stores and restaurants, or on the televisions in an electronics store.

When a movie that is all about the occult and training youth in the dark art of witchcraft, such as *Harry Potter*, is played on the big television screens across America, there is not only the obvious training aspect that is problematic, but *there is a spirit behind these things*.

In the music industry it has become widely known that groups pray and do rituals over their music and albums both throughout the recording process and before album releases. Thirty years ago this information was still largely unknown and behind closed doors. Today, the veil has been removed and the demonic forces are no longer hiding. They turned the lights out across the country as churches grew more and more drowsy under the magic spells being cast, both without and within their doors.

I think back to just five years ago and I'm stunned at how blatantly the demonic is now celebrated, preached, and demanded in all of modern media. We have lived to see mind-numbing destruction at lightning speed as if we went off a cliff's edge and are in free fall to a dark and jagged canyon floor below.

If the church in America over the past 50 years had grown stronger rather than weaker, equipping believers with the tools needed for the power of God to be active in their lives, this spiritual assault would not have been so thorough and rapid. A strong, spiritually equipped church would have been watchful, and aware, and organized appropriate responses to these attacks.

Charged Objects

In spite of the eye rolling you may receive when you try to explain this to someone in an average church, there absolutely can be power in an object.

How do we know this?

In the book of Acts, we see this extraordinary story regarding Paul.

*God was performing extraordinary miracles by the hands
of Paul, so that handkerchiefs or aprons were even carried
from his body to the sick, and the diseases left them and
the evil spirits went out.*
Acts 19:11-12

Because of the fact that the occult imitates and perverts God's structure and methods, this is one of the long list of imitations they use: supernaturally-charged objects.

Charged objects can be in nearly any form: a bookmark, voodoo dolls, a piece of cloth. Many things can be charged with supernatural power and the holy spirit works in and through us to alert us to these attacks if we are educated and in close communication with our God.

The Paranormal, Hauntings & Poltergeist Activity

How do we deal with paranormal phenomena that is outside of the definitions of science?

In spite of the dizzying popularity of ghost hunting programs and ghost tours in cities across the country, the church remains silent. If you bring up the subjects of hauntings or poltergeist activity you may be rebuked, or told those things don't exist, or mocked as an unbeliever because "those things can't happen to Christians." If you dared to bring it up you may have felt like you were put on a "watch list" to be more carefully observed by church staff.

I've had multiple clients who had full blown poltergeist activity in their homes for years and were unable to find help.

One client had cabinet doors that would open and shut on their own, and very out of place and unaccounted for noises that terrified her dog. Other clients were physically attacked at night in their beds.

Here's a story from a client that might give you insight into this phenomena.

Chris, a mature believer who worked in ministry for many years, had experienced significant trouble in his home. We took care of the house in general and then the land it sat on. We paid close attention the next few weeks to see how it was going and to be sure we hadn't missed anything.

One day after Chris returned home from work, he was unable to find his family dog who normally greeted him as he came through the door. As he walked through the house calling for him, he finally found him shaking in fear and seemingly traumatized under the bed in a room that had been a problem in the past, a room had belonged to one of his daughters when she was little. The dog was so upset that Chris had trouble getting him to come out from his hiding place. All of this was extremely unusual behavior.

He contacted me, we went into prayer, and with some intense binding and rebuking we evicted the dark side squatter that the Holy Spirit had exposed. As always, we had multiple confirmations from the Lord as we did the work and the eviction was complete, much to his now adult daughter's relief.

A few days later, he shared a dream he'd had that was totally demonic and we then felt something in another room that had been there off and on. As we were praying I heard a growl. We cleansed the room with some significant sword clanging and it has been fine ever since.

The next morning as he shared the story with his close friend and prayer partner Kevin, his friend then told him about something he had experienced there just days before.

Kevin had been helping with a repair in that second room I just described. He was working alone in the room. It was hot in the house, enough that he was sweating. Suddenly he felt a very large, dark presence and then heard a growl. Kevin said something resembling, "I'm not afraid of you," and then the room went very icy cold, the kind of cold that penetrates to the bone. He finished his work and never said anything to Chris. The next day he got very sick and ended up in the hospital for three days. It never occurred to him, however, that there could be a connection between the encounter and the illness.

Telling a demonic presence that you aren't afraid of it does nothing; it does not bind it, or cast it out, or remove its power, or prevent it from calling for assistance from other dark soldiers. As believers, we are required to use our authority over it.

If a thief broke into your home as your children slept in the next room, would you say, "I'm not afraid of you," and simply go back to sleep or whatever you were doing? Of course not! You must capture then remove the intruder.

Don't waste words with these beings. Get down to business with great specificity. I've included later in the book prayers that are very specific. We will talk more about that.

There are always dark force minions skulking about who want to steal, kill or destroy.

We have a manual and method that work. The instructions matter, the words and attitude matter. But, Kevin did not know about spiritual warfare in the way we're talking about here. He thought resisting fear and having confidence was enough, but that's just one component of spiritual warfare.

This was the first Chris had heard of the encounter, but it confirmed yet again what we had experienced as we evicted it. God always confirms. We both had felt it was very large, very dark, and we both had heard a loud growl. It put up a fight for a bit but it had no choice; in the end it was sent packing.

After this revelation from his friend Kevin, Chris shared with me that he was upset this occurred in his daughter's room. He told me how they had prayed together when she was little but that he had no understanding back then of what he has since learned.

As just a little girl of six, she had felt something in that room but it was never resolved. She had to live with that for years as she grew up. What was the impact of all that? Nearly constant fear, anxiety, and lack of rest because she didn't feel safe. It also caused her to question her faith because she and her father had prayed but the evil in the room did not leave. Her views of God were brought into question as well, laying the foundation for doubt and fear.

As of today, I'm told the rooms still feel completely different and peaceful.

One more story about these phenomena.

Long before I knew her, a dear friend endured chemotherapy treatment for cancer. She has a loving husband and two children who were very small at the time.

She kept hearing footsteps walking up and down the hallway. She prayed about it but was focused on her treatment. Praise God, she survived her battle with cancer. Later, she was talking with the couple who used to own her house; they had become friends after the transaction. She asked them if they had ever heard anything and they said, yes, they heard walking up and down the hallway all the time. When she inquired further, she found out that the house had been in the prior owners' family for generations, and that two of their family members died in that house from cancer.

There were spirits of death and cancer in that house before she and her family ever moved there.

See, we don't know what has been somewhere before we arrive. We don't know what strongholds have long been in place, what ancient occult rituals were done on the land. We don't know what spiritual darkness is present in a house or was placed in an object to cause illness or suffering.

The Holy Spirit, however, does know! If we will learn these skills given to us by our loving Father Who desires to help us through this life in a fallen world, so much of this can be avoided.

If you don't know how to bind and rebuke these things, there can be effects. We all need to know how to use the weapons the Lord gave us!

Targeted Attack

We have the testimonies of multiple kingdom warriors, such as John Ramirez[30] or Bill Schnoebelen[31] who were saved out of the dark arts, revealing to a sleeping church that there are gangs of coven members or other occult groups that walk through Christian neighborhoods or businesses, sit in church services, serve on church staff, work in the church office, and teach Sunday school as they cast spells, send curses and demonic assignments, and plant charged objects. They cozy up to pastors and their wives spewing flattery, offering assistance, and giving gifts that have been charged with dark supernatural power.

If the believers are lacking in mature discernment, uneducated in spiritual warfare, ignorant of these types of attacks and how to defend against them, the supernatural charge can be devastating. They can take the form of sudden outbursts of division in the church congregation, repeated calamities siphoning church funds, or a seemingly never-ending line of sicknesses befalling a family.

In fact, L.A. Marzulli has shared this story.

A demonically inspired dissident was compelled to uncloak during a conference presentation. They prayed over the person in the lobby then L.A. got very ill.

Even trained soldiers such as L.A. can experience retribution attack. We must be skilled with our God-given weapons.

The Enemy Is Intentional

John Ramirez[32] has a ministry educating believers on spiritual warfare, sharing his knowledge and experience from his time as a high-level Satanist.

He has described how workers of evil can sense the weak Christians from the strong *and they respond accordingly.*

Have you ever heard of a church doing a prayer walk to take back the territory from the enemy forces? That is an intentional plan of Kingdom work. Well, the dark side does the same thing in reverse.

Imagine a TV show about a gang of terrorists bent on causing harm. They stalk you to find your patterns of travel, gather all the intel they can about your fears and weaknesses, then lurking behind a carefully chosen corner they spring to attack in wicked unison as you casually walk by, throwing a hood over your head, binding your arms behind you, and tossing you in a dark van that peels off in the night. This is the kind of attack that the demonic and dark powers execute. The Bible tells us they stalk prey like a lion stalking its dinner (1 Peter 5:8).

We have effective weapons to defend against this activity but if you think you don't have to do anything for your protection or fight any battles, you are totally vulnerable and without defense. The enemy is very intentional. You must be intentional too.

Where's The Hope?

The hope is in the truth of scripture! In the person of the Living God! Never forget this: *truth is not a concept; it is a person.* Yeshua IS the truth.

Hope is also found in the testimonies of those who have been set free, those who are able to proclaim the works of El Elyon as demonstrated by the fruit born of the work, by the believers who have been forever changed.

God is exactly Who He says He is.

The Bible comprises the words of God spoken to us and it is reliable!

> *For the word of God is living and active and sharper than any two-edged sword, and piercing as far as the division of soul and spirit, of both joints and marrow, and able to judge the thoughts and intentions of the heart.*
> *Hebrews 4:12*
>
> *Jesus said to him, "I am the way, and the truth, and the life; no one comes to the Father but through Me."*
> *John 14:6*

There is also hope to be found in the testimonies of all those who have gone before you and come out the other end of the tunnel feeling freedom, often for the first time in their lives.

The end result is freedom! The fruit we see from those who do the work to get free is astonishing. It is this fruit that we need to see as one of the proofs of our faith. It not only keeps our faith strong, seeing our Father and King defeat the workers of iniquity every time, it is also one of the evidences that gets unbelievers' attention.

Just as it was in Jesus' day, so it is in our time. His miracle power is one of the ways He shows us that He is alive and the only King of Kings!

> *If the Son sets you free, you will be free indeed.*
> *John 8:36, NIV*

Roots Of Warfare

Dr. Michael Lake emphasizes how important it is to understand and interpret scripture in the light of its Hebrew culture and language.

"We do ourselves a disservice if we don't take the time to properly understand the culture in which the Word of God has been written. It wasn't written in a vacuum. It wasn't written up here somewhere in Detroit or the foothills of Tennessee. It was written among the sons of Abraham, the Hebrews."[33]

A lot is hidden in the original Hebrew, hidden in the sense that those of us who aren't fluent are unable to see the many layers of communication inherent in the language, due in part to the ancient pictographic script.

When we eliminate sections, books, or verses of the Bible, we are already disobeying God when He told us to not change a word and when He said that all of scripture is Life to those who follow it.

So, first, we must determine to take all of scripture.

When we eliminate the original Hebrew roots of the Christian faith, approaching scripture from an exclusively Greek or Roman view, we are twisting it, setting aside so much that gives the solid context on which we must form our theology.

If we are to understand spiritual warfare, indeed every biblical topic, we must place it in its proper cultural and linguistic context.

As I propose in this book, spiritual warfare is intimately intertwined with our very relationship with our Abba. So, our very relationship with God is on the table here as we more clearly define and understand spiritual warfare.

God is at war with the forces of darkness. The heavenly angels are in battle with the fallen angels. There are demonic entities and principalities on the roster. And we are told about these powers, what they are like, and what they think of humans.

Where did this start?

For us, it began with the Fall of Man in the Garden.

In Genesis 3 we read about how the serpent deceived Adam and Eve, which caused them to doubt their Father.

Elohim gave them life, placed them in paradise, brought the animals to Adam so he could name them, created a partner for Adam by forming Eve. They walked together with their Creator through the beautiful garden. They had a relationship with Him.

It seems this being, the Nachash, started the conversation and he started it with a twisting lie. We have no indication that Adam or Eve were frightened of this creature. The Nachash disparaged their loving Father Creator yet they presented no defense of Him.

The Nachash spoke, saying, "Did God actually say, 'You shall not eat of any tree in the garden?'"

This reminds me of an evil lawyer. Technically, the statement is true, but it is not true in spirit. In cross examination the attorney may say, "Did your mean mom say you could not have cookies?"

Well, technically, yes, but in spirit, no. What mom said was there was only one type of cookies you couldn't eat because they were for the company coming over later after dinner. She did not say you couldn't have any cookies, just not the box of cookies reserved for the guests. Mom was actually generous allowing you to have cookies while providing for guests as well.

Eve replies, "From the fruit of the trees of the garden we may eat; but from the fruit of the tree which is in the middle of the garden, God has said, 'You shall not eat from it or touch it, or you will die.'"

They have the pick of the entire garden, there's only one tree they were told not to eat from.

Then the hammer falls, "**You surely will not die!** For God knows that in the day you eat from it your eyes will be opened, and **you will be like God**, knowing good and evil."

The blatant lie, in complete contradiction of what the Father said. "You shall not die!" The offer of knowledge, of eyes being opened to something they can't see in their current state, and the famous line, "you will be like God."

Insert the doubt. Is God withholding good for Himself and keeping it from us? The relationship killers of jealousy, control, insecurity, and questioning the very foundation of the relationship were set loose.

The relationship.

There is no record that they even defended Elohim. After everything He did for them, they didn't have anything to say, not even, "He wouldn't lie to us. He has given us everything we need and want."

They just looked at the tree, looked at the fruit, then dove into the pool of disobedience and betrayal.

That must have broken Elohim's heart. Utter, undeserved betrayal.

Here is the bottom line. God gave us everything and we chose to betray the Lover of our Souls. We all did it.

But, God did not lie.

That original betrayal set off a reverberation throughout the entirety of creation. Death, Mayhem and Suffering screeched with victory as they were unleashed.

Our King and Creator is the loving Bridegroom, the one who peers through the lattice just to get a glimpse of His beloved. His heart skips a beat when He looks upon your face. He has written your name on the palm of His hand, like a schoolgirl with her first crush. He rejoices over you with dancing and singing.

They betrayed Him. We betrayed Him.

This whole thing is about relationship. And, the serpent hates us. He is jealous, tormented, the father of lies, desires to see us suffer, and never tires of inflicting utter devastation on us.

This was the beginning of the seed war; now it is nearing the crescendo. The Lion of the Tribe of Judah is about to return. The enemy knows his time is short. The dark forces are increasing in their use of power and assets.

Understanding The Problem

How Did We Get Here?

Original sin in the Garden sent a reverberation through all of creation that is still being felt today. But now the End Times prophecies are taking shape right before our eyes. With that fact in view, it is not a surprise that evil is increasing, and the potency of the dark ones will grow until our Lord and King puts an ultimate stop to it.

The demonic is being glorified in every sector of our culture.

In his new book *Game of Gods,* author and researcher Carl Teichrib[34] lays out the history of occult infiltration into American culture. He was interviewed by L.A. Marzulli on the release of the new book.

To the question of why he does his work of examining the occult and the cultural devolution toward darkness, Carl had this response.

> "Number one, to help the Christian community wake up and understand the context of the changes we see all around us all the time. We are in the midst of all kinds of social confusion, chaos, everything is up for grabs. Where did this come from? How did we get here? It is observable, traceable, understandable.

> "Are we willing to take the time to do it? Are we willing to be ambassadors for Christ? To be an ambassador for Christ means we understand the culture well enough that we can present the message of truth into that culture.

> "The Apostle Paul talks about us being ambassadors.

> Not a lot of people grasp what that means. To be an
> ambassador means you are the legal, official, lawful
> representative of your King, literally the King of Kings,
> regarding us as Christians. In that case, you need to
> know the King's position; that requires knowing God's
> Word. But an ambassador also studies the culture too, so
> you can effectively communicate the King's message into
> a culture that may be benign, or it may be hostile, and in
> our case, growing more hostile, it seems, all the time."

We once had a degree of covering by the hand of God as described in His Word. That covering comes from obedience by large numbers of people who are committed believers. This is how a nation can be blessed, just as a family home can be blessed with that covering when all are walking in holiness with the God of Abraham, Isaac and Jacob.

Due to an easily chartable decline over the last 50 years in the number of Americans who profess belief in Yeshua Jesus, and congruent with that, churches forsaking the very definition of Christianity, that covering has grown very thin. It grows thin because of sin.

> *Blessed is the nation whose God is the Lord.*
> *Psalm 33:12*

With the shocking but necessary undercover reporting by Center for Medical Progress[35] over the past two years which captured on video abortion doctors and clinic workers laughing and even playing with the remains of infants ripped from their mother's wombs, the American public no longer has ignorance as an excuse.

Whether the public ever accepts this truth or not, abortion is human sacrifice and it empowers the beings of darkness. That spilled innocent blood cries out to God and His anger grows.

With this mind-scarring revelation, there has been increasing exposure of the horrific nature of the abortion industry, selling baby body parts which is fully illegal though it goes unpunished, and its connections to global networks of Satanic cults.

As the dark, fetid curtain has been pulled back revealing the most repugnant iniquities in our national fabric, and the American public continues to be apathetic, it has taken the consequences to a higher level on God's chart.

> *Therefore, to one who knows the right thing to do and does*
> *not do it, to him it is sin.*
> James 4:17

Whatever covering that remained is being sucked away by the vacuum left by sin, apathy, and inaction.

Whenever believers see dark forces and sin approaching, we are required to sound the alarm and to halt the progress. The gates of the city have fallen off their hinges, the walls are crumbling. The people are no longer safe, the culture cannot survive. The enemy has been circling for a very long time, salivating for the prize of the destruction of the United States as the last speed bump on the road to the one world government. With that final global unity in place, the suffering and torment will increase, and they know it. They are very near their last crescendo before Yeshua swoops in on His white horse at the appointed time.

Sin rushes in like a flood when the people of God stop praying, walking in holiness, or are removed.

So, there is cultural pressure on every side as the individual battle of obedience continues. Christians in the U.S. are experiencing targeted persecution more every day. We are in a cultural death spiral.

This calls to the dark forces. They have worked for this for a long time. They are constantly pushing, pulling, seducing, and inspiring a public who has lost the protection of being in a largely Christian culture. Without that protection and favor which, despite our deficiencies, we receive at the hand of a loving Father, we will be overtaken by sin and destruction.

The good news, however, is that the first Christians were in that same situation and we can learn from their experiences. We have been given the tools for the work. If we will step up and use them, we will see that it not only changes our own lives for the better, it changes our neighborhoods, regions, and nation.

Why Can't I Make It Stop?

I hear this question all the time. Let me describe it this way.

We have what is referred to as a spirit-man inside us, who we are in Christ. That spirit-man has, in a very real sense, been beaten down by our own choices and by a marauding group of spiritual thugs. They wait, they plan, they use mental torture, and they are relentless. They will even leave to come back at a more opportune time. Remember when Jesus was tempted by the Devil?

> *When the devil had finished every temptation, he left Him*
> *until an opportune time.*
> Luke 4:13

This implies that Jesus may have endured further attacks of temptation. If He experienced these attacks, we will also. And, since He was the only perfect human to ever walk the earth, it wasn't because He wasn't good enough.

If you have been unable to make the attacks stop there is an open door somewhere, and usually there are multiple open doors; you may just not realize it. The dark forces must have permission to enter; they must be given authority and that either came from you or those in authority over you.

We've talked about where bondage comes from. You'll need to prayerfully go through all those things looking for any connection. Your mission is to find out where the dark forces were given authority over you and what those open doors are connected to.

What Is Your Culture?

African, Irish, South American, Russian, Asian. All cultures worshipped other gods in the past, and still do today. People purchase artifacts or reproductions of ancient statues or ritual objects thinking they're just "honoring" their roots and don't seem to understand what they are doing when they bring these cultural objects into their homes. Too often, they use these objects to express an identity they want to brand themselves with; this is powerful intent and alignment.

Later you will learn about the significance of intent and aligning yourself with something. If you surround yourself with cultural objects you could be bringing the demonic into your home.

> *About that time there occurred no small disturbance concerning the Way. For a man named Demetrius, a silversmith, who made silver shrines of Artemis, was bringing no little business to the craftsmen; these he gathered together with the workmen of similar trades, and said, "Men, you know that our prosperity depends upon this business. You see and hear that not only in Ephesus, but in almost all of Asia, this Paul has persuaded and turned away a considerable number of people, saying that gods made with hands are no gods at all. Not only is there danger that this trade of ours fall into disrepute, but also that the temple of the great goddess Artemis be regarded as worthless and that she whom all of Asia and the world worship will even be dethroned from her magnificence."*
> *Acts 19:23-27*

The first Christians had a culture; a very strong Jewish culture. Later, the Romans and Greeks. They all had to make adjustments to their lives, practices, and beliefs. They had to let go of and remove things they had done all their lives! They had relatives who were enraged with them, who taunted them for forsaking their "culture".

We have been cut off from the former vine and have been grafted into the family of Yeshua (Romans 11:17-24). Just like Lot and his family, we must leave these things behind and not long for them by looking backward. Lot's wife paid the ultimate price: the Lord sent personal angel escorts to deliver her family, but she disobeyed Him by looking back.

How can we taste of the Lord's goodness and mercy, then long for the profane?

Today, fires of cultural loyalty are stoked by mind control, exercised through every form of social media and broadcast media in part to cause division, but also because as believers we are always under assault by the forces of darkness who hunger to see us suffer and fall.

Division is not of the Lord. As the body of Yeshua we should be living in unity, of one mind and one spirit.

"One of his biggest weapons is division. Unity brings chaos into the Devil's kingdom," says saved and redeemed former Satanist, John Ramirez.

Our culture is to be of Christ! We are called to abandon all the rituals of men. Our identity it to be found in Him.

I have had friends and family, for example, who surround themselves with everything Irish or all things African: statues, symbols, fabrics, songs, all of which can be steeped in demonic power.

Many years ago, as a lover of ancient history, I had many statues, hand painted artwork, and music from cultures around the world including Egypt. At one time, I had been among those who thought all this warfare stuff related to historical objects was nonsense. Oh, how wrong I was!

When I see clients begin to realize they are rejecting Christ when they refuse to find their identity in Him, everything changes. He is your Creator! He is your Savior who bought you back from the clutches of darkness and torment! We are to surround ourselves with things about Him, that remind us of Him, voices that sing of Him, instruments that praise Him, that declare His mercy, goodness, and glory!

Technology

Technology is everywhere. 5G is rolling out to make possible the next level of the Internet of Things. And, because spiritual power can be placed in an object, high tech becomes a vehicle for dark forces.

Darkness desires to inhabit things, and more and more gadgets such as Virtual Reality and the internet are tools to use against us, seducing us with role-playing games, luring our eyes to view images we should never see, provoking curiosity into dark practices, such as witchcraft.

Due to my calling and background, I am sensitive to things connected to darkness. I guard my eyes and mind vigilantly.

Once, I was working on my computer doing research. I opened a Christian ministry video on YouTube not knowing they had included some very demonic images. I immediately felt the energy trying to come through the connection, using my eye-gate, intent, and attention.

Praise God, I knew what to do. I instantly looked away, put my hand to block it and said out loud, "No! You are not allowed here. You will get back from me in the Name of Yeshua!"

I stopped the video and prayed for a few minutes to make sure I caught everything that wanted to rush in.

I have heard similar stories from others. Guard very carefully your mind, eyes, ears, and intent. Don't allow yourself to zone out, looking and listening to things on the internet.

We have tools to stay safe. But the enemy is always looking for a way in.

Scarlet Letter Syndrome

For those who had a background that included:

- occult ceremony or practices performed over them as an infant;
- occult ceremony or practices performed over their conception;
- generational dedication from cult and occult groups such as Freemasons;
- seeking out and participating in occult ceremony, practices, dark arts, satanism, or full blown luciferianism;

There seems to be a sort of mark that can be difficult to shake. They don't like runners.

I've heard this many times. A great example of this is the powerful testimony of L.A. Marzulli.

For the first time ever, he published his testimony in his book, The *Cosmic Chess Match*. He had been drawn to the mystical and Eastern religions, followed gurus, and had his third eye opened. When he got saved, he went through a difficult time breaking the chains of occult bondage.

I have seen this too. When you've had this kind of background, it is a fight to break free from the oppression. Then, you may have heightened sensitivity to dark things for the rest of your life.

We all should set boundaries against things of the darkness, but this kind of sensitivity may be slightly more than others without this background.

This makes sense since according to scripture, God marks his own (Ezekiel 9:4; Revelation 7:3) And, the Mark of the Beast imitates God's design by marking the devil's own. In Revelation 14:9-10, those that get the Mark of the Beast are sent to eternal damnation.

How Big Is The Problem?

In our age, with the aid of technology, ministries have been documenting the spiritual enemies of our God for decades. One of the researchers in this ministry area whom I respect the most is Russ Dizdar. His ministry, Shatter The Darkness[36], has been tracking and researching both the underground occult and satanic ritual abuse (SRA), plus rescuing children from the clutches of the practitioners of SRA for nearly 40 years. I highly recommend his study materials provided free of charge on his website: shatterthedarkness.net. His heart is to educate on the subject, to equip believers for the spiritual war that is underway, and to inspire others to get involved. I am inspired in that way as well and I can't think of anyone better to include in this section than Russ.

If all of this is completely new to you, I suggest you do some homework to gain an understanding of the scope of the occult influence in our culture, media and entertainment, SRA, and the links to governments, royalty, and the ultra-elite. It is far too great a subject to tackle here. You need to know that we are absolutely under assault by a dark power that is opposed to our God and all who serve Him. Some materials I can recommend are noted in the Resources section. It is vital to get educated on what is really going on to even begin to grasp the scope of the problem.

In chapter one of his ground-breaking 1997 book, *Uncovering the Mystery of MPD*[37], licensed psychologist Dr. James Friesen described his first spiritual battle.

> The door was closed. That was not particularly unusual, but as I knocked on the door and was invited in, a strange feeling came over me. A few students sat around a small metal typing table. Their hands rested lightly on its top and their little fingers overlapped to form an unbroken ring of human contact. "What's going on?" I asked.
>
> The reply: "A seance."
>
> I did not know how seances were carried out, so I just went over to the other side of the room and quietly watched as the students continued. In subdued voices they were asking questions of a spirit. The table would tip to one side for yes, and to the other for no.
>
> To spell out a word, it would tip once for A, twice for B, and so on to twenty-six times for Z. The table was spelling out a sentence when I came in. The participants, fascinated and totally involved, hardly noticed my entry. I was not surprised at what I saw. Without any direct human help, the table tipped from side to side – and the

students were in contact with the spirit world. It was right there. I could not help but believe what I was seeing.

After about twenty minutes I realized this was more to these students than just a novel way to spend the afternoon. They were discovering. They were in contact with a spirit who had spelled out its name as "Hoz," and who claimed to have been a court magician from the Middle Ages. Spinning out its story in answer to the students' questions, the spirit drew them deeper and deeper into the mysteries of Hoz's life and death. The seance had begun about a half hour before I came into the room, and I began to marvel at the whole experience. "Hoz" had told how he died and who the king was that he worked for, and he had given a lot of incidental information about life during the Middle Ages. Those sitting at the table would never forget that day.

I had been taught the Bible throughout my childhood. My mother would read to me for hours from a Bible story book, and I had been a Christian for several years. I knew the accounts of Jesus casting out evil spirits in the New Testament and had heard missionaries from third world countries tell how they, in the name of Jesus, had cast out evil spirits. It occurred to me that I had such an entity in front of me. I found myself with a chance to discover if using the name of Jesus really would expel an evil spirit.

Thinking things through, however, I ran into a dilemma. If I spoke the words out loud, "In the name of Jesus I command you to leave," the students could take their hands away from the table, or somebody could hold the table down to prevent any tipping. I might not know if the name of Jesus could be used effectively. So, I decided to just think the command.

I directed my gaze toward the table and thought the instruction: Hoz, in the name of Jesus I command you to leave! The students had no idea that I had just cast Hoz

> out. The table was in the middle of spelling out a word, and at the very second I finished my thought-command, it stopped. The students kept their hands as they were and tried to figure out why the contact had been broken, but they could come up with nothing. The table would not move, period. They backed off from it and glanced back and forth at each other, shocked and puzzled.
>
> I told them what I had done. They expressed irritation with me and tried to start the seance again, but they could not conjure up Hoz or any other spirit. That was the end of the seance – and the power of Jesus' name had been demonstrated to me.

This powerful opening to his book describes an all too common scene in colleges and universities around the country. And, just the thought of a proper rebuke by a strong believer shut the dark spirit down! There's more to his story that you'll see in a minute.

In a recent interview on a nationally syndicated program, I mentioned a similar experience.

"You say, well, I've never practiced witchcraft. Okay. Did you ever play with Tarot cards? When you were eleven years old and you went to a sleep-over at your cousin's house, did someone pull out a Ouija board? Because most of the people I talk to have had experiences like that."[38]

A YouTube listener commented: "That Ouija board story is exactly what happened to me in middle school! It brought that hidden memory when she said it! I had totally forgotten about it!!!"

Now, back to Dr. Friesen's story. He tells us that the "innocuous" table-tipping was leading to great peril for those involved. The story spread like a California wildfire across the campus within hours and everyone was discussing what was going on.

> "Two nights later the situation had gotten so intense that at one o'clock in the morning a collection of doubters and

'experienced mediums' decided to stage a seance right in the middle of the student hall!"

He estimates that thirty to fifty students attended this witching hour seance.

> "When I came in, the table was tipping out an answer and one doubting student was on his knees, trying to figure out just how those charlatans were tricking everyone into believing that a spirit really was moving the table. He found no evidence. This was no human trick. The table was being moved by an unseen force, and there was every reason to believe it was indeed a spirit.

> "Various students would ask questions from where they were, and the table would answer. It became a forum for asking all kinds of questions about religion, philosophy and science. One very intelligent student asked the table this question. Did we really need to rely on Jesus?

> "Everyone's attention was riveted to the table. Those sitting at the table kept their hands lightly poised, waiting for the answer, which was slow in coming. Then the table started to tip, very slowly, toward the yes side. It continued to tip more and more – until it fell to the floor!"

Did you notice in this story that twice the demonic presence that was masquerading as Hoz had to obey at the name of Jesus? Yet the students got annoyed at the Christians and wanted to get back to interaction with a dark entity! Clearly, the students were either not interested in or unable to perceive logic at the time.

A mind using logic, the same type of logic required of a student in any science lab, would have observed that 1) there clearly was a dark supernatural force interacting with the students, and 2) the Name of Jesus caused the other entity to submit instantly. That should have absolutely astonished the entire group.

I want to make sure you catch that. There is a mesmerizing effect, a seduction that seems to take place. Hearts longing to be filled by the Holy Spirit seem to soak this supernatural energy up like a sponge, not realizing it's like drinking anti-freeze: it may taste sweet, but it will kill you. Colleges are full of occult influence. But behind the Hogwarts parties, Wiccan coven groups, and every séance in the student hall is the Lord of Darkness himself. Our culture at large is literally drowning in the occult. And our children are lost because we have failed to set limits and stop it.

Headlines have announced statues of Baphomet being erected outside halls of justice and the Arch of Ba'al being reconstructed on government lawns. Still, many Americans don't seem to understand there is real power behind these things; it's not just a statue or an ancient ruin.

These dark forces are all around us. And, unfortunately, their power is only growing, as interest in them continues to increase.

This is a very big problem. And, the church has not escaped the assault.

Infiltration Into The Church

Angel boards; reincarnation; Christian yoga; New Age beliefs and concepts; celebration of occult holy days such as Halloween including reenactments of Michael Jackson's *Thriller* on the church platform; communicating with angels; merging of Christianity and Islam in what is termed Chrislam; and the acceptance of those who claim to be Christian witches. Our ancestors would not recognize the modern American Christian church.

You can rationalize these choices if you believe that Christianity is just one world view among many. You cannot justify these choices if you understand that Christianity is true, that the Word of God is Truth, that when It describes supernatural power and gives us instructions to test the spirits, it is real and necessary.

Steven Bancarz is a former New Age apostle who has been redeemed. His ministry, Reasons for Jesus[39], is a great resource for reasoned evidence for faith in the Jesus of the Bible.

"Satan masquerades as an angel of light, and it's one of his favorite forms to take," said Bancarz[40] in a recent interview with David Heavener.

His new book written with co-author Josh Peck, *The Second Coming of the New Age*[41], exposes the hidden dangers of alternative spirituality in contemporary America and its churches. This is a much bigger problem than you think. The church is being consumed from within.

We're certainly seeing that deception and a failure to test the spirits in the large and mega churches today, allows for alternative spirituality manifestations, such as Kundalini spirit type convulsions, behavior that is indistinguishable from that demonstrated by worshippers in Santeria and African-based voodoo religions. It is shocking that this example of oppression or possession by dark spirits masquerading as beings of light has become common place. So, too, has the practice of talking with angels, which Bancarz' book also addresses.

John Ramirez, the ex-Satanist we talked about in the last chapter, says the devil hates unity.

"Unity brings chaos into the Devil's kingdom," he says. "The biggest witchcraft in the church [today] is the Spirit of Compromise."[42]

We have the answer the world is longing for! We must shine more brightly than ever, not try to dim the brightness in order to blend in with those lost in darkness.

With the loss of the foundations of our faith by eliminating or minimizing the Tanakh, the Old Testament, the road map God gave us through the desert on our journey toward Him, we've lost not merely tradition, but the very bedrock that keeps us firmly established in Yeshua. With all context lost, anything goes. Christian mystics twist the scripture that remains, to support things it would never support when interpreted in the full light of its origins: the God Who died for us on Calvary is the same God Who authored the Tanakh!

So, we must get our scriptural foundation restored and reacquaint ourselves with the Lover of our souls, getting to know Him, not relying on the traditions of men that forever seek to silence God's instructions.

I was taught we are to never contradict a pastor. That is not what we see in scripture! We must learn what the truth of scripture teaches us and then live it out. If the shepherd of a congregation is getting off in the weeds, it is our responsibility as mature believers to confront with love according to the biblical model. Accountability.

> *Now I urge you, brethren, keep your eye on those who*
> *cause dissensions and hindrances contrary to the teaching*
> *which you learned, and turn away from them.*
> *Romans 16:17*

> *If your brother sins, go and show him his fault in private; if*
> *he listens to you, you have won your brother. But if he does*
> *not listen to you, take one or two more with you, so that*
> *BY THE MOUTH OF TWO OR THREE WITNESSES*
> *EVERY FACT MAY BE CONFIRMED. If he refuses to*
> *listen to them, tell it to the church; and if he refuses to*
> *listen even to the church, let him be to you as a Gentile*
> *and a tax collector.*
> *Matthew 18:15-17*

This is all part of spiritual warfare. The darkness within the walls of the church must be identified and exorcised. We must establish new congregations of believers who are wise to these schemes and trained in spiritual warfare. And, we must live out the gospel. The time is short.

While You Are Sleeping... Or Not

Let me begin this section by giving you an illustration.

You are a World War II pilot, dropped by parachute behind enemy lines. During the day you must hide and wait for darkness to cover you as you make your way toward your destination. But eventually your body must do what? Sleep.

While you are awake on this journey, you have some control over what you are doing and can take precautions to protect yourself. But when are you the most vulnerable? When you are sleeping.

Sleep

Sleep is a very interesting and somewhat mysterious thing. As I was researching the subject, I discovered that science still doesn't completely understand it.

Over the years, God has led me to pray a lot about sleep. He gave me some instructions he wanted me to use in my own life and today I use those same instructions with my clients. They are extremely important and very effective.

First, here are some facts about sleep.[43]

You spend roughly one third of your life sleeping. Science doesn't understand why the body needs sleep. There are five different sleep cycles that last about 90 minutes each, and each cycle has five stages. (There is a double 5, God's number for grace. Five cycles with five stages within each cycle. Encoded within the cycles of sleep, is grace upon grace.) Your pulse drops by 10-30 beats per minute, the pituitary gland produces hormones, and with the rise in certain hormones as you sleep, the amount of urine that collects in your bladder is one third to one half of the normal daytime production. Sleep is an amazing orchestration of organs, functions, healing, repair, and detoxification all working together. There are even changes in the immune system, plus a cancer killing factor, TNF, pumps through your veins while sleeping.[44]

Sleep deprivation can be very serious. Not getting enough sleep can dramatically increase the risk of obesity, cancer, heart disease, dementia, depression, and cravings for sweet and starchy foods. It also is a significant contributor to auto accidents.[45]

Psychologist Kelly Bulkeley wrote an article for Psychology Today, titled, *Why Sleep is Torture*. You may find this shocking.

> "Prolonged sleep deprivation is an especially insidious form of torture because it attacks the deep biological functions at the core of a person's mental and physical health. It is less overtly violent than cutting off someone's finger, but it can be far more damaging and painful if pushed to extremes. The cumulative effects of sleep deprivation go beyond the loss of this or that specific function to a precipitous, ultimately fatal decline in all functions."[46] [emphasis added]

If a person is deprived of sleep longer than 24 hours, Dr. Bulkeley says, "several mental and physical problems begin to develop." In fact, he states, "**prolonged sleep deprivation will eventually kill a creature**."[47]

I happen to know a little something about this. Many years ago, after a significant trauma, I experienced severe sleep disruption and deprivation to the point where I started having visual phenomena of inanimate objects moving, a category of hallucinations.

Sleep is very important. God designed us with the need built in.

Speaking on the rewards of wisdom, in Proverbs we're told:

*Then you will walk in your way securely and your foot will
not stumble. When you lie down, you will not be afraid;
When you lie down, your sleep will be sweet.*
Proverbs 3:23-24

As we make wise choices, walk in holiness led by the spirit of God, and grow in the power a mature believer should enjoy, we are less likely to find ourselves in an unending string of adverse situations. And, when adversity does occur, we have the assurance of knowing that our heavenly Father allowed the challenge and that it will have meaning and importance in the spiritual realm.

There are problems we bring upon ourselves, problems we suffer through no fault of our own that are allowed by God's providence, or problems that are the acrid fruit of demonic bondage and/or attack, such as what Job endured.

In the book of Daniel, Nebuchadnezzar had dreams, "his mind was troubled and he could not sleep." (Daniel 2:1)

In Psalms 77:4, the author could not sleep, "You have held my eyelids open; I am so troubled that I cannot speak."

Sleep disruption and inadequacy feed anxiety, mental clarity becomes increasingly difficult to grasp, and the capacity for good decision-making declines. In addition to being a form of torture, sleep disruption affects every aspect of your life.

Recall now the illustration I gave you at the beginning of this section. Each of us is like a soldier behind enemy lines. We must be skilled in the tools of our defense and in using them effectively against enemy forces. We can't do that, however, if we don't know who the enemy is. These are all critical components of effective spiritual warfare training, knowing: what our tools are, how to use them, who the enemy is, and his most used forms of attack.

What if you were called up by your commander and told to get ready to be deployed, to be dropped behind those enemy lines. "Who are we fighting," you ask. "I don't know," He replies. "What are my weapons," you ask. "We don't have any," he says with a shrug of his shoulders. That does not sound like you are going to be victorious!

Oh, how valuable it would be if we could know who the enemy is, how they attack, and have access to accurate intel!

Wait, we do know! We have the intel! We have that in the Word of God! God loved us so much He gave us the instruction manual to becoming effective with our weapons of protection and in our skills at spotting what the enemy is doing.

What football team doesn't study the plays of the opposing team? When the tight end goes into motion just before the ball is snapped, you know to pay attention. With a good eye, because you studied the opposing team's plays before the game, you have a good chance of reading which play they're running.

Which plays do the forces of darkness run on you? You should be very familiar with them. Are you able to spot the attacks? Do you know the situations they look for as opportunities so that you are able to be proactive? You should.

The enemy gets a big bang for his buck when he disrupts sleep, and it should be no surprise that sleep disruption is a very common thing among those dealing with spiritual attack and demonic bondage. In fact, I can't think of a client who has not had significant trouble sleeping. Either anxiety overtakes them, or they are tormented with horrible nightmares. I've had several clients who endured physical demonic attack, some having dealt with it on a regular basis for decades before finding their way to me for help.

Let me remind you that my clients are mature believers, and many are in some sort of ministry. One client who is in ministry recently awoke in the middle of the night to see seven demonic entities surrounding him. Praise God, he knew what to do. They had to flee.

These attacks often occur at 12 a.m., referred to as the "witching hour"[48],[49].

There is also a lot of activity at 3 a.m. which some consider part of the witching hour. It can be in mockery of the holy trinity, or in some pagan circles it may represent the Maiden, the Mother, and the Crone aspect of the goddess, also referred to as the Triple Goddess.[50] This is a time when dark beings are thought to be the most powerful, and when black magik is said to be the most effective.

Scientific studies on dreams, psi experiences and circadian rhythms showed precognitive dreams, crisis apparitions, or sensing a presence occur most often at 3 a.m. It is also interesting to note that dream recall, when awakened at this early hour, is significantly lower than recall when awaking at 8 a.m.[51] This means that the enemy of our souls can slam you, leave you with the stress and emotional fall out, and you may not even remember much of the dream or the experience that left you so upset and shaken.

As we learn more about how the dark side operates, we find that timing matters. If you experience these issues, keep a journal of the times the encounters occur. It can help provide important clues to the source of the problem and/or eliminate the demonic as the prime suspect.

Dreams

As we sleep something called the *pons*, a portion of the brain stem, sends signals to turn off motor neurons in the spinal cord, causing temporary paralysis and so preventing us from acting upon our dreams.[52] What a great thing that God thought of that when He created us. Can you imagine if we did not have that function and acted out our dreams every night? It certainly wouldn't be very restful and could be quite dangerous.

In our dreams both the Lord and the adversary can send messages, pictures, communication, and feelings. The adversary may send to your mind a video that replays an extremely painful or traumatic event, whether physical or emotional, that inflicts torment and keeps you stuck in your life unable to move forward and completely heal. On the other hand, God may speak to you in a dream to tell you not to worry about a current problem, that He is sending the solution.

In Daniel 2:1, as we saw above, Nebuchadnezzar was being tormented with dreams and was unable to sleep. And, instead of going before the Lord for the answer, he summoned the magicians, enchanters, sorcerers, and astrologers (Daniel 2:2). NOT a good decision.

Even with a brain affected by sleep deprivation, if he had been walking in holiness as he should have been, he would have been surrounded on a regular basis by mature believers, trusted mentors, and advisors who would have been able to give him godly guidance when he was struggling to think clearly. This is how the body of Christ today is supposed to work.

In the throes of trouble and testing, whatever is hidden in the innermost parts of our hearts leaks out. This can also be true of dreams, where the subconscious plays a significant role.

For King Nebuchadnezzar what emerged was rebellion and disobedience. Without the congregation of strong believers around us, it is easy for the enemy forces to take us down.

Paul received a vision from an angel of God which was documented and later became the book of Revelation. This visitation became one of the most important ancient documents we have because it tells us what is coming and how to prepare.

Mary received a visitation from the angel Gabriel who told her she would have a baby conceived by the Holy Spirit (Luke 1:26).

So clearly dreams, visions, and visitations can be from the Lord... or they can be from the dark side.

In Luke 4, in the midst of a 40 day fast, Jesus was led by the Holy Spirit into the wilderness. He was hungry. Guess who shows up? The Lord of Darkness. He tempted Him with bread, repossession of the world that had been put under Satan's control, and he quoted the Lord's own scriptures, goading Him to do what would have been so very easy to do: to abandon the mission and call upon all of the angels to come and carry Him back to His throne. When Jesus did not fall for the twisting and lies, the Adversary left "until a more opportune time." Oh, how we like to skip past that part of that verse!

There has only been one perfect human being and it is the God-man, the second Adam, Jesus, and they tortured and killed Him. And, even though He was the only One Who ever walked out the Torah perfectly, the Adversary was lurking about, stalking, looking for any tiny opportunity to get in, to test, torment, and cause inner turmoil.

We, too, must deal with this spiritual reality of attack from dark forces, whether subtle or overt.

Let's look at an example .

I have a very close friend who endured the passing of her young son due to a disease. Even though it occurred many decades ago, she has had dreams of her son coming to her to deliver a message.

She asked me if this was God speaking to her.

What would you have said?

Aren't you glad you didn't have to answer that question? I had to gently explain that we are not to talk to the dead, that is necromancy, which is strongly forbidden in scripture. (Leviticus 19, 20; Deuternomy18)

I can't imagine what it feels like to be a parent who has lost a young child. I also find it difficult to imagine a more tempting way for the enemy to seduce someone into longing for other worldly contact. If you believe you have seen your deceased son in a so-called visitation or dream, the impact on the heart is difficult to quantify. It is the perfect scenario to cause you to forget to test the spirits (1 John 4:1-2), to be so comforted by the sight of him that you long for more of the experiences: there it is again, *longing. Longing* is very important.

> *longing :* strong, persistent desire or craving, especially for something unattainable or distant.[53]

Webster's dictionary puts it this way:

> *longing :* An eager desire; a craving; a morbid appetite; an earnest wish; an aspiration.[54]

> *For the love of money is a root of all sorts of evil, and some* **by longing for it have wandered away from the faith** *and pierced themselves with many griefs.*
> *1 Timothy 6:10 [emphasis added]*

And, in a prior chapter we talked about 1 Peter 1:12 where, certain angels *long* for, lust after, what we've been given. Longing can absolutely be an open door to the dark side.

On the positive side, the scripture refers to *desires of the heart.* It can be represented as a turning toward, as if you are turning your face and your body toward something.

> *Then you'll take delight in the Almighty; and will* **turn your face toward God.**
> *Job 22:26, ISV*

> *My son, give attention to my wisdom,* **incline your ear to my understanding;**
> *Proverbs 5:1*

In the negative, the following passage shows how setting our faces toward the wrong thing invites consequences:

> *Thus says the LORD of hosts, the God of Israel,* **"If you really set your [faces]** *to enter Egypt and go in to reside there, then the sword, which you are afraid of, will*

overtake you there in the land of Egypt; and the famine,
about which you are anxious, will follow closely after you
there in Egypt, and you will die there.
Jeremiah 42:15-16, ESV

The Hebrew word is *pə·nê·ḵem*, which is more accurately translated as *faces*, rather than *mind*, as many translations have used.

The prodigal son said, "I will get up and go to my father," in Luke 15:18. He turned from his situation and turned toward home, toward the hope of restoration, and he actually set off in that direction; he didn't just sit there and think about it.

There is a process revealed here. It involved a spark of a thought, then he embraced the thought, thinking about the aspects of the thought, then he made a choice, and his decision was to return to his father. As he got up to begin the journey, he *set his face toward* home and his father. He did not turn back.

The angels told Lot to flee and to not look back. Lot's wife disobeyed that instruction and suffered the penalty (Genesis 19). He looked forward, she looked backward. What harm could there be in just looking? Well, if you make the tragic mistake of looking at a welder doing his work, the white-hot, fiery light can blind you permanently. (A slight side note: We need to put ourselves in check if we feel we need to see destruction; it is not for our entertainment. God does not delight in it and neither should we.)

Whatever you set your face towards, the body follows.

Whatever the heartache that comes in the trials we endure, we are to move forward with the Lord. We must not hoard our pain and keep it from the Lord's healing hands.

I have seen this a lot. There are people who refuse to let go of their pain and grief. What are spiritual consequences of doing that?

First, it is disobedience, refusing to accept what God has allowed in your life, something that He clearly wants you to learn to overcome which will birth joy out of sorrow and bring glory to His Name.

Second, you are refusing total healing, healing He already paid a very high price for, which demonstrates His mercy and power. That means, you are rejecting His will of leading you through a trial to a victory.

Third, it is rebellion, the equivalent of the two-year-old stomping his foot in the grocery store because he wants something his parents have disallowed. Rebellion is very dangerous because it has both relationship and supernatural consequences. "If you're not going to give me what I want, Lord, I will play the victim the rest of my life!"

One of the spiritual consequences of this attitude could be that your relationship with the Lord won't be what it could be or what God desires it to be. Holding tightly onto the heartache declares that you don't need or want any more of the Lord in that part of your life. It's the attitude that says, "You can have this part of my life, Lord, but not this part." Over time, as you continue to choose this every day, it can become a very powerful stronghold. You will be easy to discourage or lure away from faith.

There are supernatural consequences that come with all three of these things because they are sins. Being a professional victim is not a testimony of the power of our God. All of this opens the door to bondage.

It is **intent** of you choosing to embrace and protect your pain and the painful experience that brought the pain to you, and rejection of God's authority and mercy .

But, even more, if you refuse, let's say, to forgive yourself for a mistake made that harmed yourself or someone else, you are rejecting the forgiveness purchased at such a high price by our Savior. This can mean you aren't even under the cleansing blood. Jesus paid for your sins, for you to have His forgiveness. But if you reject forgiveness, you are rejecting the sacrifice over that part of your life. This can have huge consequences and bring powerful bondage.

Remember this: *intent*.

> *Intent :* something that is intended; purpose; design; intention:
>
> the act or fact of intending, as to do something: criminal intent.
>
> Law. the state of a person's mind that directs his or her actions toward a specific object.[55]

> *As for you, my son Solomon, know the God of your father, and serve Him with a whole heart and a willing mind; for the LORD searches all hearts, and **understands every intent of the thoughts**. If you seek Him, He will let you find Him; but if you forsake Him, He will reject you forever.*
> *1 Chronicles 28:9 [emphasis added],*

The *longing* of our hearts and the *intent* of our minds are extremely important. If they are for anything other than the Lover of our souls, it is a sort of dog whistle to the dark side. We must be ever watchful and walk in repentance.

Our dreams? Must be presented before the Lord. Our struggles? Must be taken to the foot of the cross. We are to do all things in our lives WITH the Lord. We are to walk by His side, right under His arm, next to His heart, at all times.

Repentance is a turning away from, turning around from.

Webster's defines it as:

> **repentance:** the act of turning around an improper behavior; sorrow for what one has done; especially, contrition for sin.[56]

Do you see the significance of both *longing* and *intent*? Do you see how it can be a subject of our repentance?

There is amazing research on the brain, thought patterns, and health and peace in life.

In the book, *What Was I Thinking*, authors Pastor C. McCloud and Linda Lange address the role thoughts play in the body-mind connection:

> "What we think does, in fact, matter. We need to understand that our thoughts matter more than we really even completely understand at this time. As we research into the brain and how it functions, more and more evidence is showing that thousands of chemical changes occur with every single thought, and we really only know about some of them. We need to know that our thoughts will manifest in good or bad actions – and in good or bad health in our bodies. We are to take every thought captive to the obedience of Christ so that we display Christ! As we think Christ-like thoughts in our heart, we become Christ-like."[57] [emphasis added]

Thoughts, intent, and longings can play out in our sleep. There is a sub-conscious component in human beings, placed there by God's design. Ignoring it is not a good thing.

Sara Thiessen wrote in her groundbreaking book, *Splankna:*

> "Our bodies seem to store all the emotions we experience in our lives like electrical charges. When we feel intense emotion, the body and the subconscious mind seem to hold something like an imprint of them – like an energetic residue. Negative emotions that we store physiologically become a kind of fuel for dysfunction."[58] [emphasis added]

The next step for people who refuse to let go of their pain and grief is to seek out the experiences of communicating with the dead by consulting mediums, as too many grieving parents do.

It is incredible cruelty that the dark lord would use the grief of parents who have lost a child as a weapon of warfare to seduce them to inch closer and closer to the dark side and eternal suffering. But that is who he is. He *only* comes to steal, kill and destroy.

In our example, for the bereaved parent, the experience of being able to see their deceased child is like being given a highly addictive drug. That encounter is something they might long for, dream of, and spend time thinking about. If they get involved with a medium, they must block out time for the sessions on their calendars and add the expense to their budgets. They must walk or drive there. All those steps are evidence of their inward intention to do a sinful thing, to talk to the dead.

These are the same mental steps we discussed that the prodigal son went through before he stood up, turned to the right direction, then started on the journey that would lead him back to his father.

Intent. Setting our heart on a thing. Turning our face towards a desire. Longing.

This is a great example of how we make choices that invite the bondage of darkness.

Inner pain and unbearable heartache are said by many to be worse than physical pain. I must agree But, in spiritual reality, longing for someone who has crossed from life to death opens a door to the dark side, tempting the ever-willing minions who savor your destruction to minister to your pain with spiritual heroin.

There is One Who knows exactly what it is like to lose a son, made worse because it was an unjust death, and, He had to watch Him be tortured beyond description: God, your heavenly Father. He understands unbearable heartache. God wept over Israel (Jeremiah 9:1) and Jesus wept at the death of Lazarus (John 11:35).

We are to take our griefs to our Lord Who knows exactly what we suffer and, because they are so precious to Him, saves every tear.

> *You have taken account of my wanderings; Put my tears in*
> *Your bottle. Are they not in Your book?*
> *Psalm 56:8*

What we feel in our deepest being may swirl around as we sleep and offer opportunities for spiritual attack and deception.

Consciousness & Human Will

Naturalists view consciousness as merely a phenomenon of the brain. But as Christians, we believe that humans are made in the image of God, Who is the basis of all reason and knowledge.[59] Our consciousness comes from Him just as every breath we take is a gift given to us by God.

> *For in him we live, and move, and have our being.*
> *Acts 17:28, KJV*

> *The life of every living thing is in His hand, as well as the*
> *breath of all mankind.*
> *Job 12:10, HCSB*

Philosophers and scholars have debated for centuries the nature and definition of consciousness. One thing we know for sure is that without God we would not have it!

With consciousness comes will. What happens to the will when we are sleeping, when we are unconscious? What about when a client has DID (Dissociative Identity Disorder) and alter personalities none of which have memory of what another personality is doing?

Ever had a nightmare where you were trying to wake up and you couldn't? Ever had a traumatic event that played over and over in your sleep? Did you try everything to stop it?

Incredible things occur during sleep. For example, in the twilight, our bodies perform an amazing function where 40% of the usual blood flow to the brain is diverted to the muscles and extremities[60]. That seems to leave us vulnerable not just in a physical way in this dimension, but also vulnerable in a supernatural way. I'll talk more about this later.

As I was researching this subject, I found little to no material on consciousness, human will, and sleep. I sought some input from Mary Lou Lake, wife of Dr. Michael Lake, both of whom I greatly respect. Mary Lou minsters to victims of the occult and mind control. I asked her what her take was.

"At one point in my life I believed my conscious will and prayers could override anything during my sleep state, including any parts of my mind that had any automatic occult activity programmed in," she said. "I trusted Almighty God to override anything that was contrary to my conscious will."

But she has since learned that others who minister to victims of programming and SRA say that the divided will of 'back personalities' can take control of the body, and this phenomenon cannot be stopped until all those parts of the mind are set free in Christ.

What she learned lines up with what I've seen.

I had my own experience with horrific, unstoppable nightmares for decades until the Lord revealed how to cover my sleep. I've also had clients who have had programming in childhood, and I've seen what it takes to defeat and heal both.

The more we know, the more we are responsible for. When we are immature in a particular area in our walk with the Lord, He does cover us more than we realize. But, as He blesses us with more knowledge of Him and His ways, as we mature, we are responsible to do the work He's revealed to us. We are responsible to slay the forces of darkness because He gave us the tools and the instructions.

So, here are my thoughts in the area of consciousness, human will, and sleep.

Right now, I think an individual's consciousness when under demonic influence is, to some degree, suppressed or pushed to the side, off center, so to speak, because we made an agreement to let demonic influence in. For example, if a balloon is already fully inflated and placed in a hard shell, then another balloon is increasingly inflated pushing against it in the same space, there is a displacement, a pushing off center. Whichever balloon is most filled will dominate the space.

The dark forces are harsh task masters and want to rule over us, in us, and through us, in perversion of the picture we have of our relationship with Christ where He should rule over, in, and through us. God gave us free will and He will not violate that; it is a law the dark side must follow as well. That is a line they cannot cross. They can't come in or attach without permission and that permission occurred somewhere, whether from the individual, someone in authority over them, or from someone in their generational line.

At minimum, we all have degrees of bondage as an inheritance from our first parents, Adam and Eve, unless somewhere in our generations, on both sides that contribute to ourselves, they knew to break all forms of that original bondage. Then, there is still what happened since that point and what we contribute to the total picture once we take our first breath.

Consciousness and will seem to somehow be connected to DNA, the unique signature of the unique individual. We see in cases of multiple personalities, certain personalities have no knowledge or memory of what other personalities have done. There is a lot of data on this and we know from documented experiments how the mind splits and the method used to make it do so.

If this is correct, then when we sleep, the potential for both the subconscious to leap forward with its unresolved issues or for the demonic manipulation of the consciousness to provide an opportunity for dark work is very real.

Are you seeing the military advantage for the enemy of our souls to attack while we are sleeping? Or even causing disruption in the sleep process?

When we are told in 2 Timothy 1:2 that we are not given a spirit of fear but of power, love, and a sound mind, and in Proverbs 3:24

that when we lie down our sleep will be sweet, there is a clear general picture that comes into view about our walk with the Lord and our ever-increasing depth of relationship with Him. Yet, we are also clearly told we will have much trouble and tribulation in this life, in large part due to the fact that we are believers in Jesus. Both concepts are completely true.

Later we will discuss how we protect ourselves. But for now, I want you to understand this vulnerability, one that mature believers should not ignore.

The Adversary prowls, stalks, lies, deceives, is the voice of the accuser, and delights in causing torment. If he can find a way to use the sleep process against us, he will.

Protecting Your Sleep

Our sleep is very important for the health of body, mind, soul, and spirit. It is also a vulnerable time that must be protected spiritually as much as physically. And, we must learn to use the tools our Lord has given us and incorporate them so deeply into our mind and spirit that we can perform them in our sleep.

I've mentioned that I dealt with very frequent, recurring horrific nightmares since early childhood. Even after wonderful counseling and assistance to banish the demonic influence, I still suffered from the awful nightmares. Over many years, as I prayed about it, I felt as though God impressed upon me to do these things.

Dedicate both sleep and dreams to the Lord alone. Do that by first saying, "Lord, I dedicate my sleep and dreams to only You."

Then, *set the boundary* with the blood of the Lamb, "Set a boundary around me, Lord, with the blood of the Lamb, a boundary the enemy cannot cross." Say it out loud, "I do not receive any visitation, contact, communication, or dreams from any dark energy, entity, spirit, force, or dark technology."

Invite the Lord in. Now that you've declared that you will not receive any communication or dreams from the dark side, dedicate your sleep, dreams, and the time during the sleep process to the Lord for his purposes, "Lord, I only receive visitation, contact, communication, or dreams from the Holy Spirit of the Living God. Now that I've dedicated my sleep and the processes of sleep to You, I invite You to spend this time with me. Speak to me, I want to hear what You have to say. Give me any direction or correction You want to give, or just walk with me in the garden the cool of the day. I want to spend this time with You."

I began to do what I felt the Lord had instructed me to do. Guess what? I never had another nightmare. Never. Well, except for one time and we'll talk about that in a minute. And, my clients have had the same experience. It changes everything. If the nightmares don't stop immediately, they drop off dramatically and then cease altogether.

> *You will not be afraid of the terror by night, or of the arrow*
> *that flies by day; of the pestilence that stalks in darkness, or*
> *of the destruction that lays waste at noon.*
> *Psalm 91:5-6*

So, what happened, the one time I had a nightmare after the Lord revealed this covering process to me?

I had covered my sleep as I do every night since the Lord revealed the importance of this protective barrier. Not typical for me, I woke up in the middle of the night to go to the bathroom. I went back to bed and went right back to sleep. I had a horrible nightmare. When I woke up, I was asking the Lord why.

Can you figure it out?

It is because of legal authority and loopholes.

In a prior section we talked about how the enemy uses the law against us and we must understand this very well.

When I woke up and was asking the Lord what happened, it's one of the very few times I felt as though He said something to me very clearly. Here's what I believe He said. "As far as the enemy is concerned, it was a different session of sleep. You got up. Then you went back to bed. It was a different session and you didn't cover that session."

It was a huge ah-ha moment.

Can't you just see the evil attorneys shrugging their shoulders and laughing, "Hey, you didn't cover your sleep. It's not our problem."

This is how they work.

Loopholes.

They want to find every way possible through and around the legal authority we have been given to use against them.

I urge you to begin covering your sleep every night without fail. I hear from many clients that they begin having more dreams from the Lord. Often their sleep changes significantly, and because of that, it changes many other things in their lives for the better also.

The Law: How The Enemy Uses It

There is a covering that takes place with salvation. You can think of it like an umbrella. When you give your life to Yeshua, your heart is cleansed by the blood of the Lamb of God and sin is wiped away. You are given access to your heavenly Father as a son or daughter who has been cut off from the former vine and grafted into the family of the King. Your eternity just moved from a smoldering condo on the edge of the Lake of Fire to a mansion with a view built by your Savior.

But, when it comes to spiritual warfare, it is a different sort of covering. To understand this covering, you must first understand how the forces of darkness operate. It is not like the free gift of salvation, where you have asked to receive the gift, acknowledging the deity and authority of Jesus. This battlefield covering requires our participation as we move from a starting point of babies on milk, toward mature athletes, ambassadors of the King, firmly planted on the rock of the Word of God, growing in strength and wisdom, responsible watchmen on the walls of the city, and fierce opponents to the dark kingdom forces.

As the children of Israel felt like grasshoppers compared to the Nephilim who occupied the land they were instructed to take, the Nephilim are mere grasshoppers compared to Yeshua HaMashiach, the Conquering King!

The way the dark side works is by law, parameters set by God that they must work within. I describe it to my clients using this illustration. Pay close attention to the wording.

They are like very badly behaved six-year-olds.

You have two sons, one age six, another age nine. Your six-year-old comes into your bedroom and asks, "Can I get a cookie?"

"No," you patiently explain, "I don't want you to get a cookie right now, it's almost dinner time."

Five minutes later you walk into the kitchen and that same son is standing there with a half-eaten cookie in his hand and chocolate cookie all over his face.

You are not at all pleased with the disobedience. "I told you I did not want you to get a cookie because it's dinner time."

Your son, without flinching or blinking says, "Yeah. But you didn't say I couldn't have my brother get me one."

Did you catch the wording? Do you see the mental gymnastics of the opposition? And, this relatable example was just with a six-year-old!

The adult in this story understands what the child is trying to do. But because the church has removed teaching the roots of our faith and training on the reality of spiritual warfare, mature believers across this nation have no understanding that this is how the supernatural war plays out around us every minute of every day and night.

This is why, as you will see later, we must speak things in a very specific manner. It is because we can be far more effective in a much shorter period of time if we speak things a certain way, leaving the minions no wiggle room. Speed and accuracy do matter. They are critical battlefield skills against powers and entities that are stronger, smarter, and faster than humans are, and they never lack resources or motivation.

The Holy Spirit of the Living God is within us and His arm is neither too short nor lacking in strength. But, we, as His earthen vessels, are His chosen method to work against the enemy in this timeline and dimension. In part, I believe, because it both plainly demonstrates His superior authority and power, and while doing so, insults the dark forces. With all their power and aggression, they are nothing in comparison to the consuming Holy Spirit fire that dwells within us that may be unleashed on full power in an instant when we understand how this all works.

Roots & Theology

Stay with me here, and I deeply believe that you will have some ah-ha moments as dots that you didn't even know were on the screen begin to connect, as the picture becomes more clearly defined, and as you see it spring from one dimension to 3D. We must start at the beginning.

Roots

I am very adamant about using all of scripture, cover to cover, not just part of scripture, and not taking scripture out of context. When God said don't change a word, not a jot or a tittle, He meant it.

In a recent interview, Dr. Michael Lake, seminary president and author of *The Shinar Directive,* said this:

"People in church are confused about these things because the gospel is not being preached. Everything in the Word of God...the foundation is Torah and it all explodes from there. So, when you're reading the New Testament, you're talking about Torah concepts. They're expanding on definitions already given. And our confusion is when we forego the Old Testament and try to make our own definitions. Then, all of a sudden, God seems confused! He's not. There is a continuity that is supernatural in the Word of God. There are no contradictions; just some bad translations."[61]

Torah, Strong's 8451, means instruction, direction, precepts, statute.

It is literally God's manual for human life in this fallen creation. He was not confused, as Dr. Lake stated, God knew what He was writing. After all, it was written by the same God who later died on the cross for us! These are the instructions on how to stay close to Him, prevent things from getting in-between us, eliminate communication interference and cracks in the door that He designed to protect us from the dark ones. He never meant it to be ultimate salvation from sin. It is a study in compare-and-contrast style, revealing what was lost in the garden, and what is required to maintain relationship with Him in light of that tragedy.

Everything God says is important, not just some things, not just some books. God does not have afterthoughts, or experience confusion, or get caught off guard. Never has God said, "Wow, I didn't see that coming, I guess I need to come up with another plan." There is not a random molecule in the universe, or He would not be the God of the Bible! The Word of God says that before the foundations of the earth were laid, Yeshua Jesus was already the Lamb to be slain[62]. God the Father knew we would sin, and He had already planned to sacrifice His Son before He even made us. Even though we were conceived in iniquity[63] and still sinners, Christ died for us. The plan was always in place!

I had a very important journey with the Lord that changed everything; this is how it started.

I got saved at the age of four. We were sitting on the second pew at a small Baptist church in Maryland. At the end of the Sunday morning service, I was quiet and paying close attention as we all stood up. As the pastor gave the invitation for salvation, I tried to pull my hand out of my mother's hand to go forward but her hand only squeezed against mine tighter and tighter. It was obvious to everyone else that I was trying to go forward to the pastor. He saw me and he saw my mother restraining me.

"Let her go," he said.

She did. I went straight to the red carpeted steps behind the pulpit, got on my knees and prayed. I was very serious about it.

Since that day, my journey with the Lord included many twists and turns and times that I allowed events or people to pull me away from Him. But, starting at a very young age there were things that I noticed that didn't make sense, things that were preached and taught on a regular basis in most churches. One of those things at the top of the list was Easter.

Where is Easter in the Bible? Where is the reference to colored eggs? Why don't we celebrate the feasts that Jesus celebrated?

Over the years, I learned of the hideous occult essence of everything to do with Easter, from the name being a reference to the goddess Ishtar, to the eggs representing fertility in occult ceremonies, and coloring the eggs, a tradition that had come from occult ceremony where eggs were dipped in the blood from a human sacrifice. The official color of Easter eggs, according to the Catholic church, is still red. So much of it is not only not connected to the God of the Bible or His Word but was directly transferred from the devil's world, that I was horrified and I have not participated in that for many years. I encourage you to research this fact if you have not already done so. The documentary, *Truth or Tradition*, is a great place to start.[64]

At bedtime one Sunday night when I was about six years old I asked my parents why we weren't Jewish. They were shocked by the question.

"In Sunday school this morning the teacher said that Jesus was Jewish," I said.

They didn't know what to say and were silent for a moment.

I burst into tears and was very upset, "I want to be Jewish! I want to be like Jesus!"

They told me to be quiet and to go to sleep.

As that six-year-old girl, I hadn't yet understood that I didn't need to be Jewish to be saved or to please my Savior. I clearly had a heart that wanted to follow Jesus with all that was in me. But I was already beginning to sense a sad reality: the modern American church had completely forsaken the Hebrew roots of the Christian faith.

Over the years I wrote my questions down, researched on my own, took classes in biblical studies, had deep discussions with friends who were in seminary, and pursued a deeper understanding of the history of the church. I tried multiple times to go to seminary to get my degree but every time the Lord shut the door. His plan for me did not include that. So, I continued to study on my own and I still do.

Throughout this decades-long journey, I began to see my questions get answered one by one. I learned about the earliest form of the Catholic church; the Reformation and the separation that occurred; the expulsion of the Jews from Spain; how Constantine combined some Christian ideas with the completely occult culture over which he ruled; the laws he and others put forth declaring all celebration of the "Jewish" feasts must stop; and that the "Jewish" Sabbath could no longer be honored. This very short list doesn't begin to scratch the surface, but I'm sure you can see that see these events separated believers from the roots of their faith.

The enemy worked behind the scenes, binding some church leaders with a rope of pride, control, and their own views of what scripture should be, then lowering them on that rope very slowly, down into a large, dark hole in the ground, where the light of scripture grew increasingly dim.

At some point believers began to question the deletions. And when they opened God's Word without viewing it through the exclusively Greek or Roman lens, the road map leapt off the pages, revealing how much had been left behind. They began growing in numbers and sharing the beauty, freedom, and perfect and intricate weaving of scripture. Some refer to this re-establishing of the original Jewish context as a Messianic view. My fancy, ten-dollar term for it is "biblical."

Early church leaders and theologians increasingly emphasized a Greek point of view, often because of open and blatant antisemitism. (This is so strange since the very Savior they claim to profess was, is and forever will be, Jewish.) As they minimized or completely eliminated all Jewish context, the resulting views had drastic consequences, not only on what we have read that applies to the past, but also on the prophetic events which are yet to occur.

Here is an example:

> *Speak to the people of Israel and say to them, These are the appointed **feasts of the LORD** that you shall proclaim as holy convocations; they are **my appointed feasts**.*
> *Leviticus 23:2, ESV*

Did you catch that? They are *the Lord's* feasts! "*My appointed feasts.*" They are holy convocations. *Convocation* means a holy ceremony. They are not and never have been Jewish feasts or feasts of the Jews. They are the Lord's! They are invitations to have an intimate time with the King of Glory! Who would want to turn down that invitation??

They are also rehearsals for what is to come.

American Christians have a huge gap in understanding due to this one elimination. The book of Revelation refers to the Old Testament hundreds of times. In fact, 68% of the verses in Revelation refer to Tanakh or Old Testament scriptures.[65]

For example, the dead in Christ will rise in response to what sound? The trumpet described in 1 Corinthians 15:52.

In Revelation 8:2, the angels were standing before God and they were given what? Trumpets.

The trumpet was most often the shofar or the silver trumpets in the temple. The blowing of the *shofar* is very important and also symbolic, but I suggest to you that most Christians in the United States have never heard the word.

Guess what one of the seven feasts of the Lord is? The Feast of Trumpets.

Wow, wait, so maybe the feasts are actually important?

They are rehearsals for what is coming. We need to be ready.

I've already mentioned that the second greatest trick the devil ever pulled was getting people to believe he didn't exist. And that the first most important trick was separating us from the understanding of the roots of our faith. This is the biggest thing, I believe, in part because that tragic and indescribably destructive move twisted our understanding and interpretation of scripture, not just relating to the past but also to the future. And his third greatest trick was removing teaching of spiritual warfare from pulpits. You will see that these things are intimately connected in ways you may not have imagined before.

For us today, the result of the Lord of Darkness successfully separating us as believers from the roots of our faith is that we don't realize it drastically changed our context of all of scripture. In a simple term, we don't know what we don't know. It's akin to a plane taking off from an airfield and setting on a course that is one degree off from what it should be. You may not notice too much in those first moments, but when you think you should be over your destination, you will find yourself many miles off course.

One of the things that upset me as I discovered more of the Hebrew roots of my faith in Christ was that Jesus was never His name. Even if it is a translation, which is fine, why were we never taught the name given to Him by His Father God? The name the Father chose to give His Son is *Yeshua*. And it literally means *salvation*.

This feels very offensive to me. It reminds me of being at a corporate party and meeting one of those people who make it clear they have absolutely no interest in getting your name correct. Have you met people like that? Since my name is Sanda I have some experience with this.

"Hi, my name is Emily."

"Oh, yeah, Emelia, I've seen you in the lunchroom."

"No, it's not Emelia, it's Emily."

"Yeah, sure, whatever. Did you get the memo on that new project?"

If that has ever happened to you, did you feel respected, even in the most basic way? I suspect not. I didn't.

Yeshua is Jesus' real Hebrew name and it has important meaning, where the translated name of Jesus did not. Obviously, that is no accident. And, if you take the time to research the topic, God is very into names; they have great meaning to Him. If it has great meaning to God, shouldn't it have great meaning to us?

When a man meets a woman, falls in love, and wants to marry her, he wants to know what she likes and what is important to her. If she is from another country, he would want to know about that country. If her family speaks another language, he will try to learn at least some of the language. If she uses an American English name that's easier for Americans to pronounce, he would want to know her real name because he loves her and wants to know about her life and her background. Maybe on their wedding day he surprises her by making some of his marriage vows in her native language. That would be honoring to her family as well. His marriage to her certainly would not be based on how well he pronounced her original name, but it would be an act of love and intimacy on his part. *It is a matter of relationship and intimacy.*

Why wouldn't we do that with the sinless Lamb of God Who

gave His life for us? God considers names important, so we should have a desire to know and use the name God chose for His Son, the King of Kings. It is also a basic form of respect.

It does not mean, however, that you are somehow sinning or that He won't hear you when you are trying to talk with Him using the name Jesus. (There is a movement that takes the concept of The Name into what I believe to be unbiblical territory, making it a sin to call Him Jesus.) But I do think caring about knowing and using His Hebrew name can be a reflection of the depth of relationship and affection. Do you just perform the list of things you're supposed to do? Or do you know Him as the love of your life and want to treat Him that way?

That it is just one of hundreds of details that are missed in the average American church, like pixels on a computer screen that you don't even know are missing until someone adds them in. When the pixels are restored, it causes you to exclaim in utter astonishment. The picture suddenly leaps off the screen with depth, colors come alive, and definition is improved beyond description.

Yeshua kept the feasts and sabbath, as did the disciples and all the first congregations. They had scriptures. It is stated frequently in the New Testament. When they say "it is written" or they refer to the scriptures, to what are they referring?

The scriptures they had and studied were:

Torah/	**Genesis**
The Book of Moses	**Exodus**
	Leviticus
	Numbers
	Deuteronomy

Nevi'im/Prophets	Joshua	Hosea
	Judges	Joel
	1 Samuel	Amos
	2 Samuel	Obadiah
	1 Kings	Jonah
	2 Kings	Micah
	Isaiah	Nahum
	Jeremiah	Habakkuk
	Ezekiel	Zephaniah
		Haggai
		Zechariah
		Malachi

Ketuvim/Writings	Psalms	Esther
	Proverbs	Daniel
	Job	Ezra
	Song of Songs	Nehemiah
	Ruth	1 & 2 Chronicles
	Lamentations	
	Ecclesiastes	

Also, among their scriptures were: Jubilees, Maccabees (Second Temple period), and Enoch.

Yes, they had scriptures! They proved Yeshua was indeed the Messiah by quoting and reasoning from scripture, which was for them the Old Testament or Tanakh. They knew the teachings of Yeshua were of God because they aligned with scripture that came directly from the hand of God!

According to Christian theology, how many Gods do we believe in? One. Then, who wrote the Torah? God. Who gave the instructions for the feasts? God.

We do not believe in multiple Gods.

Dr. Michael Lake said this:

"After the first Pentecost when Moses came down with the ten commandments, the Bible said that Israel was playing and basically having an orgy around the golden calf. Three thousand died that day. But, on the day of Pentecost after Peter preached, is it any wonder that there were three thousand saved? There is perfect symmetry to the word of God!"[66]

Scripture was not written from a Greek viewpoint. It was written from a Hebrew view, in Hebrew culture, using the Hebrew language which is a pictorial language that adds dimension to the text which absolutely cannot be found in translations. It was written by Hebrew people, about the God of the Hebrews and the fulfillment of that same God's prophecies, in 66 books, by 40 authors writing from three continents, written over two thousand years[67], maintaining complete symmetry and combined into the Bible, creating the greatest love story of all time!

Wow!

Tim Chaffey of Answers in Genesis puts it this way, "Among all the books ever written, the Bible is absolutely unique. Actually, it is not just a book—it's 66 books. And one of its most remarkable qualities is the complete unity of the overall message despite having so many different authors writing over many centuries on hundreds of controversial subjects. Natural explanations fail to account for the supernatural character and origin of Scripture."[68]

This is a profound story of love, of a God that loved us all so much that He planned from the beginning to make the ultimate sacrifice for us, and to fill these earthen vessels with His spirit.

When scripture tells us that through the sacrifice of Yeshua and the indwelling of the Holy Spirit we are now the temple not made by human hands (1 Corinthians 6:19, 2 Corinthians 6:16), we can't possibly have a clue what that means or the significance of the statement if we don't understand what the temple is, what it was created for, and how incredibly precise the instructions were to build and maintain it. Every detail had meaning! None of this is properly understood without placing it in its Hebrew context. This same concept comes into play later with forgiveness.

Here is my favorite example of what is lost in translation.

Let's look for a moment at the name of God.

הוהי (YHWH) – The Tetragrammaton

The 4 Hebrew letters are:

Letter		Meaning
Yod	י	Hands
Hey	ה	Window; Lo! Behold!
Vav	ו	Hook; Nail
Hey	ה	Window; Lo! Behold!

So, the very name of God, using the original language, is saying:

The hands; Look! Behold! The nails; Look! Behold!

Dr. Michael Lake believes it can also be correctly interpreted as:

The God with the nailed hands that shall be revealed twice.

Do you realize the consequences of knowing this? God first revealed this Name in the Torah, in Genesis 2:4. This text is very old and predates Yeshua Jesus with a conservative estimated final compilation at the time of the exile and post exile period of 586 – 539 BC according to Professor Pete Enns[69] and 1445 – 1405 BC according to other scholars[70].

Do you see how this one fact confirms the truth of scripture?

When I first heard this, I cried from the impact. Even when we take the most conservative estimate, at least 500 years before the birth of Jesus the very name of God is written and declared in a way that both describes Yeshua and how to recognize Him as Messiah, the One and only begotten Son of God Who will come first as the Lamb to be slain with nails in His hands, and come a second time as the conquering Lion of Judah!

Let me give you another connection.

The sons of Jacob, which were to become the twelve tribes of Israel, sold their brother Joseph into slavery. He was taken into the belly of the beast, the occult center of the globe at that time, Egypt. He was innocent of charges made against him, sent to prison that was likely underground, but then raised to authority, and used to bring salvation to the entire family of Jacob.

Do you recognize the pattern of Jesus coming to save us? Yeshua was rejected and sent out by his brethren; while completely perfect and blameless, convicted and sentenced to death; sent into darkness of the grave, then raised with all authority, bringing salvation to all who believe.

God is really into patterns. In his unfathomable mercy, He has for thousands of years provided us with object lessons to help us recognize what He wants us to see.

Without Joseph's assistance, there would never have been twelve tribes or the nation of Israel and no Messiah! Joseph is one picture of the Messiah that was to come.

When you minimize or eliminate the Torah (the first five books of what Christians call the Old Testament), you are eliminating multiple pictures of Who Messiah would be! Without the Torah and the Tanakh (the rest of what Christians know as the Old Testament), you virtually eliminate every description of Who Messiah would be and how to recognize Him. There are over 300 prophecies of Who Messiah would be...and, obviously, all are in the Old Testament.

So, maybe these patterns are important?

Clearly, patterns are of great value to God. So, the Exodus story of the Hebrews leaving Egypt, a story of paramount importance, is one of the examples of God using patterns over and over again. It is a very detailed picture of the last days.

Joseph's descendants are somehow led (like lambs to the slaughter) into slavery where they endured hundreds of years of torture, falling from prominence to chattel.

Why didn't the people recognize the signs of the increasing oppression? Why did they not leave before they had their freedom of choice completely removed? There may have been a slow decent into complete subjugation. There had to have been deception as they perhaps did not want to believe what was happening to them. Maybe their prominence and favored status contributed to the blindness of the dark reality approaching like a python silently sliding upon its victim. This, too, is a picture of our time and the way the enemy works.

Then again, the Lord sends a deliverer, Moses. He is sent back to the dark dynasty where he was once a prince, to deliver the message that God wants His people set free.

From this moment in our history, we see supernatural warfare out in the open from the seat of government, against large numbers of people, supernatural blindness, and then ultimate victory, just as God had declared before the story played out.

The Hebrews were in the middle of the occult center of the world and immersed in demonically-charged ceremony and energy. They were pressed on every side by dark powers that wanted to remove them from the face of the earth, thereby eliminating the chance for the Messiah to be born and fulfill the prophecy that He would crush the head of the serpent. Let's look at this passage:

And I will put enmity between you and the woman, and between your seed and her seed; He shall bruise you on the head, and you shall bruise him on the heel.
Genesis 3:15

This is a fascinating passage. God is speaking to the deceiving serpent, the Nachash. This states that the Nachash has seed, and that the woman has seed. This is why many describe our timeline, from creation to the second coming, as a Seed War between Elohim and the Nachash and his compadres. This also is a foreshadow of what we learn in Genesis 6 when we see this play out in a way I'm sure Adam and Eve never imagined: the fallen ones combining their seed with human women.

The children of Israel were chosen and marked by God for deliverance but only if they agreed to receive it. The sign of their agreement was obeying what He told them to do. Then, they watched the supernatural acts of God through Moses be taunted and reproduced by the masters of the dark arts...for a time.

The Hebrews were there during all of this.

The children of Israel, right along with the Egyptians, endured the first three plagues, the river turned to blood along with the stench, the frogs, and the lice (or gnats depending on your translation).

Then for the fourth plague of flies, God put a hedge of protection around them and their set-apart land of Goshen as the misery continued. As God did amazing signs and wonders, so the sorcerers did signs and wonders. But when God upped the ante the sorcerers finally said, we give in, this God of the Hebrews is too powerful for us.

Guess Who won in the end? God! The chosen people, along with anyone who wanted to go with them, were taken out of slavery and deep spiritual darkness, and led on a path to a new land where they would have to get to know this God Who saved them.

God always had a plan for all nations with this instruction:

> *But if a stranger sojourns with you, and celebrates the*
> *Passover to the Lord, let all his males be circumcised, and*
> *then let him come near to celebrate it; **and he shall be like***
> ***a native of the land**. But no uncircumcised person may*
> *eat of it. **The same law shall apply to the native as to the***
> ***stranger who sojourns among you.***
> *Exodus 12:48 [emphasis added]*

This is a perfect picture of the end times which we are witnessing right now.

However, these examples are not just object lessons of the pattern of the last days, and not just pictures of Who Messiah would be, they are also instructions on relationship with our God and spiritual warfare.

We are not to be afraid of the signs and wonders of the dark side. We should have been raised to understand this from the beginning. You'll find me saying this several times in this book:

1. *Supernatural power is absolutely real but there are only two sources of it*: the Lord God Almighty and the lord of Darkness.

2. *We were made to have a supernatural relationship* but with the King of Kings not the lord of Darkness.

3. *Salvation is itself a supernatural relationship.*

In Daniel 8:24 we learn of a coming king that will become very strong, but not in his own power; he will cause deceit to prosper; and when he is finally destroyed it will not be by human power.

Supernatural power is absolutely real. And as L.A. Marzulli has described so well in his book, *The Cosmic Chess Match*, we are in the midst of a war between powers. If you will read the whole Bible, not just a few passages from the New Testament, you will see it clearly... everywhere.

Take the passage in Luke where Yeshua Jesus is speaking with two of the disciples on the road to Emmaus. They were prevented from recognizing they were speaking with Yeshua and were telling Him about all that had happened in Jerusalem. He then responded with this:

> And He said to them, "O foolish men and slow of heart to believe in all that the prophets have spoken! "Was it not necessary for the Christ to suffer these things and to enter into His glory?" **Then beginning with Moses and with all the prophets, He explained to them the things concerning Himself in all the Scriptures.**
> Luke 24:25-27 [Emphasis Added]

Yeshua Jesus began with Moses and the prophets revealing the things about Himself in all the Scriptures! Wow!

When we start at the beginning, putting things in proper context, spiritual warfare leaps off the pages. It is everywhere when we have our eyes opened.

Just like Moses and Aaron in Pharaoh's court, we are to deliver the message we are told to give as we minister healing and deliverance to the suffering, and, like Pharaoh, the dark ones may put up a fight for a time. But when we are in obedience to scripture and what God has told us to do, when we use the authority given to us, and we know how to use the weapons He's given to us for spiritual warfare, the dark forces must obey. We advance, taking the territory as the enemy forces are pushed back.

Moses met God on the mountain and God told him to bring the nation to the mountain. Dr. Lake says, "Can't you just hear Moses saying, 'I can't wait for you to see this burning bush!' But when they got there, God set the whole mountain on fire and Moses was exceedingly afraid. I can see him saying, 'Dude, I just came to show you a bush!' But God wanted to sear in their minds His majesty." (Hebrews 12)

And, also just like with Moses and Aaron in the Exodus story, God uses these things to:

Infuse believers with increasingly strong faith. Why would you doubt God's existence when He hears and responds to warfare prayer, and when you see Him supernaturally deliver others from spiritual bondage? Why would you be afraid of dark powers when you see God defeat them every time?

Demonstrate His power to believers and unbelievers alike. Both believers and unbelievers are impacted by seeing true supernatural power in action. It's one of the proofs of God's existence. It provokes a response.

Definitively prove that He alone is God. Like Elijah with the fire from heaven contest, God makes it clear Who is really God and who is the charlatan, "the God that answers by fire, let Him be God." (1 Kings 18:24)

Call to the God-created desire in all of us for the supernatural relationship only found in Him.

When we start back at the beginning of the story and stop eliminating certain books or scriptures, instructions on spiritual warfare are very obvious; we see them everywhere.

Consider Daniel 10 where he had begun praying and fasting in mourning and continued for twenty-one days. When the angelic being shows up, he informs Daniel that he had been dispensed from the first day of Daniel's prayer:

> "But the prince of the kingdom of Persia withstood me one and
> twenty days: but, lo, Michael, one of the chief princes, came to
> help me; and I remained there with the kings of Persia."
> Daniel 10:13, KJV

This is a very informative passage. Just some of what we can glean from this portion of scripture:

- these beings have names such as Michael,

- these beings have titles such as Prince,

- (which inherently means) they have position within a structure,

- (which inherently means) they have various types of authority, and

- these beings have territories such as kingdoms in Persia.

With our roots in place, we can correctly understand what was expanded upon in the New Testament and we can move forward to address our method. All of this is very important for powerful spiritual warfare.

Method

How do we discern our method from scripture?

I suggest that we take it in this order:

1. *scripture*, both what is written specifically, and the principles given,

2. *fruit of the Holy Spirit* that bears witness and confirms, and,

3. *evidence in the world around us* which includes: what we observe as we do the work, researched concepts through both science and psychology, and what we observe in the enemy as evidenced in the occult.

---

*Note: I do not suggest to anyone to study the occult. Only those who are called, with multiple confirmations of the calling, who are studying to gain spiritual warfare instruction or to rescue those enslaved in occult circles should do so. Everyone else should rely upon texts of those called to the work, such as Russ Dizdar or Charles Kraft.

It may be obvious to some that we should look to scripture

first. But there is more involved in that statement than you may at first realize. There is the category of the specific scripture itself, an obvious point, but there are also *principles* found in scripture that are expressed in multiple ways.

For example, clients often ask me how to respond to a friend or family member who won't discuss the subject of spiritual warfare or who say, with the wave of a hand, "Jesus took care of all of that."

Well, if that were the case, if Jesus really did "take care of all of that" with the very clear and strong implication that you are to do nothing, you would have to explain:

- consistent metaphor of warfare (Ephesians 6),
- consistent metaphor of armor and weapons for the purpose of that warfare (Ephesians 6),
- description of and instructions to use supernatural weapons of warfare (2 Corinthians 10:4),
- cautions that we are struggling with and wrestling against a non-human enemy (Ephesians 6),
- instructions to be strong, alert (1 Peter 5:8), alert with perseverance, wise, to stand firm against this enemy and to pull down strongholds (2 Corinthians 10:4) which are all active and not passive words (Ephesians 6),
- consistent emphasis of using authority over this enemy (Luke 10:19-20),
- instructions that we are to take back the territory from, and tear down strongholds that belong to the enemy forces (2 Corinthians 10:4),
- definitions of the enemy as inhuman, rulers, powers, spiritual forces (Ephesians 6),

And you would have to answer these questions:

- Why would God give us all this intel and instructions, and repeat it many times, if He did all the work and you were expected to do nothing?

- Why isn't there a single verse anywhere surrounding the intel and instructions that says, I'm not talking about you because I did all of this, so you don't have to?

- Why can I not find any place in the Bible where God encourages or approves of expecting Him to do the work for us, work that we are repeatedly told we are to do?

- Why can I not find any place in the Bible where God approves of seeing evil approaching and doing nothing?

- Why did Yeshua Jesus tell us He gave us the authority to do these things, caution us to not get too happy and open the door to pride when we see the demons fleeing, and purchase this gift of authority with His very life, if we were not to use it?

Well, God does expect you to do the work for the Kingdom.

There is no scripture that advocates couch potato syndrome, but scripture does make clear that we are to do these things.

Christ strengthens us to actually DO things:

> *I can do all things through Christ which strengthens me.*
> *Philippians 4:13, KJV*

We are told to work:

> *Whatever your hand finds to do, do it with all your might;*
> *for there is no activity or planning or knowledge or wisdom*
> *in Sheol where you are going.*
> *Ecclesiastes 9:10*

We are to walk, bear fruit, and increase in the knowledge of God:

> *that you may be filled with the knowledge of His will in*
> *all spiritual wisdom and understanding, so that you will*
> *walk in a manner worthy of the Lord, to please Him in all*
> *respects, bearing fruit in every good work and increasing in*
> *the knowledge of God;*
> *Colossians 1:9-12*

You can't bear fruit if you aren't doing anything.

That calls to mind the parable of the servant who hid the talent because of fear of the master.

Please read Matthew 25:14-30, the *Parable of the Talents*. The Master gave his slaves a project, something he wanted them to spend time on while he was away. This was a project he wanted them to put thought into, something that was not a onetime-drop-the-penny-in-the-piggy-bank-and-turn-your-attention-to-something-else kind of thing. The fearful slave hid his talent in the ground and spent his time on something else (we aren't told what) even though he worked at the same place with the other slaves and there had to be discussion about what they were working on.

The fearful slave received a crushing rebuke.

Was the fear just an excuse or was the fear a real issue? We aren't sure but let's assume it was a real issue.

One of the things we can glean from this passage is that God does not approve of us allowing fear to control our decisions. Clearly, as indicated by the Master's response, that slave was expected to deal with the fear (and anything else that was a hindrance), to overcome, and to have victory with the project. And, if it were not possible, then the Master would be unkind. But that is not the case. The entire point is that it WAS possible, and the servant didn't do it.

The Master instructed the others to take away what the fearful, disobedient slave had and to give it to the others who had been willing to do the work necessary.

Then, this last verse just falls like a hammer:

> *For to everyone who has, more shall be given, and he will have an abundance; but from the one who does not have, even what he does have shall be taken away. Throw out the worthless slave into the outer darkness; in that place there will be weeping and gnashing of teeth.*
> *Matthew 25:29-30*

Outer Darkness is not a rough neighborhood in heaven.

God does not want us sitting around doing nothing and claiming He did it all for us. Simply put, that is not the model we see throughout scripture. And He does not like it when we choose not to do something He has asked us to do, especially when we've been given such great instructions and object lessons that have been carefully documented for two thousand years in our Guidebook to the Supernatural.

He gave us the tools and the instructions: He expects us to learn to use them proficiently and to move forward in the battle.

Paul said he and his partners were modeling for us how we should live:

> For even when we were with you, we used to give you this
> order: if anyone is not willing to work, then he is not to eat,
> either. For we hear that some among you are leading an
> undisciplined life, doing no work at all, but acting
> like busybodies.
> 1 Thessalonians 3:10-11

He tells us to not grow weary. You can't grow weary if you aren't doing anything.

> For consider Him who has endured such hostility by
> sinners against Himself, so that you will not grow weary
> and lose heart.
> Hebrews 12:3

He gave us the authority to do the work and then told us to do it:

> The seventy returned with joy, saying, "Lord, even the
> demons are subject to us in Your name." And He said
> to them, "I was watching Satan fall from heaven like
> lightning. "Behold, I have given you authority to tread
> on serpents and scorpions, and over all the power of the
> enemy, and nothing will injure you. "Nevertheless do not
> rejoice in this, that the spirits are subject to you, but rejoice
> that your names are recorded in heaven."
> Luke 10:17-20

There is consistent reference to taking action against evil:

> *A prudent man foreseeth the evil, and hideth himself: but*
> *the simple pass on, and are punished.*
> *Proverbs 22:3, KJV*

I hope you caught that: the wise takes action when evil approaches and the one who does not is referred to as a fool. This is a potent principle. In addition to that, we can't see evil approaching if we aren't paying attention and watching, which we've already seen we are told to do.

There is also constant reference to watching for evil approaching. If you hear the warning that the enemy is approaching and you do not heed the warning, your blood is on your own head (Ezekiel 33:5). Clearly, we are expected to know the sound of warning and know what to do after you hear the alarm.

If you are the one on watch and evil is approaching and you do not warn others, God holds you responsible (Ezekiel 33:6). Clearly, we are not to just watch for ourselves, but to warn others of the danger.

God said to Ezekiel in 33:7, "I have made you a watchman," and I believe we are all called to be alert and watching, we are all to warn others of the danger approaching, and we are all to be adept at using our weapons. We are all called to ministry on an individual basis, to minister the good news of the salvation message, to pray for one another, and to engage in spiritual warfare. These are the signs of true believers:

> *These signs will accompany those who have believed: in My*
> *name they will cast out demons, they will speak with new*
> *tongues; they will pick up serpents, and if they drink any*
> *deadly poison, it will not hurt them; they will lay hands on*
> *the sick, and they will recover.*
> *Mark 16:17-18*

I don't find any examples in scripture telling us to check out of the war and take up residence in an amusement park, saying "Jesus took care of all that; we are to relax now and wait for His return."

The children of Israel were not *given* the land God had promised to them, they were instructed to *take it* from the enemy, an enemy that was much larger and more powerful than they were: they were giants.

Remember how God uses patterns over and over?

Dr. Lake said this, "When Israel left Egypt, God had already judged all the gods of Egypt. And, in those nine plagues, he stripped Egypt of the wealth it had gained by what Joseph did when they first went down there...But once you cross the Jordan you better learn how to use a sword."

And even though God sent an angel to go before them (Exodus 23:20), they still had to do the fighting. In addition to that, God said they weren't allowed to have all of the land at once, but that they would take it a little at a time (Exodus 23:29). So, it was not a situation where they could say, "Come on guys, we just have to get through this one tough battle and it will all be paradise from there."

> *But David strengthened himself in the LORD his God.*
> *1 Samuel 30:6*

David strengthened himself; he knew how to do so and he did it. It was not done for him.

God told David to pursue and overtake the enemy (1 Samuel 30:8), which he did.

So, knowing scripture is the foundation for all things, and it's not just sets of words strung together, we now realize that there are principles which apply when we take all of scripture and don't just leap to a few popular New Testament passages and take them out of context within the book, or isolate them from the rest of scripture losing overall context.

Let's go to the next point.

Why would we want to know what the occult is up to? Because we need to know our enemy, for one thing. But also, because the Lord of Darkness does the opposite of God, perverting and inverting everything God has set up, His ways, His design, His plan. So, when we think we know what scripture says on a topic of spiritual warfare, and we then discover the occult is doing the opposite of what we believe God has said in His Word, we can use that as one type of evidence that we are discerning it correctly. It is not our first order of proof, but it does become a strong consideration as we evaluate how the supernatural world works.

For example, there are those who continue to insist that there are no such things as charged objects in the spiritual war. But again, scripture says otherwise.

> *God was performing extraordinary miracles by the hands*
> *of Paul, so that handkerchiefs or aprons were even carried*
> *from his body to the sick, and the diseases left them and*
> *the evil spirits went out.*
> *Acts 19:11-12*

This is an example of supernatural power that flowed through Paul being somehow contained within an object of cloth and carried to a different location where Paul was not present, yet that supernatural power still healed and expelled evil spirits.

The enemy forces imitate God's plan, calendar, feasts, and model of the family, and they use charged objects that have been filled with demonic powers that cause various effects. As above, so below. The fallen forces try to mirror God, using darkness and deception.

Other things we see in the occult are a calendar[71] of feasts, holidays[72], rituals, prayers, indwelling, sacrifices of blood, animal and or human life, and sexual ritual to pervert God's model.

Former high-level Satanists, redeemed by the Blood of the Lamb, have shared valuable intel about what occult groups do. They look for Christians, they can tell the weak believers from the strong, and they actively send curses upon them.

As a strong believer, your supernatural radar should be sensitive enough that you recognize something pinging off your armor. You should immediately ask the Lord what is happening and check your armor again to make sure it is secure and complete. And, if you are well-trained, you will throw up some powerful prayer that will send those hexes and curses back to the sender in order to bring them to their knees in realization that it is only the King of Kings Who answers by fire, and that they are serving a liar and false god. We are to pray for these deceived servants of the dark ones. These encounters are opportunities for their salvation.

So now you know that we take scripture first, which includes what is specifically written. We take the principles given in scripture. We watch for what bears fruit by the Holy Spirit or by the dark forces (which means we have been able to see a particular point bring a consistent result). And finally, we examine what we see in the world around us that confirms our understanding and method of dealing with the supernatural.

The How: A Battle Plan That Works

Our King and Captain has not left us defenseless. He has given us tools and weapons. If we will take all of scripture, we will see the instructions, object lessons, and demonstrations everywhere.

First: We Must Be Saved

I have an extensive application I use in counseling. Within that application, I ask my clients to write down the date of their salvation and to tell the story of how they came to know the Lord.

On several occasions they were unable to tell me a date and had no description of, what should be, a life-changing supernatural encounter with the Living God. They say things like, "Oh, I grew up in church."

Only after examination do they realize they have never given their life to the Lord and we take care of that immediately.

If that sounds like you, realize that this is a major issue when dealing with the supernatural realm and warfare. You're in a battle with no right to access the winning team! Choose this day whom you will serve.

> *If it is disagreeable in your sight to serve the LORD, choose for yourselves today whom you will serve: whether the gods which your fathers served which were beyond the River, or the gods of the Amorites in whose land you are living; but as for me and my house, we will serve the LORD.*
> *Joshua 24:15*

Do you remember the day you got married to the King of Kings?

If not, seriously consider whether you gave your heart to Him or whether you just went along with the program for whatever reason, and never truly did so.

Confess with your mouth that you are a sinner in need of a Savior, and that you could never earn the gift.

Believe in your heart that God raised Yeshua from the dead, forever defeating the power of death and the grave.

Ask the Father to fill you with His Holy Spirit.

Get baptized in obedience to His instructions which also declares to the dark forces you have died to your old self and have been raised to new life in Yeshua Jesus.

Dedicate the rest of your life to serving Him and getting to know the Lover of our souls, our goel (kinsmen Redeemer), the Moshia HaOlam (Savior of the World).

Keep A Journal

This journey into freedom is full of road markers that can easily be missed or forgotten if we neglect to make note of them in a journal dedicated to this purpose. If you have a counselor, it will be very helpful for your counseling time. If you are doing this work on your own, it is still a major part of the journey.

The journal does not need to be long and detailed unless you like to write that way. A bullet-point list of the day is just fine. But dates and times are important. Don't forget to include both. You will begin to see patterns that were undetected before, for instance, dreams with a certain theme may occur at certain times of night, or on certain days on the calendar.

As often as you have the thought, multiple times a day, ask the Lord to reveal every hiding place of the darkness in your life. You will be surprised what the holy spirit brings to mind. Things you haven't recalled for years, or a childhood experience that was locked away in the subconscious may suddenly pop onto your radar. Pray about them immediately as they are presented to you and write them down.

Faithfully note any dreams. Over time, you may notice the content or the feelings of the dreams begin to change. You may notice God speaking to you more often in the nighttime as you sleep.

Make a point to note anything you believe the Lord may be speaking to your heart as you're praying. For instance, when you are engaged in prayer as you are washing the dishes or the car, suddenly you recall an old soul tie you never removed, or an action you never repented of. Write all these down and you will notice a path headed straight for the heart of our HaGoel, our Redeemer.

Also, be sure to document any time you feel you are attacked. Write down the date and what you were doing before it occurred, then describe the attack and everything you did in the battle to stop it, whether you were successful or not. After the ambush stops, begin talking to the Lord about it. Ask Him what the source of it is, where the open doors are, and to expose every hiding place of darkness in your life. Write down what you believe the Lord shows you.

This journal, you will discover, becomes the story of answered prayer, miracle confirmations, victories over the unseen realm, and the testimony of your journey to a deeper relationship with Yeshua. I've had several clients who were not journal keepers and struggled in the beginning to be faithful with the task. But before long, they began making references to their journals and how often they saw the hand of God in the process. It is the screenplay to the movie of your life. It is exciting and wonderful. It will also tell the story of how you overcame obstacles you never thought you could defeat. And, it will be your encouragement along the way. On a day you are feeling defeated, make a habit of going to your journal and re-reading the times God delivered.

Commitment Required

The process involves time, intent, devotion, and unflinching honesty. There will be fasting and tears. And, there is no substitute for the deep prayer required.

I've had a few people come to me for help saying they feel they are under supernatural attack. I speak with them, show them scripture, and the whole time they are agreeing wholeheartedly. Then, when they learn they must actually put in time and effort, they are disappointed, leave, and I never hear from them again.

What these people really want is to meet with me, tell me the events they are too afraid to tell anyone else, and then to receive some magical prayer that makes it all okay again. They want standing in the prayer line at church to be the only effort required.

This is the equivalent to expecting someone else, a spiritual surrogate so to speak, to do the work for you. This is what the Word of God refers to as the immature believer, wanting to stay on the milk of the Word rather than graduating to the meat of the Word.

> *Everyone who lives on milk is still an infant, inexperienced*
> *in the message of righteousness.*
> *Hebrews 5:14*

You can't expect someone else to do this work for you just as you can't get saved through someone else, such as your parents. You yourself have to make the decision to follow Christ, you have to learn to walk in holiness, you have to grow to maturity. This is your personal journey into the heart of your Savior.

The typical client I see has struggled for many years and tried everything, all to no avail. They are desperate for the answer. They usually do not need to be prodded to do the work; they are all too happy to do it and see results very quickly.

This is not an easy, weekend retreat kind of process. You are making a commitment not to just defeat a singular foe, but to grab hold of the tzitzit, the tassels on the hem of Jesus' robe.

Though the journey is not easy (nothing worthwhile ever is), it has the potential to be the most amazing time of your life.

You do not come through this journey unchanged. Lay everything down. Tell your King that there is nothing you will hide from Him.

> *Search me, O God, and know my heart; try me and know*
> *my anxious thoughts. And see if there be any hurtful way*
> *in me, and lead me in the everlasting way.*
> *Psalm 139: 23, 24*

The Three Pillar Model

We discussed in the Introduction the three-pillar approach. Using standard counseling alone or deliverance alone is not enough.

I believe the key to teaching the body of Christ to walk in power, love, and a sound mind for the rest of their lives is the three-pillar model.

It is not a class you take for four weeks where you collect your grade and you're through. It is training on how to live your life in Yeshua every day for the rest of your life. As we are equipped and successful, we then equip others.

In summary, the three pillars of this approach are:

1. Address the wounding and negative life patterns with *inner healing counseling* that always has in view signs and symptoms of demonic influence and attachment. In my counseling ministry this includes an extensive application and a family tree genogram that are very helpful at revealing problem areas.

2. Reveal the demonic. With prayer and fasting the *deliverance* battle plan is given by the Lord and the appropriate time is allotted for the eviction.

3. Teach, using the *discipleship* model, principles and skills of spiritual warfare, and solid foundations of the faith which require building new habits.

After the deliverance is complete, we continue inner-healing counseling for a time to effectively apply God's healing salve to all unresolved wounds revealed through the process, and we also continue discipleship to make sure healthy spiritual patterns are built and a new normal is firmly established.

Create A Genogram, A Family Tree

This is incredibly helpful. It aids in revealing patterns from multiple generations. Patterns of disease, depression, or early death, for example.

Get your papers ready for the project. Then, before you even begin, pray. Ask the Lord to bring to mind everything He needs you to remember for the picture to be complete for healing and deliverance. Do this every time you work on it.

As you write down names of family members, near each name make a note of the things mentioned above including, cancer, alcoholism, abuse, drug addiction, suicide, infidelity, divorce, and anything else that comes to mind which is in opposition to God's perfect plan. Especially note involvement in occult activities and groups, such as Free Masons and their various branches and levels. Masonic bondage was part of the powerful bondage I was not able to break on my own without support. Several of my clients have had a similar experience.

One male client has expressed to me on several occasions how surprised he has been at the level of bondage that came up connected to family involvement with the Masons. The supernatural power is real and strong. Some occult groups include dedications of future progeny. Do not neglect this part of the exercise.

The Captain Has A Plan

Because most congregations do not teach spiritual warfare, or offer support services, or even provide maturity training I refer to as discipleship, many believers are woefully unprepared for the reality of spiritual life or ministry, and they struggle to reach spiritual goals. This is not God's plan!

I need to pause here for just a moment to say a word about discipleship.

There has been a disturbing twisting of "discipleship" in recent years. I know people who have witnessed a perversion of this concept and the damage which has resulted in their congregations. This book is not addressing that problem. But I do think it is important to clarify: I am using the word discipleship in the biblical sense of mature believers leading and training younger believers in the foundations of the faith, including spiritual warfare.

In my ministry, I assist others in learning how to walk in power, love, and a sound mind, not just for a season or to defeat a temporary foe, but to walk in it for the rest of their lives, emerging from the process able to assist others and also reach a deeper level in their own ministry.

> *For this reason I remind you to fan into flame the gift of*
> *God, which is in you through the laying on of my hands,*
> *for God gave us a spirit not of fear but of power and love*
> *and self-control.*
> *2 Timothy 1:6-7, ESV*

All of the pieces of the puzzle are listed in this book and all are necessary for the deliverance process to be complete.

Stay Connected

The enemy would love to get you isolated, to cull you from the herd so you will be easy to pick off.

Sometimes it is pride or shame that makes us continue to battle alone when in fact we need to find someone within the body of Christ who understands the nature of the battle and will share the challenge and stand alongside us as we march on to victory.

Many of my clients deal with shame that is fed by flawed thinking and wrong church teaching, and the enemy adds his shame to the pot, stirring it continually.

They often feel shame because they have believed that a Christian cannot experience the types of attack for which they seek counseling. This causes them to isolate. They don't want others in their congregation to know the battle that has been raging around them, so they carefully hide or never discuss portions of their lives.

This is not the way the Body of Yeshua is supposed to function. And, it is exactly what the enemy wants to achieve because we are not created to fight these battles alone. It is not the model Jesus gave us and, because there is a reason for every instruction He's given us, we don't have the level of protection we need in battle.

Mature believers also experience significant shame because they are deeply puzzled as to why they have been unable to break the bondage or stop the attack on their own.

It is not necessarily an indication of an anemic relationship with Yeshua, though it could be. Primarily, it is because we are not designed to fight these battles alone.

We don't want to have to tell others about our vulnerabilities, our weaknesses. We are very removed from the biblical model of confessing our sins to one another. In today's church culture, we'd rather act sophisticated and aloof, or reflect whatever thing we label as cool. We much prefer acting as though we are all good and fabulous. This is not spiritual reality. It's not honesty, either.

We all have battles from time to time; that is the normal Christian life. But, until we break all of the other bondage which has come from multiple sources, it's a much greater load; it's as though we are underwater fighting for breath. We must first get the backlog of bondage and demonic attachment broken, then we only have to deal with the day-to-day stuff. Even then, however, we are to deal with these things with battle-savvy mentors.

Imagine this picture. When we have these overwhelming battles, we go through a check list, as we should. We do what we know we are supposed to do, but there is something we are unable to break. That's when we go to the mentor to uncover it and address it. As we do this, we are modeling the way Yeshua wants His body to function. This keeps us from isolating, prevents us from pretending to ourselves and others that we are without sin, plus you get free from the bondage and the mentors have fulfilled the mission and calling Yeshua had given them! It's a beautiful picture. This is how we address these things for the rest of our lives. No matter how mature we are in warfare, even after all bondage is broken, something can come up in the future when we need to get some back up for a battle.

God never works in ones!

Each person's testimony is encouragement to all the others experiencing the same thing.

If I could tell you who my clients are, you would be shocked. They are honorable and mature leaders in congregations like yours.

Can you see the lie the enemy keeps spinning here?

Many people are struggling with the same thing, because, guess what, we were told in the Bible that we would! But the enemy wants congregations to preach that real Christians can't have these problems, which is a lie. This lie keeps the sheep trapped in shame and feeling alone and isolated, when the truth is that most of the people in the congregation are dealing with the same things! It is a circle, the Ouroboros occult symbol of the snake in a circle eating its tail.

Sometimes, Yeshua just wants you to deal with another person for reasons you don't know. That happened in my own life. I've mentioned it briefly already, but let me expound. I had been studying spiritual warfare and the supernatural for many years and broken most of the bondage in my life. There was something, however, that I was aware of that I could not break. For years I prayed about it and about finding the person the Lord wanted me to work with. Finally, clear as a bell, He pointed out the person to me. Through that experience, I learned even more of what the enemy had been hiding from me, I had a fellow warrior standing with me, and we were both in the position God wanted us in at that time and in that moment. The bondage was broken, and I praise God to this day for the experience.

We must be very careful not to allow pride to keep us in bondage. Not wanting anyone to know there is a struggle we can't overcome is a tool of the enemy we are not to be ignorant of.

I hope this helps pull back the veil of lies the enemy has placed in front of the believing community. All of us deal with this!

We are instructed to live in victory *through* the battle, not just when it's over.

Find someone who can assist you during the most difficult time as you battle these forces.

Confidence In The Captain

Remember in Numbers 13 and 14 when Israel sent spies to survey the land promised to them by God? They were scared after seeing the size of the giants and God was very angry they didn't trust Him after all He had done. Joshua and Caleb tried to encourage them:

> If the LORD is pleased with us, then He will bring us into
> this land and give it to us—a land which flows with milk
> and honey. Only do not rebel against the LORD; and do
> not fear the people of the land, for they will be our prey.

> *Their protection has been removed from them, and the*
> *LORD is with us; do not fear them.*
> *Numbers 14:8-9*

When these former slaves, who were still infected with a slave mentality, had to go into the first couple of battles, they were battling fear in themselves. But after seeing the power of the Lord deliver, it wasn't so scary. They slowly began to trust Him and they did what they needed to do: they put their battle plans together, they sharpened their swords, they prayed for the Lord to lead them, then they set off on the mission to defeat another group of minions and to take the territory for El Elyon!

What was the difference? The nature of the enemy hadn't changed. The size of the enemy hadn't changed. But they had seen the faithfulness of the Captain of the army deliver victory! It was their perspective and attitude that changed.

People like to pile on after winning becomes a sure thing, don't they?

The process I am trying to describe in this book is very much like the journey the children of Israel took. God gave us a model! When they first saw the giants in the land God wanted them to take, the giants were so large that they said they felt like mere insects in comparison.

> *There also we saw the Nephilim (the sons of Anak are part*
> *of the Nephilim); and we became like grasshoppers in our*
> *own sight, and so we were in their sight.*
> *Numbers 13:33*

Yes, it's true, they were the size of a large bug compared to these enormous, evil creatures!

In addition to that, as if that wasn't bad enough, the verse before said those inhabitants devoured their human opponents.

> *A land that devours its inhabitants; and all the people*
> *whom we saw in it are men of great size.*
> *Numbers 13:32*

The Hebrew word translated as *devour* is *okelet,* meaning to devour a human subject. It's only used three times and it is the same word used in Exodus 24:17 to describe the Lord as a consuming fire. This force that was in the Nephilim consumed until there was nothing left, the inversion of our Savior's shed blood which consumes *all* sin until there is nothing left, if we accept that supernatural gift and subsequent transformation. Accepting the gift means complete transformation. There is no salvation without the expressions of righteousness and holiness.

And, don't forget that they were still full of a slave mentality that had been burned into their brains and identity for hundreds of years during which time they were never able to even defend themselves. Yet, their God, One Whom they'd just met, was telling them to be on the offensive, to gather forces and go out to attack a foe...but not just any foe, but giants imbued with supernatural evil!

God had a plan: to show them it didn't matter how big the opponent was, or how many of them showed up with all of their fierce power and noise.

> *Do not fear the people of the land, for they will be our prey.*
> ***Their protection has been removed from them,*** *and the*
> *LORD is with us; do not fear them.*
> *Numbers 14:8-9 [emphasis added]*

The Captain has a plan! He is not sending you to your destruction. The enemies' protection has been removed from them!

As He chooses to defeat this foul enemy through these tiny earthen vessels, He makes a point to the enemy forces that His power is incomparable. Imagine the insult!

He teaches us too, His earthen vessels, that His matchless power will flow through us and that all we need to do is to be prepared, follow instructions, and trust Him implicitly.

God never works in ones, remember?

Spiritual warfare is not like seeing a mouse, then calling an exterminator to get rid of that single mouse, while you go back to business as usual. In that scenario, you call someone else to take care of the problem for you while you go get lunch and when you return, the problem has been handled. You didn't change anything in your life at all. You don't need to understand and identify rodent behavior, identify signs of their presence, or know how to capture rodents and prevent them from getting in. You just call someone else to do it for you whenever needed.

To put it another way, spiritual warfare is not about defeating a single dark entity attacking you with, let's say, unwanted thoughts so that you can get rid of them and "get back to your life". It is a complete lifestyle change as a result of an encounter with the living God. It's learning Who the Captain is, allowing Him to train you, and going to the armory to get custom designed weapons that actually work. He trains you on how to spot the enemy, how to capture the enemy, how to bind them up, and how to remove the enemy. It is our calling!

The enemy doesn't change, it is you who is changed by the transformative power of the living God and by making the journey with Him!

It is all about the relationship between you and your Captain.

Once you get trained, once you see that what I'm saying is true and that these dark powers MUST obey the instructions made in the name and authority of the King of Glory, the fear melts away, you see you're on the winning team, and you enjoy winning with your faithful Captain!

Maybe you read comic books as a kid. Maybe you like the movie, Superman. This real-life experience is so much better!

When you learn Who your Captain is, the experience changes you forever, you're no longer afraid to take the territory for the kingdom, you watch the enemy run from you, and the Captain gets all the glory!

It changes everything.

Have confidence in your Captain. He is faithful to lead you in all things.

Know The Enemy

> *Your servant has killed lions and bears; this uncircumcised*
> *Philistine will be like one of them, for he has defied the*
> *armies of the living God.*
> *1 Samuel 17:26*

You can't fight an enemy you can't identify. You can't defend against weapons and tactics you have never seen or experienced.

We must know who our enemy is, understand how they work, and be able to spot indications of their presence. You can't fight skillfully if you haven't had enough practice.

We just talked about the Nephilim. We've discussed some of the evidence of evil in our culture and how that evil and deception has infiltrated the church to an astonishing level.

We are learning to more readily identify things that are not of God and respond quickly.

We've also learned who the enemy is and how they plot our destruction with a venomous hatred that we cannot begin to understand.

They use shame, self-hatred, and fear to keep you where they want you.

We've also learned that they have two main goals: 1) to cause you as much torment as possible for eternity, and 2) to stick it to God by torturing what He loves, us. By achieving number 1, they achieve number 2.

So, we must learn what our weapons are and how to use them. Much of this is not what you may think.

The Weapons

Our Captain has given us weapons to use in this supernatural battle that rages all around us. The most common scripture on the subject is Ephesians 6. We've already referred to it many times. Here is the list of the armaments.

Helmet of Salvation (found in Ephesians 6:17 and Isaiah 59)

Breastplate of Righteousness

Belt of Truth

Feet covered with the Gospel of Peace

Shield of Faith

Sword of the Spirit.

Now what?

We've already been addressing these things.

You must be saved and clothed in the righteousness of Christ which we receive at salvation.

Truth is not a concept, it is a Person: Yeshua HaMashiach, the Way, the Truth and the Life (John 14:6). The Word of God is Truth, and Yeshua IS the Word (John 1:1).

As our words explain our minds to others, so was the Son of God sent in order to reveal His Father's mind to the world.[73]

I will state clearly here and now: put on the armor every morning, every night, and every time the Holy Spirit causes it to enter your mind throughout the day. Before your feet even hit the floor in the morning, put your armor on. Put it all on.

There is literal weaponry here, but there is also a demonstration of intent every time we do so. Every time we put our armor on, we are setting our intent, turning our face towards, setting our minds upon, being fully equipped with the armor.

But our weapons are also everything in this book, such as walking in holiness. All of these things work together, are a covering, imbue us with His power, and maintain our vital connection to the Captain and King.

Here's how I include the armor in my daily prayers. There is a section of prayers later for reference, but I will also include it here.

In the morning for example:

> "Praise your name, Lord! Thank You for rest. Thank You for this day. I dedicate my day to You. Don't let the enemy waste a single moment of it. I put on the full armor of God: the helmet of salvation, the breastplate of righteousness, the belt of truth, my feet are covered with the gospel of peace, I have the shield of faith and the sword of the spirit. Lead me in all things, every thought, every word, every decision I make. Holy Spirit be in complete control."

In the Prayer Weapons section, we pull all of this together.

Intent & Longing

As you are beginning to notice, intent comes up over and over again. This is such a powerful component, both in our walk with the Lord and in spiritual warfare, that we will address it again here. We just saw how intent plays a role in putting on our armor. Now let's look at how it impacts our intimacy with God.

Intent and longing-- what we set our hearts on-- is very powerful. We must pay closer attention to what is really at the core of our actions, desires, and goals.

When I spilled my drink on you, was it an accident or on purpose? Same action, very different intent.

When I have devotions with my Savior, are my thoughts, "Okay, I have to read this chapter this morning, and then spend five minutes in prayer, then I have to get to the gym, so I'll be on time for work."

While that may be a practical thought, it is certainly not one of intimacy. That may be fine just as a thought of planning out your day, but it would not work very well if you said that to your spouse on date night.

"Okay, I have to get dressed and spend a few minutes with you, then I can get back to reading."

It doesn't sound very inviting, does it? And, I'm not even talking about the other person hearing it, I'm talking about your own intent.

Words reflect the intent of our hearts, but they also more firmly establish the direction we take. What if it was said a different way?

"I'm so glad I get to have some time with you this evening. I want to enjoy every minute before I have to get back to the kids' school project."

We know from numerous scientific studies that our thoughts and words greatly impact our feelings and health. We don't want to feed the negativity; we want to counter it with positivity and then our bodies and emotions will follow. As we feed on God's Word out emotions will eventually line up with it.

Do we even understand what it means to have intimacy with Him?

We must make the switch in our hearts to an understanding that Yeshua is real, He is not a concept or merely a world view. We have to learn to trust what we can't see, to listen to the whispers as He leads us, realize He is the love-sick teenager outside in the dew, throwing pebbles against our windowpane to get our attention.

So, intent does affect us, but it also affects things outside of us, such as our family members. Let's look at another example.

When you have a secret fantasy involving a vampire from a movie, even if you never speak a word of it, intent, what you have set your mind on, is very powerfully calling to the dark side. It may not be as blatant as performing an occult activity, like using a Ouija board. But it reminds me of a strong scent.

Have you ever been in a grocery store and someone has on way too much perfume or cologne? Sometimes the whole aisle still reeks of the scent after they've turned the corner. That scent representing intent, longing for something from the dark side, is somehow perceived by the evil ones. They are drawn to it. If these things are not put in check and repented for, it can become increasingly problematic.

This concept of intent is also very powerful as you learn to pay closer attention to your thoughts and words. Negative words spoken out loud began as thoughts in the mind. We'll talk more about words later.

Have you heard the phrase, Be intentional?

Know what city your plane is flying toward. Enjoy the journey. But know the destination, what it takes to get there, realize your companion is your loving Father. Speak to Him along the way. Every question that comes up should be directed to Him. He has all knowledge and all power, everything you need to get there safely. And, He loves spending time with His kids.

> The heart is deceitfully wicked, who can know it?
> (Jeremiah 17:9)

We need His help knowing the truth about ourselves.

Take Every Thought Captive

We talked about the flaming arrows. They are the unwanted thoughts flying in our direction from the minions behind a rock. As they land, if we do not properly deflect them, they begin to burn up and damage the target; the fire will spread.

> We are destroying speculations and every lofty thing raised
> up against the knowledge of God, and we are taking every
> thought captive to the obedience of Christ,
> 2 Corinthians 10:5

This is a critical component of this process. Begin paying close attention to thoughts that come into your head. Are they your own? Or are they from another place? Faithfully include this topic in your daily prayers.

I'm about to give you some tools to help with this. But, as you start, don't get discouraged that there are so many, many more than you ever realized. You will miss a lot of them, but you will start deflecting some. Then, as you get more skilled, the number of unwanted thoughts will begin to decrease, your response time to each one will get faster, and you'll be able to deflect nearly all of them.

You'll see the improvement in your journal.

Column A & Column B

In order to help my clients more easily identify which thoughts are from the Lord and which are not, I give them this illustration. They tell me all the time it is one of their favorite tools because of its simplicity and effectiveness. I hope it will be helpful to you.

Imagine two columns in front of you. On your right, *Column A*, which represents the Lord God Almighty. This represents everything we know about the Savior of our souls, what He desires for us and instructions given to us in the Bible.

A Side Note: We always put God on the right because of scripture where the right hand is very significant. He upholds us with His "righteous right hand" as in Isaiah 41:10. God places the sheep on His right and the goats on His left in Matthew 25:33. The occult, which is often represented by the goat (The Baphomet has a goat head and the pentagram is the Goat's Head symbol.), is called the Left-Hand Path.

On your left is *Column B,* which represents *B-Z-B,* the rap name of [74]Beelzebub, Lord of the Flies. It represents what we know of him, his behavior, his goals for humanity and his methods.

I'm going to give you a word. I want you to say which column the word should be placed in. *Column A* – the King of Kings or *Column B* – the lord of the darkness. Does the word align with what we know of God and His principles as taught to us in the Bible? Or does the word align with things that are not of God, but are associated with the Lord of Darkness?

Ready?

Okay, here's your first word.

Fear.

Which column did you place it in?

We know that the Word of God tells us in II Timothy 1:7 that we are not given a spirit of fear, and:

> *There is no fear in love, but perfect love casts out fear. For fear has to do with punishment, and whoever fears has not been perfected in love.*
> *I John 4:18*

Therefore, since it is clear that fear is not of God, the correct column for the word, *Fear,* is *Column B* – the Lord of Darkness.

Let's try another word.

Ready?

Stress.

Which column did you place it in?

> *Therefore I tell you, do not worry about your life, what you will eat or drink; or about your body, what you will wear. Is not life more than food, and the body more than clothes?*
> *Matthew 6:25*

We are told repeatedly to not worry about anything in our lives.

Be anxious for nothing, but in everything, by prayer and petition, with thanksgiving, present your requests to God (Philippians 4:6).

The word, *Stress*, should be placed in the *Column B*.

What is my point here?

This is a great generalization that helps us to quickly know the source of things and what our response should be.

The fear you feel when a car runs a red light and almost hits you is a fear mechanism placed by God in the human body to protect you. We are not talking about that type of fear. But, if you struggle with worry, stress, anxiety or fear, generally speaking, those things are from the *B-Z-B* posse.

Here's another one. Ready?

Eating Disorder.

Which column did you put this one in?

Regardless whether the issue is eating too much or eating too little, it is an addiction and is clearly out of balance.

All addictions are not of God.

Nothing is supposed to control our choices; God Himself gives us free will and He refuses to violate it. As far as our own choices, they should not be led by any spirit but the spirit of the living God.

What are you addicted to?

Prescription meds? A person? Food? A habit? Porn? Occult games? Gossip, bragging, self-pity, popularity, exercise? Unhealthy behaviors or relationships?

This very short list is rampant in every congregation I've ever been in and I suspect in yours as well.

This simple and effective tool of the two columns helps us spot what we're really dealing with.

Most of my clients deal with various shades of fear, anxiety and shame. These things are by-products of dark bondage, such as an addiction, which may include supernatural things they can't explain, especially if the addiction is to many of today's online games. But this can also be the case if the client endured significant trauma, such as abuse as a child.

While we're here, why don't you stop for a moment and pray. Ask the Lord what is out of balance in your life, what you're addicted to, what the strongholds are in your life.

Did you begin a list?

Now, let's start looking at what to do once we identify some of the problems.

Rebuke & Reject

When you have a thought that you identify as belonging in *Column B*, your instructions are to "rebuke first, ask questions later". And do so with the authority, intent, and firmness appropriate after being assaulted.

I learned this phrase from L.A. Marzulli.

Here is a sample prayer:

"I rebuke and renounce that thought in the name of Yeshua! That is not of God! I do not receive thoughts, influence, or guidance from any spirit except the spirit of the Living God!"

The next piece is critical:

Speak the light of the truth of the Word of God into the darkness of the lie.

Speak the light of the truth of the Word of God into the darkness of the lie.

Whatever the lie is that the enemy sends to you, search your Bible and put together a quiver of scriptures that speak directly to it. I highly encourage you to write them down. Some clients have put these tools and prayers on index cards and carried them around in briefcases and purses.

If you are frequently attacked with thoughts of self-hatred, for example, you can declare, "I am not worthless and unloved! My Abba says He has written my name on the palm of His hand! He says that He rejoices over me with dancing and singing!"

This is the way Jesus handled the temptation. It is our instruction as well.

> *For the word of God is living and active and sharper than*
> *any two-edged sword, and piercing as far as the division*
> *of soul and spirit, of both joints and marrow, and able to*
> *judge the thoughts and intentions of the heart.*
> *Hebrews 4:12*

Now that you understand the components, put the prayer together.

> "I rebuke and renounce that thought in the name
> of Yeshua Jesus! That is not of God! I do not receive
> thoughts, influence, or guidance from any spirit except
> the spirit of the Living God! I am not worthless and
> unloved! My Abba says He has written my name on the
> palm of His hand! He says that He rejoices over me with
> dancing and singing!"

This is your weapon! It is sharp, it is effective! It is mighty through God and will demolish those strongholds in your mind!

Smack down! Kingdom Warrior – 1. Minions – 0.

In the early stage of this process of taking every thought captive (2 Corinthians 10:5), it is vital that you are tireless in your consistency. They will try to wear you down like an out-of-control child. As a good parent, you have to be utterly consistent; the punishment will be dispensed every time the child does the bad behavior. So it is with the dark side battle. Every time the flaming arrows are sent, you must respond as quickly as possible with the instructions you have here. No matter how many times you had to do it today, you must continue even when you're tired of the battle. Don't let them wear you down. If you stay consistent, you will notice the number of unwanted thoughts lessens and lessens.

I've also seen examples where the dark side slowly loses its ability to be creative with the thoughts they send. Somehow, they seem to be reduced to a library of only one or two old thoughts that they replay over and over. This is a very interesting phenomenon and I'm not totally sure why. Nevertheless, they begin to lose the battle.

Don't give up and be as consistent as possible. You have been given the victory. You will win!

Response Time

In sports, there is something called muscle memory and muscle response time.

As you are engaged in this new assignment of taking every thought captive, in the beginning, your 'muscle response time' is rather slow. You might be halfway to work in the morning before you realize you had really negative thoughts when you woke up. That's okay, you're getting used to paying attention.

We can also look at it another way.

When you're a new parent you aren't used to paying attention to every sound that comes from the baby's room; you learn.

Give yourself time to adjust. This is a skill, just like learning to listen for your kids playing in the next room.

If you're a parent, you'll understand this example even better than those who are not. But even those who aren't parents have friends who are. We've all seen this.

You're sitting at the kitchen table talking with a friend. Your kids are playing in the next room. They're on the loud side, having fun. Despite the noise, you are fully engaged in conversation with your friend, with contributions from each side. In mid-conversation, there was a certain bang, different than the other bangs and you immediately get up to see what happened. Your parent "radar" was on the whole time, as you were doing other things, scanning for any anomaly, and it picked up on something you needed to check out.

That is how taking every thought captive works. You develop a new radar for incoming missiles. You install this new radar system with the holy spirit's help by setting your intent, including these things in frequent prayer throughout every day. At first, you may miss a lot, and you may be delayed in getting to a few. But if you are diligent with this, a couple of weeks later, you will realize you are far quicker at noticing and deflecting every thought that is a Column B arrow.

Your stats will change and it will be noticeable, just like a basketball player working on his free-throw percentages. Write it in your journal. You'll see the transformation in action.

Repentance

You're learning to take every thought captive, to use the radar God equipped you with, and to respond more quickly. A foundational part of this process is repentance.

When you notice, maybe hours later, that you didn't capture a thought, you'll want to include repentance in your Rebuke & Reject prayer.

Include:

"And, Lord, if I let that thought linger even one second too long, I repent of it. I ask you to cleanse me with the blood of the Lamb. Remove every stain so that I can stand clean before Your throne."

One day many years ago, a guy I dated demonstrated some very bad behavior. Rather than apologize, he chose to say this with a smile.

"Love is never having to say you're sorry."

Have you heard that, too?

Well, I must tell you that when he said that twisted platitude to me with that smirk, it was the final straw.

"That is the stupidest thing I've ever heard," I said in astonishment. "When you love someone, you *want* to say you're sorry!"

Needless to say, that was the end of that relationship.

So, let's think about this. Do you *love* Jesus?

Do you have to be cornered like an animal before you apologize for wrongs you commit?

We can't truly *apologize* for things we refuse to acknowledge we've done. If you try to do so, it is only words without meaning.

We can't *turn around* from something we refuse to acknowledge, either.

Let's unpack this word *repentance* by beginning with some definitions.

The ATS Bible Dictionary definition[75]:

> A change of mind, accompanied with regret and sorrow for something done, and an earnest wish that it was undone.

Easton's Bible Dictionary definition[76]:

> There are three Greek words used in the New Testament to denote repentance.
>
> (1.) The verb *metamelomai* is used of a change of mind, such as to produce regret or even remorse on account of sin, but not necessarily a change of heart. This word is used with reference to the repentance of Judas (Matthew 27:3).
>
> (2.) *Metanoeo*, meaning to change one's mind and purpose, as the result of after knowledge. This verb, with
>
> (3) the cognate noun *metanoia*, is used of true repentance, a change of mind and purpose and life, to which remission of sin is promised.

Evangelical repentance consists of (1) a true sense of one's own guilt and sinfulness; (2) an apprehension of God's mercy in Christ; (3) an actual hatred of sin (Psalm 119:128; Job 42:5, 6; 2 Corinthians 7:10) and turning from it to God; and (4) a persistent endeavor after a holy life in a walking with God in the way of his commandments.

The true penitent is conscious of guilt (Psalm 51:4, 9), of pollution (Psalm 51:5, 7, 10), and of helplessness (Psalm 51:11; 109:21, 22). Thus he apprehends himself to be just what God has always seen him to be and declares him to be. But repentance comprehends not only such a sense of sin, but also an apprehension of mercy, without which there can be no true repentance (Psalm 51:1; 130:4).

Webster's Revised Unabridged Dictionary definition:

(n.) The act of turning around an improper behavior; sorrow for what one has done; especially, contrition for sin.

I want you to see that our ability to truly repent can be stymied by self-deception if, for example, we refuse to see what's in our motivation or behavior, or when demonic deception blinds us to what we are truly doing even when we want to see it and fix it.

I've seen some people who just flat out refuse to ever acknowledge that they are wrong. That could be a spirit of rebellion, among other things.

I've also seen people who seem to want to know but are unable to see it. That could be a spiritual blindness.

I've worked with some who have experienced verbal assault from others, on a regular basis, no matter how sweetly they speak. The people to whom they are speaking, often specific relatives, strangely claim that they are rude and disrespectful. That can be the result of a twisting spirit. It twists what is spoken after it leaves the mouth of the speaker before it even reaches the ears of those listening.

That same twisting spirit can work in the reverse. No matter how sweetly others speak to you, you hear it as disrespectful and stabbing, even when others in the same room hear no such thing. I've seen this many times also, where an individual is always offended and angry because what they hear is demeaning, when those speaking had no trace of that attitude.

We must be willing to see the truth regarding ourselves as it is revealed.

> *The heart is deceitful above all things, and desperately*
> *wicked: who can know it?*
> *Jeremiah 17:9, KJV*

We must seek out the ultimate truth about ourselves that is only found in the God Who created us.

> *It is better to trust in the LORD than to put confidence in man.*
> *Psalm 118:8, KJV*

> *Search me, O God, and know my heart: try me, and know*
> *my thoughts: And see if there be any wicked way in me,*
> *and lead me in the way everlasting.*
> *Psalm 139:23-24, KJV*

Truth and correction can sometimes come through our congregational leaders, mentors, or brothers and sisters in the Lord who may try to rightly speak into our lives as the Holy Spirit leads them.

> *If your brother sins, go and show him his fault in private; if*
> *he listens to you, you have won your brother. But if he does*
> *not listen to you, take one or two more with you, so that*
> *BY THE MOUTH OF TWO OR THREE WITNESSES*
> *EVERY FACT MAY BE CONFIRMED. If he refuses to*
> *listen to them, tell it to the church; and if he refuses to*
> *listen even to the church, let him be to you as a Gentile*
> *and a tax collector.*
> *Matthew 18:15-17*

Watch yourselves. If your brother sins, rebuke him; and if
he repents, forgive him.
Luke 17:3, BSB

Repentance is something we need to learn to walk out every moment of every day.

When I first say this to clients, occasionally one will ask if it is a form of legalism. I explain that, quite the contrary, it is total joy and freedom.

They are always surprised by this. Does it surprise you, too?

It is a joy because once we get our lenses adjusted by starting at the beginning of scripture, with proper understanding of Who our heavenly Father is, who we are, the gift we've been given, and the depth of relationship Jesus desires to have with us, we can begin to see it as a true marriage. With this view, we can then see that our bridegroom hates to have anything between us. If we love Him, we would hate that, too.

Once we begin to experience the depth of that relationship, learning to walk in power, love, and a sound mind, then all correction can be a joy.

Who can discern his own errors? Cleanse me from my
hidden faults.
Psalm 19:12

Search me, O God, and know my heart; Try me and know
my anxious thoughts;
Psalm 139:23

Let me be weighed in an even balance, that God may know
mine integrity.
Job 31:6, KJV

All discipline for the moment seems not to be joyful,
but sorrowful; yet to those who have been trained by it,
afterwards it yields the peaceful fruit of righteousness.
Hebrews 12:11

The more I know my Savior, the more I love Him. I don't want anything between us. He desires to protect me, to provide for me, to lead me in all things, to give me favor. But, if I allow things to fester between us, the relationship suffers and all the blessings of relationship suffer also.

This is the joy of repentance!

I *want* to apologize, to repent. I repent daily, anytime it comes to mind because, first and foremost, I love Him.

Second, I want to cover anything that I do not know that I did.

Third, as I experience more and more of His undeserved forgiveness, as He takes me to deeper levels of healing, I find that I am compelled to repent again for some things I have done in the past, even though they are already forgiven. Why? Because as He has taken me to a new depth of healing I receive and a new depth of understanding of the event.

Let me explain.

As I've described elsewhere in this book, as a matter of principle not law, you can't forgive what you don't know took place, because you have no idea what you are forgiving. It cannot have the same depth of meaning. We do not have all knowledge as God does.

Healing comes in layers. Also, as we mature and grow, we are able to see things we were unable to see before. I've experienced this and my clients have also, as another layer is revealed then healed. We repent again in that moment because we have been given a glimpse of a whole new layer of the sin we committed.

It is the opposite of legalism but make no mistake: the devil does not want you to do it! He loses when you learn this well, so of course he lies and hopes you think it's legalism. Also, it is not the result of a belief that we were not forgiven the first time we prayed about it. It is the praise, celebration of, and humility born of going through the healing process and allowing the Master's skillful hands to gently and slowly cut away the cancerous tissue and apply the healing Balm of Gilead to every wound. It is also a mark of maturity to 'own' every part of what we do in our lives, not to make excuses for it, but to take responsibility for it and be cleansed by the blood. It is the intent that nothing is off the table before the Lord. Anything He wants to work on, we receive.

In my own relationship with Him, it is often spoken in this way:

"Oh, my sweet Lord, I see that event in a whole new way now. There is even more sin there than I was able to see when You first revealed it to me. Praise Your name, Yeshua, for loving me, for forgiving me when I hadn't even realized all that was involved in what I did. Thank You for revealing it to me so I can repent of it. Forgive me for these newly revealed levels of sin. Remove every stain as You wash me clean in the blood of the Lamb so that I can stand clean before You, so that my praise will be received, and my requests will be heard. Cleanse me completely so there is nothing between us. Praise Your Name, for Your unfathomable love, mercy, and grace!"

Here is a very interesting verse that I believe is too often neglected:

> *Therefore, to one who knows the right thing to do and does not do it, to him it is sin.*
> *James 4:17*

In God's structure, there is, to some extent, forgiveness when we don't know about it. We also see this in Torah regarding the sacrifices in the temple. It is the *asham* or guilt offering made when you aren't sure if you committed a sin or if you aren't sure what sin you committed. There is this thing of knowing and not knowing and God's mercy provides a way.

But once we know it is there, we are not to ignore it. To me, as my Lord reveals things in layers, once it becomes known to me, I believe the right thing for me to do is to repent again, even if it is regarding an event I'd already asked forgiveness for. And I do so with love and joy, praising His Name for His mercy revealing it to me.

Our King doesn't want anything between us.

We shouldn't want anything between us either.

It is similar to when your spouse says, "Can we talk? I need to share something with you...This hurt me."

Of course, if you love your spouse, you would want to hear what hurt and work it out to forgiveness and restoration.

That is what I'm talking about here.

This is not a legalistic view of beating yourself up, it is being responsible for layers of sin that our Lord reveals to us as we continue our healing journeys; it is the desire to keep our relationship with Him in good standing...and to go ever deeper.

As He reveals more, giving us the ability to see things through His eyes, as we repent more, it brings more and more maturity, being able to see different levels of offense, sin, repentance, restoration, and deeper healing, all from an event you repented for years ago. When He desires to use old experiences, we can still learn and grow from them, if we let Him cut a little deeper with His surgeon's hands.

Understanding His grace more and more, our prayers continue to change. Try adding this to the prayer at the start of this section:

"Lord, I repent for any sin I've committed. Wash me clean in Your blood. And, I also ask You to forgive me for anything that hurt Your heart. I'm sorry. Remove anything that is not pleasing to You."

Do you care about what hurts His heart?

We aren't just ticking boxes, here. We are digging deep.

I want to hear His voice clearly, at all times; I don't want anything affecting my ability to hear Him.

It is love. It is joy. It is the desire to be completely His.

Or do you despise the riches of his goodness, forbearance,
and patience, not knowing that the goodness of God leads
you to repentance?
Romans 2:4, BSB

Shut Opened Doors

As we are praying what we've just discussed, when thoughts linger a little too long before we notice we need to take them captive, when God is revealing new levels of healing and the sin attached to that level, we need to address any doors that may have been opened.

We will continue to address this subject. But this is an appropriate place to add a new portion to the prayers we've just discussed.

> "And, any doors to the dark side that were opened when
> I let that thought linger too long, Lord, I ask You to shut
> them right now in the name of Yeshua, and seal them
> with the blood of the Lamb."

This is how we live daily life in warrior mode. This is how we keep the house swept clean as dust tries to settle. If there were any dark ones stepping through the door before we slammed it shut, there may have been dirt attached to the shoes. This prayer addresses that.

This is not how we will address the old, strong bondage from the past that must be broken; these are the moment to moment, prayers we use for daily life.

Walk In Holiness

The definition of *holiness* is not a list of random things you are not allowed to do, compiled by a tyrannical Being who wants to keep you from doing things you enjoy.

Holiness is aligning yourself with your personal purpose designed by the God Who created you and aligning yourself with His gift of salvation, His methods, and His instructions that imbue you with His power, covering, and anointing.

Intent is important here, yet again. God is not interested in you ticking the box next to each task on the list: He is interested in relationship, one that has immeasurable depths which He wants us to plumb with wonder, respect, and love.

O LORD, the God of Abraham, Isaac and Israel, our
fathers, preserve this forever in the intentions of the heart
of Your people, and direct their heart to You;
1 Chronicles 29:18

The righteousness of Christ is given to us (Romans 3:22, 2 Corinthians 5:21) through the sacrifice at Calvary and the victory of the empty grave. It is a gift. Holiness is something we are to walk out, with the assistance and inspiration of the Holy Spirit.

Speak to all the congregation of the sons of Israel and say to
them, 'You shall be holy, for I the LORD your God am holy.
Leviticus 19:2

The *Matthew Henry Commentary*[77] contains this statement about that passage, "It is required that Israel be a holy people, because the God of Israel is a holy God, ver. 2. To teach real separation from the world and the flesh, and entire devotedness to God. This is now the law of Christ; may the Lord bring every thought within us into obedience to it!"

In Luke 1, the Holy Spirit prophesied through Zacharias:

To grant us that we, being rescued from the hand of our
enemies, might serve Him without fear, in holiness and
righteousness before Him all our days.
Luke 1:74-75

And:

For God has not called us to uncleanness, but to holiness.
1 Thessalonians 4:7

What is your body made for?

Now the body is not for fornication, but for the Lord.
1 Corinthians 6:13

Just a few verses later Paul says it:

Do you not know that your bodies are temples of the Holy
Spirit, who is in you, whom you have received from God?

You are not your own.
1 Corinthians 6:19, NIV

Of course our bodies are made for the Lord, because He told us we are now the temple! But, if you don't know anything about the temple from the object lesson He gave us when the temple was designed by David and built by Solomon, that statement doesn't mean all that much to you.

All of His scripture is important and brings life!

You rebuke the arrogant, the cursed, who wander from
Your commandments.
Psalm 119:21

Salvation is so stunning a gift, so incomprehensible an action by the God Who created the heavens and the earth, that there is only one appropriate response from us: to serve Him with joy the rest of our lives.

So, in a sense, holiness, is our response to the gift given to us, a response to an understanding by revelation of the Holy Spirit, that we must walk out our lives in a vastly different way than the natural, instinctive ways that are common to mankind. Let's look further into what the word *holiness* means.

The *International Standard Bible Encyclopedia*[78] describes *holiness* as used in the New Testament this way, "Christ's people are regularly called 'saints' or holy persons, and holiness in the high ethical and spiritual meaning of the word is used to denote the appropriate quality of their life and conduct," as separate from the world and bound to the pursuit of an ethical ideal.

Eaton's Bible Dictionary[79] has this offering on holiness:

"In the highest sense belongs to God (Isaiah 6:3; Revelation 15:4), and to Christians as consecrated to God's service, and in so far as they are conformed in all things to the will of God (Romans 6:19, 22; Ephesians

1:4; Titus 1:8; 1 Peter 1:15). Personal holiness is a work of gradual development. It is carried on under many hindrances, hence the frequent admonitions to watchfulness, prayer, and perseverance (1 Corinthians 1:30; 2 Corinthians 7:1; Ephesians 4:23, 24)."

For a simple explanation that fits our purposes, here is Webster's definition:

1. (n.) The state or quality of being holy; perfect moral integrity or purity; freedom from sin; sanctity; innocence.

2. (n.) The state of being hallowed, or consecrated to God or to his worship; sacredness.

Yes, this is a journey, one that never ends until we transition from this life into the heavenly realm with our Savior.

If you truly pursue holiness, your relationship with Jesus deepens and causes you to catch your breath on a regular basis. As you do this, you seek all of His Word with a hunger planted in your heart by Him. He desires for you to seek Him out.

Let's look at some passages from Psalm 119:

30...I have chosen the faithful way, I have placed Your ordinances before me.
33-35...Teach me, O LORD, the way of Your statutes, and I shall observe it to the end. Give me understanding, that I may observe Your law and keep it with all my heart. Make me walk in the path of Your commandments, for I delight in it.

Walking in holiness means we have to make choices everyday with that in mind, with intent:

46...I will also speak of Your testimonies before kings and shall not be ashamed.
47...I shall delight in Your commandments, which I love.
48...And I shall lift up my hands to Your commandments, which I love; and I will meditate on Your statutes.

97…O how I love Your law! It is my meditation all the day.
98…Your commandments make me wiser than my
enemies, for they are ever mine.
127…Therefore I love Your commandments above gold,
yes, above fine gold.
165…Those who love Your law have great peace, and
nothing causes them to stumble.

We must surround ourselves with those who love the Lord.

63…I am a companion of all those who fear You, and of
those who keep Your precepts.

As we choose to walk in holiness, our Savior meets us, the relationship deepens, and we are transformed by His faithful presence.

Pray Without Ceasing

The Bible tells us to do this, but in my experience, no one takes it seriously. Let's look at the scripture in context.

We urge you, brethren, admonish the unruly, encourage the
fainthearted, help the weak, be patient with everyone. See
that no one repays another with evil for evil, but always
seek after that which is good for one another and for all
people. Rejoice always; ***pray without ceasing;*** *in everything*
give thanks; for this is God's will for you in Christ Jesus. Do
not quench the Spirit; do not despise prophetic utterances.
But ***examine everything carefully;*** *hold fast to that which*
is good; abstain from every form of evil.
1 Thessalonians 5:14-22 [emphasis added]

With all prayer and petition ***pray at all times*** *in the Spirit,*
and with this in view, ***be on the alert*** *with all perseverance*
and petition for all the saints.
Ephesians 6:18 [emphasis added]

In this process, we must examine everything carefully. And, we also need to pray without ceasing.

How can we possibly do that, you may ask?

It's like a cell phone. If there is an emergency, do you want your cell phone to be off or on?

If there is an emergency and you have to find your phone, turn it on, wait for it to load, then dial the appropriate number for help, it may be way too late.

Using the metaphor of a cell phone, that phone connection with our King should always be open, on, and active. Think of it like the secret service members protecting the president, who have their ear pieces on at all times.

One way we can do this by utilizing our prayer language. When I'm busy with things such as grocery shopping where I have to read the list and search for items while negotiating through a sizeable crowd, I am whispering in my prayer language.

When I'm cleaning my house, doing the dishes, or driving alone in my car, in a place where I can hold a cogent thought, I whisper in prayer all the time or sing out loud to Him. Praise Him that you ate today, that you have a roof over your head. Ask Him what He would like you to do with the ministry project you have on your plate. Ask Him to search your heart and to reveal every hiding place of darkness.

That last one is especially important while you are in a process of breaking bondage. You are seeking help to remove all the things that clutter or obstruct your relationship with Him.

Talk to Him as you would your closest friend:

> *There is a friend who sticks closer than a brother.*
> *Proverbs 18:24*

I've had times where I'm praying nearly constantly. And, it is no surprise, that the day goes so much better!

This is our goal, to pray without ceasing. Like when your mind gets stuck on a song and it plays over and over, and you sing it off and on, all day long; sing praises to Him.

This keeps the connection open and active. He can ale something you can't see, and you can ask for help in inst necessary. The extra special icing on the cake is that you will walk in divine favor.

In this type of battle, ordinary measures are not enough. To take a castle captive and tear it down, it takes purpose, intent, consistent prayer, and fasting.

Prayer is not a last resort.

Prayer is conversation with our Captain!

Praise God, we don't have to know everything and He doesn't expect us to. We serve the One Who does know everything! We must stay in communication with Him at all times so that when He tells us to pay extra attention to something, we hear Him. When we do that, the enemy has a very difficult time sneaking up on us.

Fasting

In the average church, it is rare these days to see anyone fasting to seek the Lord.

> *"Yet even now," declares the LORD, "Return to Me with all*
> *your heart, and with fasting, weeping and mourning; and*
> *rend your heart and not your garments." Now return to the*
> *LORD your God, for He is gracious and compassionate, slow*
> *to anger, abounding in lovingkindness and relenting of evil.*
> *Joel 2:12-13*

> *And I set my face unto the Lord God, to seek by prayer and*
> *supplications, with fasting, and sackcloth, and ashes.*
> *Daniel 9:3*

Fasting is a very interesting subject. Many major religions utilize fasting to connect with their gods -- which are really the dark entities in the supernatural realm. It is another inversion of the pattern God has set for us to connect with Him. Fasting our hearts, changes situations, helps us to hear from our Lord more clearly, and it is a sharp, effective weapon of spiritual warfare.

But this kind does not go out except by prayer and fasting.
Matthew 17:21

"This kind cannot come out by anything but prayer."
Mark 9:29

Clearly there are times when the rebuke is not enough. We've seen how there are different dark side types, species, and authorities, all in a structure that resembles the military. They are intentional, and they have a plan written against us. In spite of their selfishness and pride, they will cooperate to destroy us.

Just as in my own case, the last attachment I could not get free from was a high level, very powerful entity that had been there for a very long time, through generational bondage. It had authority because someone somewhere had given it access to my family.

I did intense prayer and fasting and worked with a trained spiritual warfare person. As I was fasting, the Lord revealed in a dream what I was dealing with and then we knew what to do about it.

The constant prayer and regular fasting as I sought the Lord over many months was a major key in breaking the stronghold of that massive 'general from the dark-side'.

We had total victory! But it put up a fight. It was angry. It didn't want to lose hold of another person. They don't like losing anything; they know that they are ultimately losers! But it had to bow to the authority of Yeshua!

I wish I'd known years ago what I know now, what I'm writing in this book. It would have been so much easier and quicker!

Learn to pray without ceasing and make fasting a regular part of your relationship with our King.

Tearing Down Strongholds

This is where it all starts coming together. All you've been learning is needed to turn that stronghold wall to dust.

The Word gives us a plan.

> *For the weapons of our warfare are not carnal [of the*
> *flesh], but mighty through God to the pulling down of*
> *strong holds.*
> *2 Corinthians 10:4, KJV*

> *Jesus summoned His twelve disciples and gave them*
> *authority over unclean spirits, to cast them out, and to heal*
> *every kind of disease and every kind of sickness.*
> *Matthew 10:1*

If we are going to tear down strongholds, we must first be able to recognize them. My simple definition is: something not of God that you are not able to remove.

If you've tried to remove it with considerable effort and it isn't leaving, you might have some attachments or strongholds. Once you've identified a stronghold (or many strongholds, as the case may be), you must be very intentional. Use everything you are learning here.

Explore the genogram to search for patterns. Begin seeking God with prayer and fasting, asking Him to reveal every hiding place of the enemy. Start praying without ceasing. Make notes of what you believe He tells you. Keep a journal so you can spot clues and also see the deliverance in motion. Write in your journal as you explore your life, including childhood, looking for any opportunity the dark side had to enter. And for difficult or resistant oppression or attachments, connect with a trained ministry person to assist you with the battlefield confrontation.

You can't do it by yourself. Hopefully by now you understand that is the way our Lord wants it done.

Expertise with any weapon doesn't just overtake you against your will. Nor is it acquired by association just because you spent time around someone else who was trained in it. I know someone who is a nationally ranked marksman. I have received none of that expertise just by having lunch with him!

And that doesn't mean you must be a weak Christian.

We've talked about the secret shame and guilt so many believers carry, thinking they should be able to deal with it by themselves even though they have never had proper training. This guilt and shame is more than just a form of spiritual torment. Because it is not of God and it began with thoughts that were not taken captive, it became an open door that gave dark spirits access to your life. The more shame you hold onto, the stronger the dark forces become, because they have an open, active, access point giving them a steady stream of power. This is a very important point.

We've also looked at how shame and guilt cause those suffering to isolate or distance themselves from others, hiding the thoughts from spouses and best friends. Even those who have had some training in spiritual warfare could find themselves really struggling, trying to understand why they can't deal with it themselves.

So, then why is it that you can't break it yourself?

Let's expand a little more on this point.

Mostly, it's just because that's how the Lord designed it to work -- together with a brother or sister in the Lord, edifying one another with instruction and love.

This is the way the body of Yeshua is supposed to work!

Many of us would prefer to keep our dirty laundry to ourselves. Yet, scripture says that we are to bear one another's burdens and pray for one another. So, in some cases, even if you have had some training and have been successful at other times, it may be that the Lord wants you to work with someone else on this challenge.

What is gained by that?

First, it is the way the body of Christ is to function.

Second, we are not to isolate.

Third, it is pride that we don't want a single soul to know we are struggling with something.

Brrrr, that nasty SIN word. This is a huge tool of the enemy! Nearly every client I see, after they tell me their story, the story that has kept them saturated in shame, is astonished when I tell them I have multiple other clients with the same story.

They look at me with their eyes wide with shock, "Really?"

Fourth, it prevents ministry. God uses our most difficult challenges as our most powerful ministry. If we refuse to share the struggle with a trusted and trained brother or sister, we are preventing the work of God in our own lives, we are preventing those called to this ministry from doing the work God called them to do, and then we are not able to share that victory with others who need to be encouraged as they battle a similar thing.

God never works in ones, remember?

This is how we are to deal with it: things not of God, found in Column B with origins from *B-Z-B* must be bound, rebuked, and cast out! We must get so adept at this that this action takes place at the very instant the dark thought comes to us, effectively extinguishing the "flaming arrows of the wicked one." (Ephesians 6:16)

As you find someone you can trust who has knowledge and training in this area of ministry, the Lord is glorified, you've been obedient, the bondage gets broken, and you and the ministry team you work with deepen your relationships as brothers and sisters in the body of Yeshua. Then, the victorious testimony is used, somewhere, somehow, with someone who needs to hear it.

What a beautiful picture!

Here's another important point: You cannot effectively solve a spiritual problem with fleshly actions. by trying to be logical or by using positive thinking. We must put on our spiritual armor and get in the battle. The battle is raging all around you, whether you admit it or not, whether you like it or not. You can either be victorious by using the weapons of your warfare given to you through Yeshua, or you can be trampled by the dark powers and live in torment and defeat.

Thin Walls: Real Estate & Property

In a story that was unfolding as I wrote this book, a client who lived in a condo duplex had a very good relationship with her neighbor, an elderly, single, retired military man. For over a year, the neighbor had been spending a lot of time away from home, due to the extended recovery of a loved one in another town. He had only been home a few times a month for a day or so at a time.

When my client saw him in the driveway, she wished him a Happy New Year.

Within only a minute, he said very casually, completely out of the blue, "You know, something very strange happened last night."

She could tell he was concerned about something and needed to tell her. He was fairly reserved and this was a little unusual. She instantly paid closer attention.

"I was sleeping. Around 2:30 or 3 a.m., I heard a voice say, 'Hey, there.' I sat up and went through the house, but no one was there. I didn't feel like I was in danger or anything but nothing like that has ever happened before. I've never experienced anything like that."

He added that the voice was male, not a young voice, and was in the room with him near the bed, not in another room in the house.

Because of her long-standing affection for her neighbor, my client encouraged him and then shared, "Be very careful with these voices. They may act or sound harmless, but they aren't. They may act friendly but they're only trying to draw you into talking with them."

"Yeah, they're all evil, right?" he asked.

"Yes," she said, "they are."

Knowing he was a praying man, she gave some suggestions that he very gratefully received.

His prayer needed to come from a place of authority that the property he owned was a gift from God. And, because he belonged to God, he, therefore, had authority over the property that God had given to him.

He nodded as she spoke.

"Tell them they must leave, that they are not allowed here, but be sure you do it in Jesus' name. Humans have no authority over those beings; only Jesus does. And, say it out loud; you need to say it out loud."

He seemed relieved and glad to have the encouragement and thanked her.

As she turned to go inside to get dinner started, she was contemplating what the information meant for her and her home.

This can be a neglected subject. Apartments and condos have some unique things we must watch for. Shared walls, shared roofs, and sometimes shared attic spaces make a perfect playground for deceiving and twisting spiritual entities who will delight in creating havoc when the homeowners don't understand proper authority and how to lay down and defend boundaries.

She was praying as she thought about the spiritual principles and how to properly deal with it. Since the neighbor was gone so much, that could be an open door that otherworldly beings may take advantage of.

She shared with her neighbor that vacancy can be associated

with other beings moving in. He told her that he prayed over his home and property boundaries on a regular basis, which, I must say, is extremely rare! So, she just reminded him to make sure he did it in Jesus' name and he was happy with that.

Empty or abandoned buildings, or apartments or homes vacant due to its occupant being in the hospital or for any other reason give dark forces an opportunity to move in.

Also, shared spaces can present an issue if you don't deal with them properly. In condos and apartments there are shared walls. In some condos an attic space is shared. In all cases the boundaries must be set by the blood of the Lamb and vigilantly watched.

There is also the issue of covering and ownership authority. Since her neighbor was the owner of his space that was adjoining hers, she had authority to set the boundaries over her own space, but she did not have authority over his space or to evict any trespassing spirit in his space...that is, unless he gave it to her.

She ran back outside where he was working in his yard.

"I have a quick question," she said. "Since you're gone so much, would you be willing to give me spiritual authority to pray over your property?" Without hesitation he said, "Absolutely!" and he reached for her hand to shake it in gratitude.

She walked back into her own home smiling and so excited that she now had the authority over the whole property, not just hers!

As she walked through the garage toward the inside door, she said out loud, "Okay, that's it. I have been given authority by my neighbor over his property. In the name of Yeshua, any dark entity that is in, on, or around his property must leave now in Jesus' name and never return! You have no authority here and are trespassing. Leave now."

When dealing with property, there is another important step in the prayer.

"The air space above, and ground beneath, from the very
center of the earth, to the heavens."

I felt the Lord give me this phrase very specifically. More than
a year later, I found out from a friend who works in real estate that
phrase is used in real estate legal contracts.

This is a three-dimensional space that includes the air, ground,
and the structure of the home or building.

Set the boundary of the property with the blood of the Lamb.
Then notify the dark side they are trespassing and not allowed "in,
on, or around" the property or the building. Announce who gave the
property to you.

Make sure you have done a thorough house cleansing and
anointed every door and window. Walk the boundary of the property
in prayer and dedication, evicting anything on the property. Once
everything is cleared out, don't forget your spiritual maintenance.

Once you take back territory, be prepared to defend it.

"This home was given to me by the King of Kings for
Kingdom purposes. It has been dedicated to Him and
His work. The blood of the Lamb is on my forehead and
on my doorposts and lintels. You are trespassing. You are
not allowed here."

Remember in the beginning of the book I told you the Lord
showed me a path that was a shorter distance between two points,
that we have to be very specific to leave the minions no wiggle room?
Well, now you're seeing part of that.

You will learn more about prayers as we go.

Let's look at the results of this initial spiritual battle that began
with my client seeking help for a significant spiritual warfare issue:

The client received help, discipleship, and training which resulted
in victory in her own life and home.

Praise God, now she has spiritual authority over the entire property, not just over her home! This means she can take authority over any dark presence who may try to take up residence there and she is well-trained in how to do it! There will no longer be an empty space on the other side of her wall that provides shelter to demonic forces.

In addition to that, the neighbor, who clearly had been concerned about the experience with the external, audible voice, enough to bring up the subject, received encouragement, and he received it without a long process or heavy conversation. It was quick and pleasant, totally led by the Spirit of God.

He also will feel, in a new way, the presence of Jesus as he prays with more authority, through and over his home, which will strengthen his faith.

If the client had not been trained in spiritual warfare for issues in her own life, she could not have received victory in her life -- forever changing her relationship with Yeshua, and she would not have been able to minister to her neighbor who is now receiving encouragement and a deepening of his own faith! All of this, as a result of some demonic minions trying to bother somebody!

GOD NEVER WORKS IN ONES.

What we work through with Yeshua becomes a ministry to others.

Territory was won! Territory that was in the grip of the enemy forces was just returned to the camp of the righteous!

If we are watching and praying as we should, with eyes trained on the process, we will not only recognize the demonic forces, but also, as we follow God's instructions, evict them!

Energy Fields & DNA

Energy Fields

Our bodies have energy fields around them. The heart generates a powerful electromagnetic field.[80] We still don't understand everything about the body's energy fields. But they are very important.

Instead of allowing the New Age movement to usurp the term, as Christians we should acknowledge the fact that our Creator put them there for a reason and pray over them! Cover them with the blood of the Lamb!

I teach everyone to include it in their prayers of covering every day.

> "Lord, I dedicate myself to You today, body, mind, soul, spirit, and energy fields. Anything that is missing, replace it. Anything that is damaged, fix it. Anything out of order, reorder it. Protect my body and my health from all forms of attack, in Yeshua's name. Send your rafua shelema, the perfect healing of God, down to the cellular level, to the DNA level and beyond. I do not give authority to any dark energy, entity, spirit, force, or dark technology to alter my fields or my DNA in any way. You created it, Lord, it belongs to You, and You are the only one I give that authority to."

Energy fields may play another important role in spiritual warfare.

In the chapter, Understanding the Problem, we read the story, from the book *Uncovering the Mystery of* MPD by Dr. James Friesen, of a college séance.

In that story, he described his first spiritual battle. He walked into a room where students were engaged in a séance. There was verified supernatural activity taking place by an entity that called itself Hoz. Friesen, thinking logically, wanted to know if the Name of Jesus would work in that situation. He decided speaking it out loud would make it difficult to gauge the effectiveness.

"So, I decided to just think the command. I directed my gaze toward the table and thought the instruction: Hoz, in the Name of Jesus I command you to leave!"

The very minute he thought this command, the supernatural activity stopped.

I've seen this type of evidence myself. But it presents an issue we must deal with.

Can these entities read our thoughts?

I do not believe they can. Let me explain.

One of the best descriptions I've ever heard about dark side foreknowledge is the corn field analogy. I heard it from L.A. Marzulli.

He wondered, when people go to a medium who is channeling a demonic spirit, how do these spirits get some future things right?

It's as if you are in a cornfield. Corn is tall and thick. You can only see a couple of feet in any direction. God is omniscient, above all, seeing all of time, from beginning to end, equally and perfectly. He can see the entire cornfield from beginning to end, the very boundaries of time and space. The fallen entities do not have the vision that God has, but we already know that we are created lower than they are. They are stronger than we are and have abilities that we don't. They are different creatures. It's as if they are in a deer stand in the cornfield. They can see farther than we can, but not everything that God can.

Here is what I believe is going on. In the supernatural realm, there is another type of communication possible, a type of understanding, or access to information between us in these earthly bodies and the supernatural entities of good or evil.

I've come to suspect that these creatures that seem to possess a type of vision, whether with a form of eyes or a perception of some kind, are able to see or perceive information in our energy fields. Our thoughts themselves may play a role also, whether they are set upon dark things or blazing with the presence of The Son of Man.

What we set our minds on, our intent, shows in some way and to some extent, in these energy fields.

If you sit in a dark room for hours with the intent to contact dark supernatural beings, you just might do so. That happens with various religions on 'vision quests' and other practices such as sweat lodge encounters, some using drugs that give access to these beings. They sense, perceive, and are drawn to the intent for contact.

We see this type of behavior and interaction with UFO groups that sit in fields at night with the intent to make contact with lights in the sky, and they do.

I've referred to it as a type of dog-whistle that they hear. It also reminds me of the film, *The Lord of the Rings*. When Frodo puts on the ring, something he should not do, the dark spirits are immediately able to perceive him and they start charging in his direction. The ring functions like a homing beacon leading them to his location. That beacon is in the ON position by default until we get redeemed by the Blood. When we walk in power, we are able, by the mercy and grace of our Father and power of the Holy Spirit, to keep it in the OFF position. But as we waffle in our relationship with our Beloved, the beacon begins sending a signal, even if a weak one. The more we don't access our weapons or we reject our calling to powerful battle, the more the power of the beacon's signal increases.

We can also look at it another way. We are a captured bride of the Lord of Darkness when we are born. That ring I referred to is the ring of attachment, marriage, utter slavery, to him. It is only when we take off that ring and marry the Lover of our souls that the former ring is removed. When we don't align ourselves with Him (and the only way to do that is by following everything He's told us to do), we are, in essence, putting on the old wedding bond to the Dark One and it calls to him. He wants to re-capture us or make us as spiritually anemic as possible.

I believe our energy fields in some way reflect what is going on within us. When you are drowning in despair, they are drawn to your suffering and they descend upon you like a pack of wolves on the hunt. When you feel overcome with fear, they surround you, taunting and sending unwanted thoughts to lead you into further torment.

And of course, since the devil has the power of death and is the author of confusion and evil, he might seem to 'know' the future because of what he is planning to do in it.

Intent is very powerful.

We've discussed how our Abba is not interested in box-ticking. In fact, one of the few times in my life I can say I believe I heard God speak clearly to me was when I was praying about ministry and how to help people understand His heart.

He said, "I am sick of these polite affections."

It's offensive to Him. It breaks His heart.

In Revelation it says,

> "I know your deeds, that you are neither cold nor hot;
> I wish that you were cold or hot. 'So because you are
> lukewarm, and neither hot nor cold, I will spit you out of
> My mouth."
> Revelation 3:15-16

Learning to take every thought captive, paying attention to the intent of our hearts, these are not small things. They just haven't been addressed in the typical church.

DNA

Our DNA is being assaulted in so many ways. With the roll out of 5G it is only going to get worse. Do you actually think it is altruistically designed to help you connect faster with old friends? The slightest bit of research (see below) will show not only its dangers but other sinister capabilities.

There is good reason to believe that part of the function of the

Mark of the Beast will be to change DNA. Multiple movies, such as *Elysium*, foretell of the alteration of DNA via a mark required by the global government.

Though many people claim there is nothing to worry about with chip implants, I strongly disagree. Chip implants are not benign. The tech we are allowed to see is at least 20 –50 years behind the tech possessed by elite cabals. They are doing far more than they want us to see.

More than a decade ago, when watchdog groups warned that new televisions were spying on us in our homes, they were called crazy. In recent years, however, it has been revealed that their warnings have proven to be true and accurate. The advanced tech already in play now, such as chip implants, nano particles and 'smart' meters, etc., have the ability to work together and are upgradable. Nano particles and insect-sized drones may be able to work cooperatively on goals set by programmers or AI.

So, even if you think a chip implant is not a danger right now, 1) you will have no way of stopping all the upgrades they force through wireless delivery systems, and 2) we don't know what these implants are releasing into the body: micro-doses of mind-numbing drugs, contraceptives, hormone disrupters, frequencies, nanoparticles that attack or attach and then modify parts of the human brain such as the part that perceives God?…the possibilities are frightening. Oh, and 3) you have no way of knowing how implanted chips will cooperate with other forms of technology, such as nanoparticles that have been sprayed in the sky for decades, and, again, the 5G system.

In my research, the possibility exists that the Mark of the Beast might not be a singular object implanted or a singular action implemented on a singular date. It could be components released in a scheduled project roll-out, with varying forms of delivery.

The nanoparticles sprayed in the air can communicate with each other and form shields or antennas. They gain access to our bodies through inhalation, ingestion of food containing the particles, and by contact.

Chip implants or other micro-tracking devices are very likely to have abilities we don't even know about yet, just as the Samsung televisions delivered years ago, that were spying on us before we were aware of the danger.

The 5G wireless system is the final web that connects all of the components.

For more information on 5G, refer to the Resources section.

Now is the bell going off in your mind why I include in protective prayers "dark technology"?

> *The LORD is my rock and my fortress and my deliverer,*
> *My God, my rock, in whom I take refuge; My shield and*
> *the horn of my salvation, my stronghold.*
> *Psalm 18:2*

Start covering your energy fields and DNA in the blood of Jesus every day, and any time it comes to mind.

My Name Is...

I stated at the very beginning of this book that I have no intention to disparage any ministry. I am only responsible for what I believe the Lord has led me to do.

Having said that, there are some ministries which teach that you need to discover every name and occupation of every entity that is oppressing someone. They engage in supposed conversations with the demonic, demanding answers to questions to gather information.

Generally speaking, I do not work in that way.

How can you reliably use information from a known liar? A being that is smarter than humans and a master at twisting both the mind and scripture?

In my view, we are not to engage in conversation with the voices of darkness. We are to train our ears to hear the voice of our Captain. I take my battle instructions from Him alone. He knows all that the enemy is doing and the names of those involved. I do not give them the room and time to grandstand, to feel important, to control the situation, or the strategy.

I have been led to be strategic. It's akin to the *work smarter, not harder* idea. If I have done what I need to do as I am led by the Holy Spirit, and I strategically plan what I need to say, it leaves them little room to argue or resist.

I have had occasions when they will try to tell me their name. My response?

"I don't care what your name is. Be bound and be silent right now in the name of Yeshua."

If, for some reason, God needs me to know their names He will tell me. That has happened a few times but, in my experience, it is the exception to the general rule.

Can you see the military tactic they're using here?

They can see what's going on and they know they are in the process of being bound by the blood. They know that, at some point, whether at that moment or a later time, they will be cast out. So, what are they doing? Stalling and trying to get you to engage with them.

Here we are again with the metaphor of unruly six-year-olds.

It is the equivalent of you telling your son to go to bed and he then says, "Mommy, can I have a glass of water?" You give him a glass of water that he doesn't really want, then he says, "Can I ask Daddy a question?" Or, "Will you read me another story?" "Can I check on my pet turtle?" To which the answer is, "No, go to bed; *now.*"

These minions know what they are required to do. What they are testing is if YOU know what they are required to do.

Some of the consequences of engaging with these entities in this way could be that you waste time, you are led in the wrong direction by talking with a liar, or they could cause an emotional reaction in you that you don't expect. Here's an example.

This just came up in a counseling session today.

Let's say you are a parent with a child who has experienced manifestations of demonic attack or oppression, such as hearing voices instructing him to do violent things. Your son is asleep in his bedroom; you are in the living room praying, binding, and rebuking over him. A demonic presence presents itself and tries to engage you in conversation. It says that a relative was sexually abusing your child. That is very difficult for you to hear and it causes a strong emotional reaction of anger, even if what it said is not true.

It would be difficult for a parent not to have a strong reaction to that kind of a statement. And that emotional response could knock you off center, make you miss what God is trying to tell you and you could go in a totally wrong direction.

If, in fact, there is intel that I need to get the job done, my Father, Jehovah Nissi, my Banner for Victory, will tell me himself. We do not want the spiritual drama to go on for one minute more than it has to. We do not need theatrics or acting out. Shut it down immediately and keep asking the Lord for all information that you need to complete the eviction.

Let's look at the passage in Mark 5:1-13 where Jesus was approaching the Gerasenes.

> *They came to the other side of the sea, into the country of the Gerasenes. When He got out of the boat, immediately a man from the tombs with an unclean spirit met Him, and he had his dwelling among the tombs. And no one was able to bind him anymore, even with a chain; because he had often been bound with shackles and chains, and the chains had been torn apart by him and the shackles*

broken in pieces, and no one was strong enough to subdue him. Constantly, night and day, he was screaming among the tombs and in the mountains, and gashing himself with stones. Seeing Jesus from a distance, he ran up and bowed down before Him; and shouting with a loud voice, he said, "What business do we have with each other, Jesus, Son of the Most High God? I implore You by God, do not torment me!" For He had been saying to him, "Come out of the man, you unclean spirit!" And He was asking him, "What is your name?" And he said to Him, "My name is Legion; for we are many." And he began to implore Him earnestly not to send them out of the country. Now there was a large herd of swine feeding nearby on the mountain. The demons implored Him, saying, "Send us into the swine so that we may enter them." Jesus gave them permission. And coming out, the unclean spirits entered the swine; and the herd rushed down the steep bank into the sea, about two thousand of them; and they were drowned in the sea.

This possessed man was so violent that no one could even walk in that area which means it was clearly known by all, which is also confirmed later in the passage when the herdsmen ran to the city to tell everyone what happened. Jesus was obviously not concerned about what they called danger. He knew exactly where He was going and what would play out.

The possessed man ran up "from a distance" to Jesus and bowed before Him because...this is often missed...Jesus was *already*, from a distance, saying to him, "Come out of the man, you unclean spirit!" Before He even got up to the man!

The quote from scripture uses an exclamation mark, so Jesus was saying it with some heft. I don't think that our Lord was yelling at him. But, if He was not, then it makes the case that in the supernatural realm, they can feel the power and authority of Yeshua from a distance, even before the voice could be heard in human terms.

I have seen this myself. I have helped others even over the phone and seen complete eviction of a presence from a house. The text also implies that Yeshua could have said it more than once.

Yes, when the man was bowing before Jesus and the demons were imploring Him not to send them out of the country, He did ask their name. But I chose this passage anyway (there is a similar story in Matthew 8) because of all of the other important points. There is no record that Jesus had a conversation with them.

In my mind, I can imagine the story unfolding. Even at a distance, probably before the demons were even aware of Him, Jesus may have had His eyes fixed on the possessed man. Then He began to speak, "Come out of the man, you unclean spirit!"

I bet it hurt those demons!

Doesn't that remind you of Dr. Friesen's story?

Jesus' intent and command got their attention! The demons in the man probably began shrieking and causing a ruckus. Because they must bow at the very name of Yeshua, they ran to bow before the King of Kings present in human flesh, full of resentment and hate, begging all the way.

Yeshua granted the request to enter the pigs, but the end for them was and is still destruction.

Not being omniscient, I doubt they realized the pigs would run off the cliff to drown in the sea leaving the demons to search for new bodies to inhabit. I also wonder if Yeshua's power and intent focused on them shut down their ability to see even two feet into the future timeline.

They drowned in the sea, which is also interesting. Kind of like what happened with Noah and the infestation the earth was suffering before the flood. The Nephailm were drowned in the sea also. But I digress.

See, it's all connected.

It is very telling that the residents of the country were so frightened by this display of healing and delivering power that they begged Jesus to leave the region.

That sounds like many believers today. We don't want to see any of that stuff, they say. They ignore the cries of the tormented and go about their business pretending it has nothing to do with them. The Gerasenes in this passage reflect, rather well, the attitude of many in the U.S. church today.

In battles with these spirits, God will help us to adjust to the battle as necessary, just as he did with Moses.

In Exodus 17 before the battle with Amalek and the Rephidim, the people had been crying out for water. The Lord told Moses to take his staff and some elders and go to the rock at Horeb, before all the people. Then, the Lord said this:

> *"Behold, I will stand before you there on the rock at Horeb;*
> *and you shall strike the rock, and water will come out of it,*
> *that the people may drink." And Moses did so in the sight of*
> *the elders of Israel.*
> *Exodus 17:6-7*

The Lord stood with him there!

Then in the next section, Amalek attacks the people. There is no record, even in the Hebrew, of God instructing Moses in a direct way what to do when they were attacked.

> *So Moses said to Joshua, "Choose men for us and go out,*
> *fight against Amalek. Tomorrow I will station myself*
> *on the top of the hill with the staff of God in my hand."*
> *Joshua did as Moses told him, and fought against Amalek;*
> *and Moses, Aaron, and Hur went up to the top of the*
> *hill. So it came about when Moses held his hand up, that*
> *Israel prevailed, and when he let his hand down, Amalek*
> *prevailed. But Moses' hands were heavy. Then they took*
> *a stone and put it under him, and he sat on it; and Aaron*

and Hur supported his hands, one on one side and one on the other. Thus his hands were steady until the sun set.

So Joshua overwhelmed Amalek and his people with the edge of the sword.

Then the LORD said to Moses, "Write this in a book as a memorial and recite it to Joshua, that I will utterly blot out the memory of Amalek from under heaven." Moses built an altar and named it The LORD is My Banner [Jehovah-Nissi]; and he said, "The LORD has sworn; the LORD will have war against Amalek from generation to generation."
Exodus 17:9-16

Let's take a closer look at this passage.

I find it very interesting that, when they got attacked, Moses made a plan with no direct instruction from God. He did not say, let me fast and seek the Lord. He did not say wait and God will do it for us. He told Joshua to gather his men and start fighting. He brought his guys with him to the top of the hill with his staff. And, as the battle ensued, he saw that whenever his hands dropped Amalek's forces began to win, and whenever his hands stayed up, Israel overtook the enemy. We have no record that God told him this. When they got attacked by evil forces, he knew what he had to do! They had to go to battle! How did he know that every time his hands dropped Israel began to lose the fight? He was paying attention! He was keenly watching the battle!

Here are just a few points from this encounter:

- Moses was already in the flow of conversation and relationship with God. He didn't wait for an emergency to try to speak with Him.

- Moses took action.

- He had people already in positions to handle battle needs, such as Joshua in charge of the fighting forces.

- Joshua had worked out his emergency plan and trained his forces in what to do when they had to fight; that training had already been in place. They knew what the battle call was, the shofar blast. *Teru'ah* is the nine short, staccato blasts of the battle cry.[81]

- Moses knew what his role was; he did not grab a sword and run to the battlefield. He needed to intercede and guide the people.

- Moses had his support staff to aid him. He knew whom to take with him in emergencies.

- They went to a place where they could see what was going on. They didn't go hide under a rock; they needed clear, unobstructed vision.

- Moses was not a spectator! He did NOT say, well, the soldiers will deal with it, I'll relax until I get word of how it turns out. He did not watch it like entertainment or a sporting event.

- Moses was *involved* in the battle from his position on the hilltop. They paid attention to the battle, interceding for the people, and noticed subtleties. It's not such an easy thing to see who is winning moment to moment from the top of a hill a distance away. It takes careful analysis and unrelenting attention. And to recognize the connection to his hands being up or down, that is paying attention and the wisdom of God.

Moses could not have done that alone. He needed his support team to help him adjust to the intel he received as they watched the battle.

Moses had to stay there all day; it was not over in a few minutes.

Battle is dirty, challenging, and dangerous. The troops were exhausted even though they won. If you've ever fought hard for something, like a collegiate wrestler using physical strength, strategy, and instinct, then you know that you don't emerge victorious from an intense battle without breaking a sweat.

In the battle of Jericho (Joshua 6) they were told to march around the city with the ark, blow their shofars, and shout. They never had to even raise a sword!

They were commanded to *shout*. Sometimes we have to get a little loud with these dark beings. Some ministries teach that we never have to raise our voices in spiritual warfare encounters. I find that to be untrue. As a former athlete myself, I'm pretty sure that Joshua and his troops fighting for their lives against Amalek and the Rephidim weren't using soft voices.

When you are working hard at your sport, let's say, you sweat, you make noises as you do weight training to strengthen your muscles, and sometimes in the moment of competition there are noises made. Think of the Olympic shot-put competition. When you are pushing that much weight, there is a sound of exclamation made at the release. This is also true with some tennis players.

For years I never had to raise my voice when confronted with the demonic. And, I teach that they are definitely not hard of hearing. But in the throes of a big battle, I have in recent years found that sometimes you do have to say it with more volume and emotional energy, and it can get intense.

It reminds me of another scene in *Lord of the Rings*. When Gandalf confronts the demonic beast inside the mountain, a creature that seems to recall the size of the Nephalim, he stands his ground, looks the minion in the eye, and with absolute resolve says, "You shall not pass!"

In retrospect, I find that the times years ago that I never had to raise my voice were the times that the entities were smaller or less powerful. I've since encountered a number of bigger beasts and staying quiet and dignified is just not always the way the battle plays out.

We cannot expect that just because we turn and glare our eyes at one of these minions they will always turn and run the other direction. That is not the model we see in scripture. After all, these maniacal minions know exactly who Yeshua is, yet they plan to go to battle with Him at the end of time! When God uses the language and vocabulary of battle in His Word, there is a reason!

Sin On A Curve

According the Bible sin is not graded on a curve. You don't get a lesser penalty because everyone in your particular group was doing it.

I went to a Christian high school. During that time in weekly chapel services, as I heard the testimonies of others who had been dramatically saved and delivered out of something like drugs, or as one person I knew had been delivered from prostitution, I was amazed. I had an unspoken longing to be so fully known, yet chosen, and dramatically and forever changed by the loving Creator God. I had never experienced what they described.

"I got saved when I was four," I thought to myself.

Other students expressed this observation after a poignant service. A few of us talked about it, that we were raised in church and don't know what that feels like, to be loved that way in spite of all the wrongs committed, to experience the supernatural changing work of the Holy Spirit in a way that everyone around you can see.

As we tried to understand the difference, feeling we were missing out on the Father's love somehow, we could only come up with the idea that dramatic salvation was something we weren't given, something we could not experience.

> *You did not anoint My head with oil, but she anointed My*
> *feet with perfume. For this reason I say to you, her sins,*
> *which are many, have been forgiven, for she loved much;*
> *but he who is forgiven little, loves little.*
> *Luke 7:46-47*

It is true, that he who is forgiven little, loves little. But in our immaturity, we hadn't realized it is not salvation that is different: *it is the perception of sin.*

It is the lack of recognizing sin in our own lives. And for those of us who have grown up exposed to a biblical congregation and principles, we can become numb, falling prey to the idea that we are "good".

There are not separate types of salvation for people, one for those who never committed murder and one for those who did, or one salvation for those who never had sex before marriage and those who did.

And, there are not different types of love from our Father. He loves each of us as much as the other.

> *For all of you who were baptized into Christ have clothed*
> *yourselves with Christ. There is neither Jew nor Greek,*
> *there is neither slave nor free man, there is neither male*
> *nor female; for you are all one in Christ Jesus. And if you*
> *belong to Christ, then you are Abraham's descendants,*
> *heirs according to promise.*
> *Galatians 3:27-29*

There is neither Jew nor Greek – racial and cultural.

There is neither slave nor free – socio-economic; the haves and the have nots.

There is neither male nor female – men are not loved more than women, and vice versa.

> *For there is no distinction between Jew and Greek; for the*
> *same Lord is Lord of all, abounding in riches for all who*
> *call on Him;*
> *Romans 10:12*

Our Abba loves us all! He has more than enough love to go around.

Our issue was that we were unable to recognize sin; especially in our own lives. And, there was also arrogance attached to it.

That basic error in our thinking has profound implications and consequences, both theologically and in the life of the believer.

As it is written, There is none righteous, no, not one.
Romans 3:10, KJV

The fool says in his heart, "There is no God." They are corrupt; their acts are vile. There is no one who does good.
Psalm 14:1

The fool says in his heart, "There is no God." They are corrupt, and vile in their ways; there is no one who does good.
Psalm 53:1

Do not bring Your servant into judgment, for no one alive is righteous before You.
Psalm 143:2

If we say we have no sin, we deceive ourselves, and the truth is not in us.
1 John 1:8

We don't like to think about how sinful sin really is. Sin is sin. As we've mentioned, God does not grade sin on a curve.

There is a tendency for us to think, "Oh, that little thing? Come on, that's not sin. I just sent a digital download of a song I like to friends who did not pay for it. That's not sin. Everybody does that."

Sorry, that is stealing. Theft. You gave someone else a copy of something they did not pay for. Or maybe, you wanted to give a gift and act thoughtful, but you didn't want to pay for their gift, so you just copied your own.

Especially with the Internet of Things, there is a real problem right now with being able to recognize stealing.

We must guard our hearts and minds to prevent this kind of deception. We can become numb to conviction of the heart. When we allow the veil of delusion that we are good to become a comforting blanket, it shuts down the power of the Holy Spirit in our lives, and it also affects our relationship with Jesus at the very foundation.

We are all sinners. We all needed the work of redemption by a sinless and holy Sacrifice. He did that work for us. That transformative work in us is an ongoing, everyday unfolding of the gift of righteousness that blooms like a rose.

When we allow this numbness to holiness, we take up residence in a place filled with the blissful smoke of forgetfulness. The joy that springs forth as we are rescued from the grip of darkness is not allowed to flow through us. That expression of joy glorifies Him, is wonderful for us, and regular joy causes healing and amazing body system effects proven by science[82].

God never works in ones.

When we don't understand the depth of the sin, we can't comprehend the magnitude of the gift of salvation. As we've discussed, this deception causes distance between us and our bridegroom, and it cuts off the joy we should be walking in every moment of every day.

Here's one more scripture just in case you're still fighting this one.

> *Surely I was sinful at birth, sinful from the time my mother*
> *conceived me.*
> *Psalm 51:5, NIV*

We weren't that bad, we thought, and it was somehow different for us. Dramatic salvation was something we weren't given, something we could not experience.

Fasten your seat belt; this will be tough for some of you.

What it actually is, is arrogance. It is automatic in humans. It's like the saying, misery loves company. We group together with those somewhat like us and we say, we're not as bad as the other group is, as we think of some other group that is worse. It's very comforting gathering together with the other pigs in the pigsty. We've all got mud caked on us. But that other group over there has more mud on them than we do!

It's so easy to look behind at someone we perceive as worse than ourselves. Yet, if we would just turn our heads and look in the other direction, what we would see is God's perfect holiness. Perfect. That is the target we are to shoot for. Holiness.

Anything, no matter how small, other than God's perfect holiness, is sin. And, sin cannot be in His presence! Sin brings with it consequences and repercussions, it sets things in motion in both the physical realm and the spiritual, and it affects far more than the sinner.

We've looked at sin is a sort of beacon that calls to the forces of darkness, drawing them nearer to us. And this iniquity can be passed on through our progeny through God's concept of covering and covenant.

That is exactly what it is: arrogance, thinking we are better than someone else, that our own sin is somehow not as bad as someone else's sin; that we are above others and that others are below us. There is an automatic assumption, "I've never done anything that bad." This reveals an utter lack of comprehension of what sin is and how it affects us.

What Is Sin?

This book is not a theological treatise on the subject. But a basic understanding is very necessary. If we don't have the foundation of the basics of our faith established, whatever else we attempt to build upon it, including and most especially spiritual warfare, will be fundamentally flawed.

The sons of Sceva made a critical mistake on the use and authority of the Name of Jesus with a demon-possessed man and it got them a ticket to the woodshed (Acts 19). All seven of them were beaten and bloody and fled back to town naked.

Generally, sin is anything disobedient to God. But, just like with lies, there are sins of omission and commission. Though most people tend to emphasize the sins of commission, there are still sins of omission.

An article by Lehmen Straus[83] gives us an easy to understand description. He quotes and refers to work by Charles Ryrie.

There are at least eight Hebrew words used for sin, and twelve words used in the New Testament in Greek.

> "The usage of these words leads to certain conclusions about the doctrine of sin in the Old Testament. (1) Sin was conceived of as being fundamentally disobedient to God. (2) While disobedience involved both positive and negative ideas, the emphasis was definitely on the positive commission of wrong and not the negative omission of good. In other words, *sin was not simply missing the right mark, but hitting the wrong mark.* (3) Sin may take many forms, and the Israelite was aware of the particular form which his sin did take."

Regarding the New Testament usage, he says:

> "From the uses of these words several conclusions may also be drawn. (1) There is always a clear standard against which sin is committed. (2) *Ultimately all sin is a positive rebellion against God and a transgression of His standards.* (3) Evil may assume a variety of forms. (4) Man's responsibility is definite and clearly understood.

> "God has a high and holy standard of what is right, and so long as man follows the Divine standard he will see himself as he truly exists in God's eyes. *The flat statement of the Almighty is that all men have fallen far short of God's required standard.* It is the popular and common practice of men to create their own standards; however,

God has established His standard of perfection for entry into Heaven, and all men have 'missed the mark' as an archer's arrow would fall to the ground because it fell short of its target.

"Let no man ever think that he comes anywhere near the standard set by God. God *has demanded absolute perfection, and no matter how one measures himself, he falls far short.* Some men measure themselves on the basis of human intelligence, some by educational attainment, some by financial success, some by cultural environment, and others by religious performance. But God refuses to accept man on any of these grounds. *He has established His perfect standard, and by that standard He measures every man.*

"The Divine verdict in every instance has been the same, 'You have come short, you have missed the mark.' And when the best of men have done their best, our Lord would challenge each with the words, 'Which of you by taking thought can add one cubit unto his stature?'" [emphasis added]

Sin can be stealing your best friend's crayons and then when confronted, pretending you forgot. It can be the sex before marriage that you dismiss as, "it can't be a sin when you love someone."

But Jesus took it to a whole new level from what the law stated. Yes, you read that right; Jesus did not come to abolish the law but to fulfill it, and He took it to an *even higher level* when He said:

> Let your light shine before men in such a way that they may see your good works, and glorify your Father who is in heaven. **Do not think that I came to abolish the Law or the Prophets; I did not come to abolish but to fulfill.** For truly I say to you, until heaven and earth pass away, **not the smallest letter or stroke shall pass from the Law** until all is accomplished. Whoever then annuls one of the least of these commandments, and teaches others to do

the same, shall be called least in the kingdom of heaven; but **whoever keeps and teaches them, he shall be called great in the kingdom of heaven.** *For I say to you that unless your righteousness surpasses that of the scribes and Pharisees, you will not enter the kingdom of heaven.*
Matthew 5:16-20 [emphasis added]

And:

You have heard that it was said, 'YOU SHALL NOT COMMIT ADULTERY'; but I say to you that everyone who looks at a woman with lust for her has already committed adultery with her in his heart.
Matthew 5:27, 28

Jesus set the bar impossibly high for lowly humans. He made it clear we could never pay the penalty. It's wrong to break the law with action, but He declared that you've already sinned by even allowing a sinful thought to linger.

The story of scripture, cover to cover, is the greatest love story of all time, ever written or conceived of. The greatest mystery of the universe is why God loves us so much.

This story, that begins with Genesis 1:1, does not end in writing until the last word of the book of Revelation, and does not end in reality until Yeshua returns with the blow of the shofar and defeats the forces of darkness in the final battle. Our story with Him will go on for eternity, for those of us who give our lives to Him. But our God is omniscient (knowing all), omnipotent (all powerful), and omnipresent (being everywhere at the same time). He did not make a mistake in explaining His instructions to us. He explains in kindergarten terms how our reality works, that when we do something it doesn't just affect us, and that there is a spiritual alignment whether with the good side or the bad, with everything we do.

*You shall not worship them or serve them; for I, the
LORD your God, am a jealous God, visiting the iniquity
of the fathers on the children, on the third and the
fourth generations of those who hate Me, but showing
lovingkindness to thousands, to those who love Me and
keep My commandments.*
Exodus 20:4-6

We should be praising God for Torah! Thank you, Lord, for loving us so much that you showed us what sin is! For saying, I love you so much I want you to know what causes separation between us, and how ultimately it will be repaired by the fulfillment of the prophecy in Genesis:

*And I will put enmity between you and the woman, and
between your seed and her seed; He shall bruise you on the
head, and you shall bruise him on the heel.*
Genesis 3:15

As mature believers, it is our responsibility to have our behavior, choices, thoughts, and desires come into alignment with the scriptural description of a mature believer, with what scripture calls walking in holiness.

This story that began in Genesis describes what is going on in this life that sins of the ancestors affect the following generations.

*What then? Are we better than they? Not at all; for we
have already charged that both Jews and Greeks are all
under sin; as it is written, "There is none righteous, not
even one."*
Romans 3:9-10

*The LORD is slow to anger and abundant in
lovingkindness, forgiving iniquity and transgression; but
He will by no means clear the guilty, visiting the iniquity
of the fathers on the children to the third and the fourth
generations.*
Numbers 14:18

This passage in Numbers is not a threat from a vengeful, angry God. He is telling you the consequences of sin! He is not saying to an innocent, perfect, sinless person, "Sorry, dude, you will have to pay for the sins your father committed." He says clearly in Ezekiel that is not the case:

> The soul that sins, it shall die. The son shall not bear the
> iniquity of the father, neither shall the father bear the
> iniquity of the son: the righteousness of the righteous shall be
> on him, and the wickedness of the wicked shall be on him.
> Ezekiel 18:20

He is showing us all what happens when we sin. We put things in motion in this dimension and in the spiritual dimension that involve spiritual powers of either darkness or light. There is an element of works that is established in scripture, works which are the fruit of our salvation, or works which reveal a sort of sin alignment. When we sin, we are aligning ourselves with a dark power that is ever pressing on the boundaries set by the blood of the Lamb.

Where do you have your blood boundary set? Is it right up against the throne of your heart? Or is it at a safe distance because you are the mature watchman on the wall walking in holiness, ever vigilant of the approach of enemy forces?

The deception and dysfunction that repeated over and over in the life of the patriarchs exhibits this. Abraham lied about Sarah being his sister, then Isaac did the same thing with Rebekah. Rebekah and Jacob schemed to deceive Isaac as he was on his death bed. Then, Jacob makes an agreement with Laban to work for seven years to have Rachel as his wife and Laban deceives him. The deception infests the lineage. Sin sets things in motion in both dimensions.

To have never committed any sin would be sinless, and there is only One Who lived among us Who committed no sin.

For all have sinned and fall short of the glory of God.
Romans 3:23

*He made Him who knew no sin to be sin on our behalf, so
that we might become the righteousness of God in Him.*
2 Corinthians 5:21

*You wouldn't even know what sin is without the law God
gave us.*

For through the Law comes the knowledge of sin.
Romans 3:20

My point here is not that the law brings us righteousness; it does not. But in the haste to view scripture through a Greek mindset and minimize the difficulties of the law, the law has been viewed in a twisted way. The law reveals, it brings light, it is guidance, it is wisdom, it shows us how to live, and it shows us Who God is. And, God is all about relationship. He's not interested in ticked boxes. He wants us to be connected to Him, to talk with Him, to walk with Him, to bring our burdens, hurts, fears, and anger to Him.

He is the Lover of our souls Who has been incorrectly attributed with being an angry, lightning bolt thrower, Who delights in punishing mortals. All of this is a lie!

We have to come to understand Who He is and that is revealed in His Word; all of it, not just part of it. He is the same loving Creator Who surrounded His beloved Adam and Eve with breathtaking beauty and freedom.

He does not want to be loved because you have no choice. Who wants that? No one wants to be loved because you had no option.

*I have loved you with an everlasting love; Therefore I have
drawn you with lovingkindness.*
Jeremiah 31:3

He has left evidence of His presence, of His power, of His love for you. He leaves breadcrumbs that lead you to Him.

He wants you to know Who He is and to become aware of the evidence showing who the dark beings are and He wants you to choose Him. We are born in sin and iniquity; we are already enslaved to it. True freedom is only found in God! It is His mercy that is new each morning that gives us each breath. In addition, the Word of God is not ink on paper; it is the person of Yeshua Jesus! He *is* the Word!

> *In the beginning was the Word, and the Word was with*
> *God, and the Word was God. He was in the beginning with*
> *God. All things came into being through Him, and apart*
> *from Him nothing came into being that has come into*
> *being. In Him was life, and the life was the Light of men.*
> *The Light shines in the darkness, and the darkness did*
> *not comprehend it. … And the Word became flesh, and*
> *dwelt among us, and we saw His glory, glory as of the only*
> *begotten from the Father, full of grace and truth.*
> *John 1:1-5, 14*
>
> *He is clothed with a robe dipped in blood, and His name is*
> *called The Word of God.*
> *Revelation 19:13*

It's one of the things we need to repent of: Lord, I repent for believing lies about Who You are!

Sound familiar? That's just what happened in the garden to Adam and Eve. They believed a lie spoken by a liar, about the Lover of their souls.

Is this helping you see the sin we all need to have cleansed from us?

It is very important that you do.

If we can't comprehend the height, breadth, and depth of the debt, the blackness of the sin, our sin, then we can never begin to understand the magnitude of the gift we've been given.

This same sin, sin that we participated in, is the very reason there is evil in the world, why all of creation was spun into pain and warfare. We participated in it; it wasn't just somebody else.

This is where the well-spring of joy lies! When you get this, you are never the same.

And, there is only one appropriate response: to serve the Lover of our souls completely, forever!

What Feeds Dark Forces?

If we are to be effective, we need to understand what feeds the forces of darkness.

Does that make you uncomfortable?

Since spiritual warfare training has been removed from the teaching in many pulpits, congregants no longer realize that they themselves can be feeding the problem rather than the solution.

Dark forces are made stronger or weaker by things we do. With our thoughts and behavior, we can either welcome them in, or maintain an environment that is so godly that they have a difficult time sticking around.

By this point, you have been learning about sin, arrogance, and the dangerous numbness of apathy. All these things contribute to the problem. We feed these forces with negativity, not spending time with the Lord, unforgiveness, rebellion, disobedience, and a big one, intent. If our intent isn't on the things of God, it may be on things that either glorify or feed darkness.

When you do what I've written in this book it removes the barriers to the intimacy we need with our Savior. When you get plugged into that and the exchange of the love and power He has for us, the enemy has a hard time getting a toe-hold.

Set your mind on the things of God. You will see the change.

Doubt Can Masquerade As Wisdom

It's not only doubt that can masquerade as wisdom. There is a litany of Christian phrases, words, actions, and platitudes that get thrown around way too often. If we're not careful, they can be a mask covering our true thoughts and feelings and lead us into a habit of living a lie.

Let's look at this very subtle deception in a common illustration.

Let's say you have a wonderful, Christian son who has been trying to make a decision about which college to attend. At the family table you and your husband listen to him as he describes how he prayed about the options, felt he had multiple confirmations of what the Lord wanted for him, and then came to a decision. He clearly has spent time in prayer and has carefully evaluated the pros and cons of each possibility.

Your husband agreed.

But you respond with, "Yes, that's a fine school but I'm not sure that's where the Lord wants you. I think you should pray about that some more."

What you didn't admit to your son or your husband is that the real motivation in your heart is that you don't want him to go to school in another state. It has nothing to do with what is best for him or what the Lord wants.

This is just one example of how we can use Christian language and phrases that may sound good to those who don't know the real story. And, it can masquerade as wisdom.

If you shared with a friend an oversimplified version of the conversation, saying only that your son chose a school and you told him to pray about it some more because you don't think that's what the Lord wants for him, your friend might say, "Oh, that's so wise. Maybe he just isn't hearing the Lord the way you did."

But the truth is, the whole thing is a lie because you don't want to deal with your own feelings about your son being in another state.

Can you see the problem here?

And this is not just a problem in the relationship between a mother and her son.

If the mom in this story stood firm in her opinion, that could open up to a lot of sin. If it was a momentary lapse as she struggled with the emotions of her son leaving the nest and being at a distance, it still presents things for which to repent. Let's look at a list of sins that could possibly play out in this scenario that, at first glance, seemed so innocent, so common, and all about love:

Arrogance – God's plan can't possibly be better than yours.

Fear – What if something happens when he's so far away?

Doubt – He and his dad can't be right. (That's actually doubting God's position, qualifications and sovereignty.)

Lack of Trust – You can't trust God with your son and his life... or your own.

Rebellion – You asked Him and God gave an answer, but you just don't like the answer and refuse to do it. Recall Job?

Idolatry – Your thoughts and plans are better than the plan of the omniscient God, putting yourself on the throne of your heart and removing God from His proper place.

Lying – Using the name of God and false Christian behavior as an excuse for your rebellion.

The mom in this story is living in doubt of God's sovereignty, not trusting that the Lord has a better plan for her son than she does, and in rebellion against the instructions the Lord has given. To make it even worse, she lied using the Lord as an excuse, letting her friend believe she was being so wise.

This inner healing work cuts deep, doesn't it?

We don't like to think that what we do is sinful.

We need to deal with our emotions in a healthy way, but we must never allow those emotions to prevent us from doing what we are called to do. As we are obedient to God's plan, our emotions will come into alignment with Him. Sometimes it hurts; but God is faithful and we grow from the experience.

And, we are told by Paul:

> *We destroy arguments and every lofty opinion raised*
> *against the knowledge of God, and take every thought*
> *captive to obey Christ.*
> *2 Corinthians 10:5, ESV*

Do you see how it is absolutely true that even our righteousness is as filthy rags?

> *All of us have become like one who is unclean, and all our*
> *righteous acts are like filthy rags; we all shrivel up like a*
> *leaf, and like the wind our sins sweep us away.*
> *Isaiah 64:6, NIV*

This whole take-every-thought-captive-thing really exposes our thoughts and motivations.

How can her son learn to trust God when she doesn't?

How can she have a solid relationship with him when she is more interested in what feels good for her than what is best for him?

We all have done these things without much thought, failing to recognize the connection to our spiritual life. But there IS a connection to our spiritual life.

When we willingly commit sin like this without being willing to take every thought captive or to face things that scare us when the Lord has told us to move forward, we are living in rebellion and we are shutting down the communication with our Savior, and that is an opportunity for the Lord of Darkness to sneak in and set up an operation in your heart and home.

212

*Search me, O God, and know my heart; Try me and know
my anxious thoughts.*
Psalm 139:23

On the other hand, when we begin the process described in this book, to ask the Lord to search us and know us, to remove everything that is not pleasing to Him, when we begin to truly understand the mercy and love of our King, we melt into tears that we ever doubted Him.

*Surely the arm of the LORD is not too short to save, nor
His ear too dull to hear. But your iniquities have built
barriers between you and your God, and your sins have
hidden His face from you, so that He will not hear. For
your hands are stained with blood, and your fingers with
iniquity; your lips have spoken lies, and your tongue
mutters injustice.*
Isaiah 59:1-3, BSB

Palms Up

There is a natural human response, both in the body and in the spirit, of tightening up and drawing in when we are stressed or afraid, when we don't feel safe, and when we feel a need to control.

I teach all of my clients to use the Palms Up technique as a part of daily spiritual life.

Just so you understand what I mean, I'll give you a picture of this prayerful position.

In a seated position, place your hands on your knees but with the palms facing up.

What does this mean?

It signifies that you have no desire to have your hands on the steering wheel of your life, that you want God to be in complete control. It signifies to yourself and to God that you are trusting Him, and that you are receiving all that He has for you.

As you learn to lay things at the foot of the cross and leave them there, we have moments when we realize that we have picked them up again, the fear/stress, the lack of trust, the desire to control, or whatever your struggle is.

Immediately upon recognizing that you have stopped trusting the Lord for the outcome, turn your palms up and talk to your Savior.

"Lord, I'm sorry, I did it again. I started worrying about something I already gave to You. I repent for not trusting You, and for thinking my plan is better than Yours. I repent for thinking my method and timing is better than Yours. I repent for the unbelief."

You will feel Him surround you with mercy. He is so pleased when we correct ourselves, maintaining relationship with Him.

Even when you struggle with trust, *speak the truth and light of the Word of God into the darkness of the lie*, in this case, the feeling that you aren't secure.

Say out loud, "Lord, I've been struggling with feelings of insecurity. No matter what I feel right now, I *choose* to trust you. Your Word says You have my name written on the palm of Your hand. Cause my emotions and feelings to come into alignment with your Word."

Kryptonite To Dark Forces

There are certain things that are kryptonite to the forces of darkness.

> *But if serving the Lord seems undesirable to you, then
> choose for yourselves this day whom you will serve,
> whether the gods your ancestors served beyond the
> Euphrates, or the gods of the Amorites, in whose land you
> are living. But as for me and my household, we will serve
> the Lord.*
> *Joshua 24:15*

Here's the kryptonite:

Walking In Holiness

This leaves them very little room to get comfortable. As we do this, we are obedient to God, and at the same time it repels dark forces.

Speak The Truth Of The Light Of The Word Of God Into The Darkness Of The Lie

The lies may be things said over you and about you, as the forces of darkness worked through people who had authority over you such as abusive parents and family members. Whether or not they realized it, they were being used by the forces of darkness.

All of the emotional and thought connections that were developed as those lies and abusive actions were directed at you during childhood and early adult development must be torn down and removed. Replace them with the truth of what God says about you, the blessing He speaks over you.

Here is the blessing God told Aaron to speak over His people:

Then the LORD spoke to Moses, saying, "Speak to Aaron and to his sons, saying, 'Thus you shall bless the sons of Israel. You shall say to them:

> *The LORD bless you, and keep you;*
> *The LORD make His face shine on you,*
> *And be gracious to you;*
> *The LORD lift up His countenance on you,*
> *And give you peace.'*
>
> *"So they shall invoke My name on the sons of Israel, and I then will bless them."*
> *Numbers 6:22-27*

It's like an old switch board with an operator, like you might see in a movie from the 50's. The Lord has to unplug connections from certain places and then plug them into the place they were supposed to have been connected in the first place. He does this work lovingly and it takes time.

If you are working to overcome childhood abuse or another situation that damaged your view of yourself in the Kingdom, a good resource is *Victory of the Darkness*, by Dr. Neil T. Anderson.

Humility

In the section, *My Name Is*, we discussed the power of humility. This is something the evil forces abhor. Use this same prayer I gave you earlier about rejoicing that it is not your power that has authority over the power of darkness.

"Praise Your name, Yeshua, that it is Your power and Your authority that these entities must bow to! Praise Your name, that it is not my power or authority! I rejoice that I don't take a single breath without You and that I am a servant of the Most High God! I rejoice in Your perfect plan to work in this way through earthen vessels to declare Your glory!"

Communion

This is so important. It is deep warfare that shines a laser beam of light that blinds them. Do not reserve this reminder of the work of our victorious Savior for once a month or holidays. I do this nearly every day. This is one of those things where intent really shines. As you line yourself up with the work Yeshua did on the cross and when He rose from the grave, it is the black eye to the Lord of Darkness himself! If you are able, make it a part of your daily time with your Redeemer.

I use the Hebrew blessings for the bread and the wine. Here they are if you choose to use them.

Bread

Barukh atah Adonai Eloheinu melekh ha'olam, hamotzi lechem amiti min hashamayim ba'mashiach Yeshua. (John 6:32)

Blessed are you oh Lord our God, King of the Universe, who brings forth the true bread from heaven in Messiah Yeshua.

Wine

Barukh atah Adonai Eloheinu melekh ha'olam boray p'ree hagefen haamiti boray brit chadasha ba'mashiach Yeshua. (Jeremiah 31:31)

Blessed are you oh Lord our God, King of the Universe, Creator of the fruit of the true vine, creating a new covenant in Messiah Yeshua.

Music & Authentic Worship

Music is incredibly powerful and influential. We must choose carefully what we listen to, especially when we're not thinking about it. That can get into the realm of the sub-conscious and subliminal programming.

We have an unprecedented assault on us from media and entertainment in general, but music is an especially dangerous weapon of the dark side. The repetition is like chanting, driving it deeper into our being. This occurs on both a psychological and spiritual level within us, but because it is connected to supernatural power, it changes the atmosphere around us as well. It can call upon and welcome the Holy Spirit into the room or the car where you are worshipping, or it can invite darkness.

Worship is NOT: songs of encouragement to the frustrated, songs about Christian life, your challenges or pain. Authentic *Worship* is about Him.

So many believers are completely confused about what worship actually is, I believe in large part, because so many churches have adopted the seeker-friendly model with concerts every week. If it's on the platform on a Sunday morning, or sung or performed by someone who is *supposed to be* a believer, then they think it's worship.

In addition, not all musicians or song writers take the time to make sure the theology expressed in their lyrics is correct.

When we use true worship and when we sing scripture, it is a very powerful weapon of war.

I recommend to every client to create playlists of true worship, and fierce spiritual warfare music. And use them daily!

> *The sound of joyful shouting and salvation is in the tents of*
> *the righteous;*
> *Psalm 118:15*

What is the definition of *worship*?

Worship: reverence offered a divine being or supernatural power[84]

What is the definition of *praise*?

Praise: to glorify (a god or saint) especially by the attribution of perfections[85]

Worship our loving God Who redeemed us and Who gave us authority to tread on serpents!

Here are some lyrics of true worship from a public domain hymn:

> *And when I think that God His Son not sparing*
> *Sent Him to die - I scarce can take it in*
> *That on the cross my burden gladly bearing*
> *He bled and died to take away my sin.*
>
> *When Christ shall come with shout of acclamation*
> *And take me home- what joy shall fill my heart!*

Then I shall bow in humble adoration
And there proclaim, my God, how great Thou art!

"How Great Thou Art", Carl Bober, 1859-1940; English Translation; Stuart K. Hime, 1899-1989; public domain.

Here is another of my favorite worship songs:

"You Are Holy"

As for me and my house we will serve You, Lord
Lifting holy hands in worship
We will not bow down to the gods of men
We will worship the God of Israel

You are Holy, Holy, there is no one else like You
You are Holy, Holy, there is no one else like You

Choose this day whom you will serve
Choose this day whom you will serve
But as for me and my house, we will serve You, Lord
We will serve You, Lord

We will not bow to the gods of men
We will not bow to the gods of men
We will worship the God of Israel

Holy, You are Holy
Holy, You are Holy
There is no one else like You

Kadosh, Kadosh atta
Ein kamocha Adonai
Kadosh, Kadosh atta
Ein kamocha adonai

Holy, You are Holy
Holy, You are Holy
There is no one else like You

We will not bow to the gods of men
We will worship the God of Israel

Words & Music by Joshua Aaron, copyright 2012
From: *You Are Holy* (2012)[86], *Roar From Zion* (2019)
Reprinted with permission of the author, Joshua Aaron

There is a video of *For Your Name Is Holy*[87], sung by Paul Wilbur, available on YouTube and end noted here, that I highly recommend you make time to include in your next personal worship appointment with the Lord.

I cannot stress enough to you that worship is a very powerful weapon of our warfare. Shout praise to the Lord and sing to Him, even in that moment of despair, even when you are exhausted from fighting, even when you are resisting depression. Your body and emotions will come into alignment with the Word of God and things will change. Plus, the forces of darkness are enraged when we worship our Lord while we are struggling.

Stop thinking about yourself for a few minutes, stop asking for things, stop thinking of anything else... and just worship Him for a while, because of Who He is and what He's done for you.

Guard Your Mind

Take every thought captive.

When voices of shame and accusing come, or anything from Column B, the first sound I want those minions to hear from you is, "shwiiiinnnggg!", the sound of that gleaming, razor sharp sword being pulled from its sheath! After all, that is a sign that the minions are afoot, stalking, so wouldn't that be the proper response? Step into a classic movie character for a moment and say, "This is the forest of King George! Leave now or die!" That's actually the right attitude.

Guard Your Speech

There are several things we need to learn about our speech. If it seems foreign to you, just give it a try. You will find you can learn this just as you learn any of the other things I've given you in this book. It is just a matter of creating new habits. With all of this work on our journey with the Lord, the Holy Spirit helps us and gives us the ability to do what we cannot do on our own.

Speak It In The Positive

> *Whoever keeps his mouth and his tongue keeps himself out of trouble.*
> *Proverbs 21:23*

> *Whoever restrains his words has knowledge, and he who has a cool spirit is a man of understanding.*
> *Proverbs 17:27*

> *Anxiety in a man's heart weighs him down, but a good word makes him glad.*
> *Proverbs 12:25*

> *There is one whose rash words are like sword thrusts, but the tongue of the wise brings healing.*
> *Proverbs 12:18*

> *And whatever you do, in word or deed, do everything in the name of the Lord Jesus, giving thanks to God the Father through Him.*
> *Colossians 3:17*

> *Death and life are in the power of the tongue, and those who love it will eat its fruits.*
> *Proverbs 18:21*

> *But no human being can tame the tongue. It is a restless evil, full of deadly poison.*
> *James 3:8*

> *And the tongue is a fire, a world of unrighteousness. The tongue is set among our members, staining the whole body,*

setting on fire the entire course of life, and set on fire by hell.
James 3:6

*Righteous lips are the delight of a king, and he loves him
who speaks what is right.*
Proverbs 16:13

*With his mouth the godless man would destroy his
neighbor, but by knowledge the righteous are delivered.*
Proverbs 11:9

*The mouth of the righteous utters wisdom, and his tongue
speaks justice. The law of his God is in his heart; his steps
do not slip.*
Psalm 37:30-31

*For by your words you will be acquitted, and by your
words you will be condemned.*
Matthew 12:37

*He who guards his mouth protects his life, but the one who
opens his lips invites his own ruin.*
Proverbs 13:3

*May these words of my mouth and this meditation of my
heart be pleasing in your sight, LORD, my Rock and
my Redeemer.*
Psalm 19:14

We must be extremely careful about our words, not only over others but also over ourselves. Most of my clients have had curses spoken over them by parents, whether those parents knew it or not. We must break those curses, of course. But we also have cursed ourselves by using phrases and terminology that is common to our culture both within the church and outside of it.

This is a concept that is often overlooked. How we say things is often as important as what we say.

If, for example, a client has been healing from a childhood trauma that created a stronghold of the expectations of failure, rejection, and attack around every corner, their speech can develop around that traumatic experience and the connections made in the brain.

As they live in underlying constant fear and preparation of the next attack, they may have habits of saying very negative things without even realizing it.

Here is a scenario to illustrate the concept.

You have received approval from your insurance company for the minor dental surgery you need. But, your history of abuse dictates how you think and talk about it with your friends.

"Well, the insurance company approved the dental surgery, so I guess I'll have to deal with it now. You know I don't do well with doctors," you repeat very negatively at every opportunity.

The reality is, you prayed for months asking God to provide the surgery. It is a total gift from God so you should be praising your Abba for answering your prayer. Instead you continue to talk about how much you hate surgery and how difficult it will be.

"I hate surgery. This is going to be a very difficult week and there's no way to get through it without being unconscious as much as possible."

Let's break this statement down.

This is voicing hate for something you had prayed for, something your Abba just gave to you as a gift. There is no gratitude. He is due praise and authentic praise includes joy.

There is an expectation and proclamation that it will be very difficult, even when it is a minor surgery. This is actually a curse you are speaking over yourself. If a witch from a local coven was sending curses to you, he or she might say something very much like that, "it will be very difficult, miserable, and you will desire to be unconscious or die."

No, it doesn't *have* to be difficult. I've experienced times myself when God gave me miraculous grace where even major surgery went off rather easily.

There is also a negative prophecy stating, "there's no way to get through it," which is a lie. First of all, you are not omniscient; you do not know what tomorrow holds. You made an absolute statement, that there is no way through it, when you have nothing factual to base that on. And even if you had evidence of such, you are to speak the truth of the Word of God into the darkness of the lie! You can do all things through Christ.

This statement ends with a longing and intent to be made unconscious by *pharmakeia* as much as possible. That brings up a whole other level. Desiring to or longing to be unconscious is very closely aligned with desiring a type of death. You are saying that for a time you want to not be alive, to not experience anything, to be absent.

That does not sound like walking through a battle with confidence and complete trust that your Captain has equipped you with all you need to come through it beautifully and victoriously, especially since he is the One Who gave you the gift!

And, that intent and longing for drugs opens a very dangerous door to the demonic. You could find yourself living the results of a self-fulfilling prophecy as you realize you have become addicted to the drugs from that same surgery.

The overall attitude and tone are very negative. And, guess what? That is not aligned with God's Kingdom. It is, however, lined up with the kingdom of darkness and it invites their company.

These thoughts and attitudes cause the body to secrete specific mixes of chemicals that can do anything from adding to stress to drastically altering the immune system or creating and feeding depression.[88]

For as he thinketh in his heart, so is he.
Proverbs 23:7, KJV

Do you believe God gives you gifts to set you up for failure? The way you sound in this first example shows that is a core belief whether you realize it or not. If that is a core belief, that would have an obviously negative impact on your faith.

It would also greatly impact your overall attitudes, stress levels, joy levels, and ability to receive unexpected blessings in your daily life.

Are you seeing how speech can really be a problem?

In another way, you may be saying the right words but with obvious sarcasm or negativity with, not only your tone, but also with facial expressions for emphasis, "I guess I get to have surgery. Yea."

This is not how to praise our loving Abba for showing us that He not only hears our prayers but also answers them! And we do this more often than we realize.

Let's switch the setting and look at a different scenario.

Your ten-year-old son has begged you for a bike. He pointed it out on websites, talked about the health benefits, and how he was the only one of among his friends who didn't have one. Without this bike, he would not be able to join his friends on the group day trip to a bike a trail in a national park. That trip was coming up the following week and he was very sad he couldn't go.

Unbeknownst to him, you had already bought the bike, had it stashed at a relative's home, and had just notified the group trip leaders that your son would be going.

While he was at school you set the bike up in the garage. You arranged for a few of his closest friends to walk him home and join in the surprise. He comes home from school with his friends, you ask him to get something from the garage and he sees the bike, polished, outfitted, and ready to go.

He turns to you in front of his friends and says flatly with sarcasm, "Wow. Yea. I guess I'm going on that trip. I hate exercising, I don't like being outdoors. There's no way to get through it but just to get through it."

You may be shocked, possibly angry. Maybe discipline would even be required.

Sometimes the way we treat our Abba is just plain rude.

Do we believe in the personal, loving God of the Bible? Or do we believe in some impersonal, universal force as Eastern religions do? The behavior, above, suggests the latter.

So, how can we change the way we talk about the surgery, while honoring the way God made the body to function? Could we acknowledge that it is a bit scary, but still stand firmly on the Word of God with joy and positivity?

Yes. Here's an alternate response:

"Praise God, He answered my prayer! The insurance company has approved the dental surgery! In the past I've struggled with things like this, but God has been healing me. Since He has given the gift, I know He'll walk with me through the experience. After all, the Word of God says, I can do all things through Christ!"

As we heal from past wounds and negative life patterns, our speech patterns begin to change, and it shuts down the demonic dog whistle we've been blowing with our negative words. So, the oppression from the dark side continues to melt away, and our relationship with our Abba is transformed. Instead of giving major attitude when He gives you a gift you asked for, you are now praising Him and running to hug Him.

That's a dramatically different picture of relationship, isn't it?

Speak It Out Loud!

When dealing with spiritual warfare, some things must be said out loud.

Declare this frequently and loudly with joy:

"I serve only Yeshua! I receive guidance only from the holy spirit of the Living God!"

Scripture teaches us to declare our salvation, declare the works of God, and praise Him for His goodness.

When in the midst of intense battle, this is a powerful weapon. Don't just think the positive thought in silence, declare it for all of creation to hear, and so that any dark forces near you can hear, too.

> *I shall not die, but live! And declare the works of the Lord!*
> *Psalm 118:17, KJV*

Speak It Silently In Your Heart

We must also train ourselves that some things should only be said in our hearts and minds. What do I mean by that?

For example, if you have a real struggle with fear and anxiety, train yourself not to say out loud things such as:

"Uh oh, I can feel the panic attack coming on. I hate it when I hear that alarm. It always starts a panic attack!"

Once we understand there are enemy forces about, watching for every opening to cause torment, we give way too much intel away when we do not guard our speech.

Watch for your own vulnerabilities, how you confirm and strengthen your weaknesses, and how you tell the scouts for the Lord of Darkness exactly how to effectively torment you.

Pray over your speech and over renewing your mind. Ask the Lord to do it with His hands, according to His perfect blueprint.

The Way God Made The Body to Function

We've discussed how this type of ministry usually offers only one of two approaches. Here is a brief recap.

First of all, most congregations no longer offer ministry such as inner healing or spiritual warfare with deliverance. If they offer any ministry at all, it is usually a counseling program for inner healing.

Here's the problem: Inner healing ministries do not address the demonic roots of bondage, spiritual warfare, or deliverance. The crippling bondage of severe anxiety, for example, is rarely a chemical or genetic problem alone. It is rooted in spiritual bondage. At the very least, it is both. There is always a spiritual component to that type of bondage.

Secondly, if the congregation does offer spiritual warfare and deliverance ministry, it is usually focused on deliverance and does not fully address the inner healing portion which leaves deliverance incomplete because the client never discovers how the problem developed in the first place. And, it's not usually that they played with Tarot cards at a slumber party in seventh grade. That may be a contributing factor, but in my experience that is not the common cause. The real problem is much deeper and almost always involves generational bondage and/or childhood experiences; a wounding or childhood trauma is often what really throws the doors open to the dark side.

I propose that childhood trauma always involves demonic attachment. The Devil's minions prowl around looking for these types of opportunities to get in and cause mayhem.

So, these things need to be addressed, along with a strong discipleship model so that all three pillars are in place.

With inner healing counseling, we address the roots of the bondage and apply healing salve to all broken places. With spiritual warfare, we address the bondage and minister deliverance as it is revealed. With discipleship, I clearly tell clients what I am thinking as I am praying, as we are talking, as we discuss spiritual strategies and tools to empower them. They then learn not only how to stop the attacks right away, but also how to think through it. That way, when they are through the process, they are not only free, they are trained how to stay free for life if they maintain their relationship with the Lord. They leave the counseling experience trained and comfortable with the process in a way that prepares them to be able to minister to others, whether individually as God sends people to cross their path, or in a more formal calling.

These things are intimately intertwined. Also, with this approach, we cannot ignore the body.

I teach every client that we must work with the body the way God made the body to function. Here's a real counseling example:

My client has been growing and healing for well over a month and suddenly finds himself attacked by overwhelming fear. We get on the phone to discuss what is going on and he tells me that he's done all the things he is supposed to do such as binding and rebuking and praying but the fear is not budging. I then ask for more information about what he was doing before the attack, which reveals that he was having a perfectly innocent conversation on the phone with his mother --- one of his childhood abusers. Though there was nothing out of line in the phone conversation, it can still cause a trigger response from the wounded child still working on healing and, in that case, it is the human emotional side that needs addressing.

So, with that information, we then address the emotion that needs to be processed and released, then again address any spiritual component, and then the fear is removed.

Another example is this: A woman was abused by her husband, ended up in the hospital, and then went through a divorce. At church, she had a reaction to a man walking toward her who at first glance looked very much like her ex-husband. Some ministries or churches might accuse her of not having faith, not being strong in the Lord, or not taking every thought captive. This tragic behavior only re-traumatizes the wounded person. She needs to deal with the emotions and the trauma of the abuse before her body can release the fear.

God made the body to work a certain way. We are fearfully and wonderfully made (Psalm 139:14). And God chose to weave together our physical bodies, our minds, and our emotions in a beautiful and complex system where each component works in harmony with the others. Part of the way we are made to function is the function of denial and dissociation. It is a safety valve that helps us survive trauma. But if we are to help people heal, we cannot just quote scripture at the wounded. We must honor the way the body is made to function by properly dealing with the emotional and psychological aspects of the trauma, then dealing with any demonic attachment that occurred with the trauma.

Yes, we deal with the demonic. But we must first find the broken places, discover the roots of the trauma, process the emotions and memories related to the trauma, and then we can address the demonic.

When we approach it this way, the demonic loses its food source. As the client heals and grows stronger, the demonic loses what has kept it strong and it begins to weaken. At the right time appointed by God, we then cast out whatever had gained access from the traumatic experience.

I have had the joy of seeing amazing transformations. I have worked with more than one woman who absolutely argued with me when I told her she was truly a lovely person with so much to give in the body of Yeshua. Months later, both ladies were thriving with newfound joy and hope. This is the work of our Savior!

R.A.D.

Through the healing process the Lord is lifting the lid on the box that has long been locked and hidden away. Repressed memories, painful events, and emotions associated with them begin to surface. In order to properly process emotions, I use the acronym R.A.D.

Recognize

Acknowledge

Deal

Recognize you are feeling a certain emotion. You can't recognize you're feeling an emotion if you aren't paying attention, so pay attention to changes in your emotions.

Acknowledge the emotion you're feeling in a very specific way, and out loud if possible. "I recognize I am feeling shame right now. Lord I ask You to reveal the sources of the shame." You said you wanted to heal, so the broken places begin to surface. Receive them, pay attention to them, and take each one to the Lord.

Deal with it. The way you deal with it is to spend some time in a quiet place thinking about it, exploring what the source of it may be, what the trigger may have been, praying about it, and writing in your journal about it. Are there any memories associated with it? Is there a certain event that you recall associated with that emotion? Write about any event that comes to mind and how it is connected to the emotion that surfaced.

As you work through the emotions and memories that needed to be addressed, you are working your way to the root of the bondage. We don't want to remove part of the bondage; we want to remove all of it!

Let's look at a very interesting passage.

> *And He took with Him Peter and the two sons of Zebedee, and began to be grieved and distressed. Then He said to*

> them, *"My soul is deeply grieved, to the point of death;*
> *remain here and keep watch with Me."*
> Matthew 26:37-38

If we take the time to think about what is said here and not just read past it, we discover some very important things.

Jesus was fully God, never relinquishing His deity, and fully man, choosing to condescend to human level experience and to limit all He had at His disposal.

So, in this passage we see the Creator of the universe, while in human flesh, distressed to the point of death.

First, He was able to be severely distressed. Second, it was able to go to the point of death. And, He was praying late at night in the garden and the disciples couldn't stay awake. This passage shows the power of emotion, of a mind which knows what is coming because He is omniscient wrapped in a human limitation, and that being distressed has a profound impact on the human body.

Trauma (and even surgery, which is a type of trauma) can create demonic bondage that can have physical, emotional, and spiritual effects. If you only do biblical counseling trying to heal wounds and traumas, the healing may not be complete, such as with my clients who had been on anti-depressants for years from the bondage of trauma-based anxiety. Demonic bondage can't be broken when it's not even acknowledged.

Forgiveness With Inner Healing

We talked about unforgiveness in the early part of the process. But let's address daily walking out forgiveness.

Forgiveness doesn't mean much if you don't know what's involved. To look at it another way, you can't forgive what you don't know.

What I mean by that is best illustrated by two examples.

You come home after a Saturday morning trip to the home store for lawn care items. As you get out of your car in your driveway, your next-door neighbor walks up to you, saying, "I'm so sorry." At first you have no idea what he's talking about, so you ask him.

He replies, "I just accidentally mowed over a couple of the new flowers you planted in the back yard last weekend. I'll pay for what I damaged."

Now, that may be annoying, but the neighbor is honestly taking responsibility, apologizing, and notifying you at the first opportunity. That's all we can expect of each other. It should not be a difficult challenge to forgive his mistake.

But, now let's look at something completely different.

You had some childhood trauma as a young girl. There is some time during elementary school you have very little memory of, mostly first grade.

You receive a call from a well-liked aunt and uncle in a neighboring state. They want to stop by for a visit. You haven't seen them for a couple of years and you are glad for the opportunity to visit with them.

When they come over, you have a wonderful dinner prepared and everyone enjoys the fellowship. Your uncle shares that he gave his life to Jesus a few years ago and that he is discovering new joy, has stopped smoking, and their marriage has never been better.

You are so delighted to see Jesus working in their lives.

After dinner, your aunt asks if she can put your children to bed and you are glad to let her share that with them because they love her as much as you do.

As you sit at the table with your sweet uncle Roger over a cup of coffee, he shares more about how his life has changed after his salvation. He was raised in church but never truly gave his life to Jesus.

But as he talks, you sense there is something more.

"I want to apologize to you," he says.

"What for," you ask, smiling. You can't imagine what he could need to apologize for, he's always been kind, even though you never saw him often.

"That time when you were in first grade and you were alone with me and I molested you."

Suddenly, in an instant, the air is sucked out of the room and you feel dizzy as the memory comes flooding back. In a millisecond you can remember the room, the smell of the peanut butter and jelly sandwiches you'd had for lunch still hanging in the air. You suddenly experience it all over again, the fear, the confusion, the shame. You think you may start to hyperventilate.

"Excuse me, I need to get some water," you mumble as you stand up and go to the kitchen to remove yourself from the room for a moment.

You stand at the kitchen sink staring out the window while the ringing in your ears whines, trying to deal with the memory that was just recovered, and the feelings that are swirling around inside you like a tornado.

Forgiveness.

What would forgiveness look like in that situation?

This is a very different thing.

You can't forgive something when you have no knowledge of it. You can issue general forgiveness, as when someone has had a cold for two weeks and has been a bit grumpy and hard to be around. But specific forgiveness for inner healing issues as illustrated in this story is a very different thing.

I address this in this book about spiritual warfare because there are so many professing Christians, and at least some well-meaning, who say the most hurtful things to people who are already working to heal from trauma.

One of the things they say is, "You need to let that go. You aren't having faith if that is still bothering you."

That is not only utter nonsense, it is damaging. It would also be denial, a sign of a lack of healing if a traumatized person did that!

God did not make the body to work like that.

There are times that through prayer, spiritual warfare, and inner healing work, God delivers in an instant, or very quickly. But, most often He wants us to work through the pain and fear. And that journey requires that we work with the body the way God made the body to function.

God created our bodies with a safety valve to deal with traumatic experiences and that is a key to the healing process. In this case, healing will involve dealing with dissociation and missing memory. We must bring the healing of Yeshua Jesus into all aspects of the healing journey, to the body, to the spirit, and to the soul.

It is an amazing thing that the human body does in a traumatic event. There is an ability to dissociate in the moment of the trauma and the body kind of tucks the memory away, sometimes completely forgotten for many years, in order to survive the traumatic event.

Let's look at another example of forgiveness.

You left your two children, including your six-year-old son, Justin, in the care of friends from church who have children of similar ages. You came to pick them up in the evening after a full day at a work conference. Your friend, the mother in the care of your children, Marcia, chats with you for a moment in the kitchen before you gather the kids to leave. In the course of the conversation, she tells you there was a conflict between her nine-year-old son Brian and your Justin.

"I'm sorry, I don't know what it was about. Justin cried but it wasn't a big deal. He's fine now," she says, as if it was a momentary scuffle about who got to play with the toy truck.

You have no reason to be alarmed by the very common report and Marcia helps you gather the kids and their things.

When you get home, as you put the kids in bed, there is a problem with Justin. Your normally well-behaved, mild-mannered child is clearly upset, seems angry and agitated.

As you spend some time with him trying to get him settled and ready to go to sleep, you ask him how his day was.

"I don't like it there," he says.

"Why not," you ask.

"Brian hurt me. He's mean."

"How did Brian hurt you?"

Your sweet, well-behaved child then tells you how an older child sat on top of him on the ground, pulled up his shirt and repeatedly stabbed him with a sharp pencil. He then shows you where the red puncture marks are over his stomach and chest.

He also tells you that Marcia walked in on them, yelled at Brian and sent Brian to his room for time out.

This scenario is very different because Marcia said the words, "I'm sorry," but withheld information that you as a parent need to know, and she blatantly lied by telling you nothing out of the ordinary happened, when she knew something major had taken place.

You had received Marcia's apology based on what she had told you happened between the boys, but that information was a lie. Her apology was false, and your receiving the apology is nullified because you have now discovered it is a completely different situation.

See how forgiveness can be very different depending on the situation?

Since I work with clients who have had significant trauma, this understanding is very important.

Have you experienced a situation where someone claimed you had no right to be upset about something because they had technically already apologized, even though it was under false pretenses?

Whether you have experienced trauma in your own life or not, we need to be better at not making sweeping statements about forgiveness that only re-injure the wounded.

Body & Spirit: Family Connections

Family units are not just a handful of people under one roof; they reflect our relationship with God. And, the connections are beyond what we think we understand.

As you are on a journey of healing and deliverance, never forget that family members are affected along the way. Keep them in your prayers, offering protection, favor, and healing for each of them. Recognize that what comes up during the process could impact them as well.

This could be a time to train your children how to seek the Lord on a spiritual journey, how to battle effectively in the supernatural realm, and how to support each other with prayer.

Here's an example.

A former client had been working on her healing for nearly two years. She was putting it all together: spiritual depth, counseling, breaking bondage, walking in holiness, spending daily time with the Lord, and taking better care of her temple with cleansing and purification. Powerful things were happening! Genetic bondage was being broken!

Her kids were doing the body cleanse along with her. She taught them as she learned spiritual tools and how to battle effectively. They were growing closer as a family and began manifesting the same physical issues at the same time. She went through shoulder pain, neck pain, and then hip pain. Each time, one of the children manifested the same symptom. The children did not know that she was dealing with each of these pains. They simply manifested the same pain in the same shoulder, part of the neck, or the same hip.

You have the power and authority to break this generational bondage so it will no longer continue in your children.

Training Children

How do you train children in spiritual warfare?

Some parents think the best possible demonstration of good parenting is to shield their children from every challenge or disappointment. But that is not the picture we see in scripture.

David was only a teenager when he said, "For who is this uncircumcised Philistine, that he should taunt the armies of the living God?"

> *"This day the LORD will deliver you up into my hands,*
> *and I will strike you down and remove your head from you.*
> *And I will give the dead bodies of the army of the Philistines*
> *this day to the birds of the sky and the wild beasts of the*
> *earth, that all the earth may know that there is a God in*
> *Israel, and that all this assembly may know that the LORD*
> *does not deliver by sword or by spear; for the battle is the*
> *LORD'S and He will give you into our hands."*
> 1 Samuel 17:46-47

One client has taught her children these skills since they were infants. They are some of the most well-adjusted children I've ever seen. Here is a recent example.

Eleven-year-old Joshua came to his mom, Laurie, in the morning. He said he'd had trouble sleeping last night.

"Mommy, I had trouble sleeping last night. You know how you taught us that when we can't sleep to talk to God? I did and He said something to me."

"What did he say," she asked?

"He said, 'I love you.'"

She was thrilled her son had a personal encounter with the Living God.

Her kids have learned to pray for each other, and to listen to the Holy Spirit because she taught them scripture and the whole of the Word of God including spiritual warfare. The youngest was just five.

Recently, when pulling into a parking space at the grocery store, there was a man that seemed to be conducting a drug deal through the window of an open car nearby. As they pulled into the parking space, Laurie's nine-year-old daughter said, "Mommy, I'm getting out on your side."

Another victory!

This young girl felt the urging of the Holy Spirit to exit on the other side of the van and she acted on it!

As a result of that statement, the family had another impromptu discussion about listening to the Holy Spirit and then heeding the instruction.

This kind of training is not for adults only! It keeps our kids safe, builds the wisdom of the Lord, and teaches confidence to act when they believe the Holy Spirit is leading them.

The kids I've known who are raised this way operate on a different level, spiritually. We are created to have a supernatural relationship: with the living God not with the powers of darkness. They are already wondering about these things. These children are getting their questions answered as they grow and will be less likely to be deceived by or to cozy up to dark powers.

They know how to cover their sleep and their dreams. When they have a bad dream, they know how to bind and rebuke, and call upon holy spirit power for protection, discernment, and power.

Whole House Cleaning

Every time you move, I strongly recommend that you do a whole home cleaning before you take a single possession or box into the new home. I have done this for years and it really prevents a lot of unnecessary drama. It is the same process when there is something going on in the home.

Once you know how to do it, it doesn't take long at all unless you uncover some dark forces that don't want to leave. That can take a bit longer. If it's just a quick walk-through cleansing of a house you already own that has been fully cleaned before, it takes approximately 15 minutes for a small home, a bit longer if larger.

If you have never done this before, plan accordingly. If you know there is demonic activity in the home, plan on at least two hours.

Do the home first, then walk the property line, dedicating the property to the Lord and occasionally drizzle some olive oil as the sign of dedication.

I have used various methods over the years. This method is the one that I have found to be the most effective and easiest to perform.

It needs to be done by whoever has the authority over it, which would be the owner or the renter. Because of the covering revealed in scripture, couples should do this together, unless the husband doesn't want to, and he gives his authority to his wife to conduct the cleansing on behalf of both of them.

I used to have a weekly Bible study in my home. As people come into your home, they bring all their spiritual baggage with them.

Since you open the door and invite them in, legally and technically, from the dark side's point of view, you let the dark forces in too. It gives them an opening to come in and stay unless you notice their presence and evict them.

One night as people were coming in for our Bible study, the Lord alerted me instantly to a presence that came in with someone and darted into a corner. I was praying silently as everyone came in and got settled, asking the Lord what He wanted me to do. I felt He was telling me to be vigilant, and not to forget to tell it to leave after the study was over.

During the study, that person who brought in the spirit, started an argument with someone else. That had never happened before.

As soon as everyone left, I cracked the front door and prayed and evicted it. It only took a couple of minutes. They tried to sneak in, hoping I wouldn't notice. If I had not been paying attention and listening to the Holy Spirit, who knows what havoc it would have tried to create.

Get the house clean, and then always be vigilant with the knowledge that these entities are attached to people who haven't been set free yet. Don't give them an opportunity to sneak in and stay.

Do not bless a house that is infected with dark spiritual forces. Get the house cleaned out, then bless it.

If there has been any ungodly supernatural activity in the home, have at least one trained person with you.

If there is no demonic activity in the home, you can do this yourself.

Instructions

Prepare with prayer and fasting. Have your armor on and be in prayer before you even walk in the new home, or before you begin in your current home.

You need: olive oil, selected worship music, and something to play the music.

Use a stereo, a Bluetooth speaker, boom box, or set your phone on *Speaker* and play intense worship music. Sing along and praise Yeshua with joy and do it loudly!

Clap your hands in praise. I am not totally sure why this is important and effective, but it is. They hate praise and the clapping of hands.

Be full of joy before you begin.

Enter the home and leave the front door open just a crack until you are finished.

With the front door at your back, begin to your right, moving around the walls of the home, going into each room. As you enter each room, anoint (seal) every window and closet door, pausing to evict anything you sense in closets and storage spaces. Once you feel the closets are alright, close the door and anoint the door frame with olive oil in the sign of the cross.

Once you feel the room is clean, as you exit the room, if it has a door, shut the door and anoint the doorframe of the room with the olive oil in the sign of the cross, sealing the room.

Move to the next room, going around the home to the right.

Go through each room of the home on the first level, then move to the upper level in the same manner.

Once the upper floors are clean, move to the basement.

Go through the entire home until all doors and windows have been anointed.

What you are doing is driving any dark spiritual entity or force ahead of you around the house until there is nowhere else for them to go.

As you reach your starting point at the front door, pause and pray, commanding anything you've bound by the blood of the Lamb to be cast out, that they must go to the dry places, and they are never allowed to return to you, your family, or property. After you feel you are finished, close the front door, and seal it on the inside with the olive oil in the sign of the cross.

Then, dedicate the home and property it sits on to the Lord for His purposes, praising Him for blessing you with it, whether you rent or own. Even with a rental, it is a legal agreement that it is your home or room as long as you are keeping your end of the agreement of paying the rent.

Here is the prayer to cleanse the home:

> "I serve notice to any dark entity, energy, spirit, force, or dark technology that may be in, on, or around this home that this home now belongs to me. Yeshua gave me this home for His purposes. You no longer have any authority regarding this property. You are no longer allowed here. You are not allowed anywhere in, on, or around this home, and that includes the air space above, and the ground beneath, from the center of the earth, to the heavens. In the name of Yeshua, any dark energy, entity, spirit, force, or dark technology that is in, on, or around this home, the Lord rebuke you, the Blood of the Lamb be upon you. You must all come together into one group to be bound in the Blood of the Lamb right now. Your communication is cut off, both within the group and outside the group. Your power is cut off, and by the authority of Yeshua, I cut off any access to future sources of power. Staying all bound together in the Blood of the Lamb, you are now cast out as a group. You must leave, all together, as a group; now. You must go to the dry places and you are never allowed to return to me or my family or my property, in the name and authority of Yeshua Hamashiach."

Here is a prayer of dedication once the home is clean:

"Lord, You gave this home to me for Kingdom purposes. I now dedicate it to You. There is no dark entity, energy, spirit, force, or dark technology allowed anywhere in, on, or around this home or property, and that includes the air space above and the ground beneath, from the center of the earth to the heavens. The only spirit allowed here is the Holy Spirit of the Living God. I now invite the Holy Spirt to fill this home, every corner, every crack and crevice. Yeshua, I ask You to fill this home with Your presence. The blood of the Lamb is on my forehead and on my doorposts and lintels. Lord, I ask You to set a strong boundary around this home defining the property line with the Blood of the Lamb. I ask that You send angels to guard the property and to do battle on my behalf. If any action or error creates an opening to the forces of darkness, alert me and instruct me. May this home and all who live in it, glorify You. In the name of Yeshua, the King of Kings, Amen."

Remember, whenever you take territory, be prepared to defend it. Always have your radar on. Remember to pray over your home and the property it sits on frequently. Remember to praise God for your home on a regular basis. Frequently declare loudly that there is no spirit allowed in your home but the Holy Spirit of the Living God.

Auto-Cleanse

I must confess I did not come up with this term, but I instantly declared I was adopting it! It makes your home very inhospitable to dark spirits.

This can be a great help if: you've had a problem in the home, if you are on a deliverance journey breaking bondage, or if you just like to keep your home feeling full of the light and shalom of our King.

There are multiple audio books available on YouTube of spiritual warfare prayers. I found one that is several hours long of nothing but prayers against darkness. I turn my computer on, start the video, and turn up the volume. After running errands, I come home to my house full of the Light of Jesus!

I also have a playlist I created of worship that is related to spiritual warfare, full of songs of victory, the authority of Yeshua, and that He alone is Holy. I will set that to play while I'm gone or even while I'm cleaning.

This is very effective. I encourage you to use this simple tool regularly.

Act On What You Know

Don't focus on what you don't know; act on what you do know!

Sometimes we can get too focused on what we don't know. This can keep us bound and unable to move forward.

What do you know that scripture says?

When engaging in the healing process and dealing with spiritual warfare, if you have a moment where you feel stuck with what you don't know, remind yourself of what you do know.

What does scripture say?

What is our armor and how do we put it on?

Start there and the Holy Spirit will lead you.

Casting Down Arrogance

There is a whole lot of power and authority at our disposal, purchased for us by the sacrifice of our Savior when He defeated all the powers of darkness. There is no demon from the pit of hell, no matter how big it is or how loud it growls, that can stand against the Lord. We are covered: *if* we are in obedience to His Word.

Yet, we are commanded not to rejoice in this.

> *Nevertheless, do not rejoice that the spirits submit to you,*
> *but rejoice that your names are written in heaven.*
> *Luke 10:20*

Arrogance or pride, in any form, is a huge open door to the forces of darkness. It was Lucifer's original sin and is detestable to God.

To make it more difficult to spot, one of the most used tools of the enemy is the *Christian Language* tool. Satan gets you to use this tool to further his agenda when you use language that sounds, on the surface at least, very Christian-like.

Some churches have counseling programs. Many people won't use them because they report that there are major issues with confidentiality. Most of us have experiences where someone who has inside information due to a position on church staff begins praying out loud at a prayer meeting in completely inappropriate ways.

"Oh, Lord, please bless our sister who is struggling with her marriage. I rebuke that spirit of adultery that inspired her husband to cheat on her with the Sunday School teacher!"

Clearly, most of the people in that group now know exactly who has done what she is talking about. People will often tell themselves that they're interceding for someone when they are really operating in pride and engaging in gossip, trying to dress it up in Christian-like behavior. They use the excuse that they were praying at a prayer meeting at church. Dressing up a pig in a dress and lipstick doesn't change the fact that it is still a pig. That pig represents sin.

There are stories I've heard of believers who run ahead of their experience, training, and God's instructions, and start rebuking principalities and high-level spirits. They then suffer sudden illness or destruction explodes in their lives and they wonder why.

We are not to tempt the spirits. Apart from a directive from the throne of God, with multiple confirmations by the mouths of two or three witnesses, we are not to go looking for trouble with high-level entities. We need to learn how to deal with what happens around us every day. When supernatural trouble crosses our path, we are to respond in a careful, thoughtful, thorough, and completely obedient way.

Not long-ago during prayer and intercession I was shown a principality. I knew exactly what it was, and I asked the Lord what He wanted me to do. I already knew that we are not to rebuke or mess with principalities, so I immediately asked the Lord for instructions.

I asked, "Lord, I stand fully covered in the armor of God, ready to do what You command. What do You want me to do with this one? Do You want me to rebuke it? Or do You want me to set a strong boundary?"

Hey, if my King tells me to stab some minion with the Word of God, I will do so without hesitation. If God is the One giving me that instruction, He will also cover me. But, I'm mature enough to know that we need to wait for confirmation of big things or things that may be a little close to the edge of what God normally commands.

I don't often say that God told me something. My clients would tell you I usually say I felt as though the Lord was leading me to do something. But, in this case, I clearly heard the Lord tell me not to rebuke it, that He wanted me to set a strong boundary as I continued with the intercessory prayer in which I had been engaged at the time.

There is a method, there are instructions, and we must learn how to battle correctly. We must not get cocky.

Arrogance is fertilizer to the lie that we aren't very sinful. It is the dam against the river of joy.

Staying Free

Now that the power and mercy of Yeshua has broken the chains that had you bound, you must be vigilant to protect the territory you have recovered from the enemy.

The enemy doesn't like to lose territory and he will try to get it back. You must be prepared to defend it at all times!

You may feel very different inside, you may have behavior changes that others notice, you may have life pattern changes.

For at least a month, devote your time to pressing in to Yeshua and spending time with your spouse if you are married. Many things will be different so stay in it as much as you can to get adjusted to your new normal.

It's as if you have new glasses on that give you vision about your life that is very different. You can see things you couldn't see before. It's clearer and sharper. The enemy should have a harder time sneaking up on you.

But this does not mean that the enemy has decided to leave you alone! The enemy is like a roaring lion seeking whom he may devour. Scripture tells us the situation; it does not give us platitudes.

The Holy Spirit may give you more revelations of things for which you need to repent. Repent, repent, repent!

And when you repent of sin, it doesn't mean just saying a quick, "I'm sorry". Rather, it means sincerely admitting it, taking responsibility for it, and, if possible, making it right. It means asking Yeshua to cover you with His blood to make you clean before Him, to remove every stain so that you never have anything between you and your Savior.

You should be asking the Lord to reveal sin to you that you can't see, not just fielding the sin you do see.

You may feel some spiritual attack as those spirits kicked out of the house try to get back in.

You must be very fierce about protecting all gates: eyes, ears, mouth.

You must guard against, identify and cast down the thoughts that are not from God.

You must put on your armor daily, first thing in the morning and upon retiring at night, and throughout the day as it comes to mind.

What are the fiery darts of the enemy? The unwanted thoughts! Take every thought captive immediately with the Word of God! The most intense battle ground is in the mind.

You may need to rearrange your time, your commitments or your friendships as the Lord leads you to stop spending time on some things and to start spending time on other things.

You may find yourself drawn to a ministry you'd never considered. Or be interested in something you never cared about before.

You should be able to hear the leading of the Holy Spirit more often and more clearly now that the interference from the enemy has been cleared out of your heart and your spiritual ears.

Spend time in the Word, not reading books about the Word.

Spend time pressing in to Yeshua, not reading books about others pressing into Him.

You may find you are more sensitive to something that didn't bother you before, such as TV, your DVD collection or books on your bookshelf. There may be things in your home or car that need to get the boot!

Don't expect the Holy Spirit to tell you repeatedly; learn to listen and to move in obedience immediately.

You should be able to spot the enemy and their plans more easily, recognize thoughts that are not of God, and immediately rebuke, cast out, and seal the completed work with the Blood, always forbidding them to ever return.

If there is something that comes up that is not responding to you or that you aren't sure how to deal with, contact someone trained in spiritual warfare ministry and ask.

Inner Healing and deliverance are not an end to something as much as they are a beginning. This is the beginning of walking your life out in power, love and a sound mind, and dealing with the spiritual darkness as necessary.

Spiritual darkness and warfare have always been raging around you, but now you are learning how to recognize it, deal with it, war against it, and therefore, be able to walk in power every day.

We do not look for battles with the forces of darkness but when they challenge us in any way, we are to have an immediate and strong response.

There is no god like Jehovah! Through His mighty power and mercy, you can walk in freedom!

If something comes up that you need help with, don't let the enemy lie to you, saying it's because the Word isn't true, it doesn't work, or God isn't real. Remember that our Lord wants us to work together as the body of Christ, and often that is why we need assistance, because we are not made to be an island unto ourselves. We are made to work together and support one another.

Walk in holiness, keeping your armor on at all times, and stay alert to the spiritual forces around you. That is how you stay free. The enemy gets back in through sin, so it is a necessary redundancy to say, repent, repent, repent! Moment to moment!

You will find that this way of living, as is instructed in the Bible, will produce more humility and the fruits of the Spirit, and the Potter's hands are able to shape you into the vessel He has designed for you to be.

> *For God did not give us a spirit of fear, but of power, and of love, and of a sound mind.*
> 2 Timothy 1:7

> *For you have not received a spirit of slavery leading to fear again, but you have received a spirit of adoption as sons by which we cry out, "Abba! Father!"*
> Romans 8:15

Nothing in this walk is a once-and-done thing. God does not like box-ticking. It is an unfolding relationship journey where He knows the future and we do not. We must trust Him in the next moment, and the next moment after that.

Boundaries must be set, re-set, strengthened and guarded. We must stand -- and having done all to stand, stand therefore!

> *...and having done everything, to stand firm. Stand firm therefore...*
> Ephesians 6:13-14

Prayer Weapons

I had no idea that my background as a project manager and business analyst would be useful in this ministry. But our God wastes nothing. He had a ministry purpose for those skills from the beginning.

God began teaching me to take the shortest distance between two points. Efficiency. After all, who wants a battle to be longer than necessary, or to battle the same forces over and over again because we weren't fully effective?

I don't need to know their names, I will not have a conversation with them, I will listen to the leading of the Holy Spirit and get them bound and evicted as quickly as possible. Leaving them loopholes to use prolongs the process and wears us out unnecessarily. That is not efficient use of our time.

> *See then that ye walk circumspectly, not as fools, but as*
> *wise, Redeeming the time, because the days are evil.*
> *Ephesians 5:15-16, KJV*

This means we must be very specific. The enemy wants to find openings or twist the Word of God to confuse us or scare us. But, if we know what we're doing, we can pray in such a way that leaves very little wiggle room for the enemy to escape and later return with an even greater attack force.

In this section, I've included prayers that will be effective right from the start.

Morning

This morning routine is easy to do, it sets the tone of your day, and you greet the day fully equipped. Once you train yourself in the pattern it takes only about a minute. And, once in the habit, you may notice things don't go well if you forget to start the day with Him.

First Fruits – Thoughts

We must train ourselves to offer the first fruits of our thoughts to our Lord. If this sounds strange to you, I promise that you will be able to do it. You just have to be intentional.

Here's what I mean.

Train yourself so that every morning, as you are just beginning to come awake, your first thoughts are praise to the Lord. Even in a very sleepy state you can develop the habit of saying words of praise. Here is a suggestion.

"Hallelujah. Praise Your Name, Lord."

Then, continue to the next stage of offering the first fruits of your words.

First Fruits – Words

Continue the praise as you are becoming conscious and then speak them out loud, offering the first words of your lips to Him.

"Praise Your Name, Lord. Thank You for sleep. Thank You that I had a safe place to sleep. Thank You for waking me up this morning. Thank You for Your mercy."

This is how you greet full consciousness as you sit up in bed.

Armor

Next, as you are still in praise, before your feet even hit the floor, begin putting your armor on.

"In the Name of Yeshua I am fully covered in the armor of God. I put on the helmet of salvation, the breastplate of righteousness, the belt of truth, my feet are covered with the gospel of peace, I have the shield of faith, and the sword of the spirit. I serve only You, Lord."

Dedicate The Day

After you've got your armor on, dedicate your day to Him.

> "Holy, holy, holy, is the Lord God Almighty, Who was,
> and is, and is to come. Blessed be the Name of the Lord,
> for the Lord is good and His mercy endureth forever!
> Lord, I dedicate my day to You, I dedicate my life to You.
> Guide every thought, every word, every decision that I
> make. I want to walk in Your perfect will, not just Your
> permissive will. Don't allow the enemy to steal a single
> minute from my day. Place a wall of fire around me,
> protect me from attacks of the dark ones, and give me
> divine favor in all I do today. Give me sharp discernment
> and wisdom in all things."

This routine will get you headed in the right direction and give you better defense against the daily assault by the evil ones.

Throughout The Day

Anytime the thought of the armor of God comes to mind, pause and immediately put it on again. It may be the Holy Spirit alerting you to minions plotting to trip you up. No matter how many times it comes to mind, just put it on again and praise God for the warning.

Bubble Of Protection

> "Lord, I ask You to place a bubble of protection around
> me right now, so that the forces of darkness cannot
> understand or perceive anything I say, do, or write, or
> any communication I receive from You. In the Name
> of Yeshua."

Nighttime

The night routine is like the morning routine, simple and effective. Be faithful to do it every night and you will be more protected from assault.

Dedicate Sleep & Dreams – Set The Boundary

"I do not receive any dreams, voices, communications, contact, or visitations from any dark energy, entity, spirit, force, or dark technology. I set a boundary around me, and my sleep and dreams with the blood of the Lamb."

Dedicate Sleep & Dreams – Dedicate To The Lord

"Lord, I dedicate my sleep and dreams to only You. During this time, I will only receive dreams, visions, and communication from the Holy Spirit of the Living God."

Invitation To The Lord

"Now that I've set the boundary and dedicated my sleep and dreams to You, Lord, I invite You to speak to me in my sleep and my dreams. Please spend this time with me. Give me Your direction, Your correction, or just be with me as we walk in the cool of the day in the garden. I dedicate this time to You and I want to spend it with You."

Armor of God

"I put on the full armor of God: the helmet of salvation, the breastplate of righteousness, the belt of truth, my feet are covered with the gospel of peace, I have my shield of faith and the sword of the spirit. Place around me a wall of fire to protect me from the attacks of the evil ones and send Your angels to protect me through the night/day. In the Name of Yeshua, Amen."

Receiving Correction

"What? I'm so sorry, I didn't realize I was wandering too far away from Your arms. Thank You, my Lord, for alerting me to the danger! Thank You for loving me so much that You called to me. I repent of the sin and anything that even hurt Your heart. Wash me clean by the blood of the Lamb so I can stand clean before Your throne, so my praise will be received, and my prayers will be heard. Search me and know me, my King, and remove anything that is not pleasing to You. I've learned of Your character, Who You are, and how much You love me. I've learned I can trust You more than I can trust myself or anyone on this earth. Show me, I'm listening. And I joyfully receive Your correction so I can be back in your embrace."

Warfare

In times of battle, the Lord led me to be very specific, helping me to create a shorter distance between two points. If you are afraid this might be legalistic, it's possible you may be missing the lesson.

The enemy uses every loophole they can find, and they twist the Word of God to use it against us. If we can't spot it, they might be successful.

We are lower than the angels, as we've already discussed: we are not that hard to figure out. The dark forces study you to find your flaws and weaknesses and they will use them.

In order to accomplish a tighter knot in the prayer that they can't get out of, in less time, we need to be specific. We want to leave as little room to maneuver as possible.

Here are some prayers to get you going. You can add more detail, if you like, to be even more specific to your situation.

This is my general warfare prayer. Read through it, then we'll dissect it.

General Warfare Prayer

Sometimes you have to do this several times with strong authority and fire. It is a real battle! Remember, they are very much like badly behaved children who annoy a parent who refuses to take authority.

Once they start seeing the evidence that you mean what you say and that you will stand in the authority of Yeshua until they leave, they start leaving more quickly and with less of a battle. They begin to see that the tricks they used to use on you aren't working anymore.

> "In the Name of Yeshua Jesus, I speak to every dark energy, entity, spirit, force, or dark technology that may be in, on, or around me. The Lord rebuke you, the blood of the Lamb be upon you. You must come together into one group right now to be bound by the blood of the Lamb. Your communication is cut off, both within the group and without. Your power is cut off, and I cut you off from any future access to power. You will be silent; you will be still. Lord, I ask You to send blindness, deafness, and dumbness upon them so they cannot plan or strategize against me or my family. Now, all bound by the blood of the Lamb, staying bound together as a group, you are cast out. You must leave right now and go to the dry places. You are never allowed to return to me or my family. Leave now in the Name of Yeshua."

> "Holy Spirit reveal every hiding place of any dark energy, entity, spirit, force, or dark technology. Expose any hidden darkness that has me bound."

When you aren't sure if there is a demonic influence in a situation, you can phrase it like this:

> "If there is any dark energy, entity, spirit, force, or dark technology causing [fill in the blank], you are trespassing. The Lord rebuke you, the blood of the Lamb be upon you. You are now bound by the blood of the Lamb and staying bound you are now cast out in the Name of Yeshua Jesus. You must go to the dry places and you are never allowed to return to me, my family, or my property. In the Name of Yeshua."

If you feel there could be more than one spirit you are dealing with, even if you aren't sure, you can say:

> "I speak to every dark energy, entity, spirit, force, or dark technology that is causing [fill in the blank]. In the Name of Yeshua, you must all come together into one group to be bound by the blood of the Lamb. The Lord rebuke you, the blood of the Lamb be upon you. Your communication is cut off, within the group and outside the group, your power is cut off, I cut you off from access to any future sources of power. And, Lord, I ask You to send blindness, deafness, and dumbness upon them so they can't strategize against me or my family. Now that you are all bound, staying bound together as a group, you must leave now and go to the dry places. You are never allowed to return to me, my family, or my property, in the Name of Yeshua."

The Lord gave me this prayer and I have found it to be very effective when a spirit is being stubborn.

> "You have been exposed by the true Light of the true Word of the Living God!"

Then do the above.

Declarations

> "I serve only Yeshua! The blood of the Lamb is on my forehead, and it's on my doorposts and lintels."

> "You are trespassing! You have no authority here! You must go now!"

The Lord is holy and the enemy hates hearing that. Shout it out with joy!

> *"Holy, holy, holy is the Lord God Almighty! Who was, and is, and is to come!" (Revelation 4:8)*

> *"Worthy art thou, our Lord and our God, to receive glory
> and honor and power; for Thou didst create all things,
> and because of Thy will they existed, and were created."*
> *(Revelation 4:11)*

> *"Blessed be the name of the Lord! For the Lord is good and
> his mercy endureth forever!" (Psalm 100:5)*

Dark spirits hate to be reminded that the Lord reigns on His throne. Hit them with this.

> *"Yeshua Hamashiach is King of Kings and Lord of Lords!"*
> *(Revelation 19:16)*

> *"At the Name of Yeshua EVERY knee must bow and
> EVERY tongue confess that He alone is Lord!" (Philippians
> 2:10, Romans 14:11)*

Commit this Hebrew phrase to memory. They really hate this. Declare it out loud with joy frequently. It is also very effective when in the midst of a battle.

"Ra-ooey oo-hassey!" This is a transliteration which means, "Worthy is the Lamb!"

House Cleaning

Do not bless a home that is infected with dark spiritual forces. Get the house cleaned out then bless the home.

Prayer To Cleanse The Home:

> "I serve notice to any dark entity, energy, spirit, force,
> or dark technology that may be in, on, or around this
> home, that this home now belongs to me. Yeshua gave
> me this home for His purposes. You no longer have any
> authority regarding this property. You are no longer
> allowed here. You are not allowed anywhere in, on, or
> around this home, and that includes the air space above,
> and the ground beneath, from the center of the earth,

to the heavens. In the Name of Yeshua, any dark entity, energy, spirit, force, or dark technology that is in, on, or around this home, the Lord rebuke you, the Blood of the Lamb be upon you. You must all come together into one group to be bound in the Blood of the Lamb right now. Your communication is cut of, both within the group and outside the group. Your power is cut off, and by the authority of Yeshua, I cut off any access to future sources of power. Staying all bound together in the Blood of the Lamb, you are now cast out as a group. You must leave, all together, as a group now. You must go to the dry places and you are never allowed to return to me or my family or my property, in the name and authority of Yeshua Hamashiach."

Prayer Of Dedication Once The Home Is Clean:

"Lord, You gave this home to me for Kingdom purposes. I now dedicate it to You. There is no dark entity, energy, spirit, force, or dark technology allowed anywhere in, on, or around this home or property, and that includes the air space above and the ground beneath, from the center of the earth, to the heavens. The only spirit allowed here is the Holy Spirit of the Living God. I now invite the Holy Spirt to fill this home, every corner, every crack and crevice. Yeshua, I ask You to fill this home with Your presence. The blood of the Lamb is on my forehead and on my doorposts and lintels. Lord, I ask You to set a strong boundary around this home defining the property line with the Blood of the Lamb. I ask that you send angels to guard the property and to do battle on my behalf. If any action or error creates an opening to the forces of darkness, alert me and instruct me. May this home and all who live in it, glorify You. In the name of Yeshua, the King of Kings, Amen."

Real Estate & Property

"I am speaking to any dark energy, entity, force, spirit, or dark technology that is in, on, or around this house/property. You are trespassing. The blood of the Lamb is on my forehead and on my door posts and lintels. The Lord rebuke you, the blood of the Lamb be upon you. In the Name of Yeshua, you will all come together into one group to be bound by the blood of the Lamb right now. Your communication is cut off, both within the group and outside the group. Your power is cut off. I cut off access to any future source of power. Lord, I ask You to send blindness, deafness, and dumbness upon them so they cannot strategize against me or my family.

This group must leave, staying bound, and you must go to the dry places. You are never allowed to return to me or my family. Leave now in the Name of Yeshua."

Taking Back The Land

You must do the home first, get that cleansed and sanctified. Then, address the property the home or business sits on.

Use worship and the prayers above as you walk the property line drizzling olive oil. Bind, cast out, and dedicate.

It Changes Everything

The journey described in this book is not a short one. And it takes effort. That perfect vacation you'd love will not materialize with a few clicks on your computer and no work on your part. But, your work in this arena brings you a life-altering, transformative way of living that changes everything.

It changes the way you view God, the way you view the world, the way you view the supernatural, the way you view yourself, the way you view yourself moving through this temporal world, the way you view spiritual warfare, sin, adversity, military war strategy against dark forces, your own attitudes...and it forever changes your relationship with Yeshua Jesus.

It changes everything.

In 1 Chronicles 28:9 David delivers an address about the temple and the plans to build it. These are powerful scriptures in light of what we have studied here.

> *As for you, my son Solomon, know the God of your father, and serve Him with a whole heart and a willing mind; for the Lord searches all hearts, and understands every intent of the thoughts. If you seek Him, He will let you find Him; but if you forsake Him, He will reject you forever.*

Then in verse 10, in front of the crowd, David told Solomon, "the Lord has chosen you...be courageous and act."

Just a few verses later in verse 20, David again said to Solomon:

Be strong and courageous, and act; do not fear nor be dismayed, for the Lord God, my God, is with you. He will not fail you nor forsake you until all the work for the service of the house of the Lord is finished.

Know Whom you serve! Pastor Mark Biltz recently said, "If people really knew God, they wouldn't run away from Him: they would run to Him!"[89]

On the other hand, if you now understand that there are only two sources of supernatural power, the Living God and the fallen cherub, Lucifer, and that there is no gray area here, then you'll understand that all the psychic, channeling, New Age, and occult powers are NOT from God, they are from the imitator. Don't be deceived! The Devil has no friends! Run away from that stuff like Joseph ran from Potiphar's wife. Have nothing to do with it.

I hope I've given you enough of a glimpse of the heart of the Lover of our souls to encourage you to run to Him, get on your knees, repent, and ask Him to let you know Him in a deeper way.

Know His heart, His character, His love.

We have been called. Our King has equipped us. He has not left us defenseless. We are empowered by the ruach hakodesh, the Holy Spirit of the LIVING God. And, through the battles, as our muscles grow stronger with each thrust of the sword piercing the enemy's armor of deception, we develop skill, and knowledge of the enemy's tactics, which makes us stronger in both body and spirit.

Having many victories behind us, we grow in confidence, understanding the truth of what we have believed, that we serve the King of Kings, and Lord of Lords! He rescued each of us from the grip of darkness when He came as the suffering servant, but He is also the Conquering King, the Lion of the Tribe of Judah Who works in and through us as we do battle preparing the way for his return!

We are responsible to share this with others, to share salvation with others, to equip and disciple them so they are not left defenseless and with the mistaken idea that this Christian life is just another religious view. No!

This is a way of life, a lifestyle of victory that devastates the armies of darkness! They have nothing! All of the minions from behind the gates of hell can't stand against the Lord and his anointed!

> *Then the seventh angel sounded; and there were loud*
> *voices in heaven, saying, "The kingdom of the world has*
> *become the kingdom of our Lord and of His Christ; and He*
> *will reign forever and ever."*
> *Revelation 11:15*

Because we have been divinely adopted as sons and daughters of the Most High, we conquer and take back the territory in the Name of Yeshua with joy, singing, and blowing our shofars as the walls of Jericho disintegrate into dust!

Here is a public text from a ministry in Nairobi that a friend sent to me as I was finishing this book. It perfectly stated what I wanted to say here.

"God healed you so you could become a healer, so you could become a blessing. He favored you so you could show people favor. He brought you through that loss, He gave you a new beginning, so that you could help others make it through their loss. It's not enough to just bask in what God has done, just go around thanking Him. That's good, but you have a responsibility to help someone else in that same situation."

The time is short, and the enemy forces are gathering weapons, power, and assets. We must learn what they wanted us to forget: how to walk in power, love, and sound mind, while we devastate their end-time plans of utter mayhem, as earthen vessels flowing with active, supernatural power of the King we serve!

He is always the victor! He wants you to learn how to be the victor. He wants you to share the victory with others.

Change From The Inside Out

As you go through this process you will notice things begin to change.

Recently a former client, Laura, asked me for input regarding a conversation she'd had the day before with her childhood friend, Maggie.

The two had been close since high school though the relationship had experienced some distance in adult years due to multiple factors, including thousands of miles of distance between them and life choices that had them on wildly different and opposing tracks.

Laura was tearfully recounting to me this latest example of Maggie's behavior that has over the years consistently been highly self-centered, unsupportive, subtly insulting, and at best very inconsiderate. I was already familiar with the troubling nature of this friendship because it had come up several times when Laura had been in counseling.

Yet, even as she recounted this latest exchange that began with texts, she blamed herself for being what she assumed was unforgiving, declared that no matter what Maggie does she cannot distance herself from her, and was asking why this continues to hurt her so.

In a setting that was unrushed, safe, and loving, she was able to describe the situation and her feelings.

After she finished, I said, "It sounds like the very kind of destructive behavior you have worked hard to get out of your life and to heal from. And it sounds like you have less tolerance for it than you used to."

I saw the lights coming on as she thought for a moment, then she said, "Yes, I think that's right!"

I reminded her how, for several years now, she'd been diligently working to be able to more quickly spot these very same destructive and selfish behaviors in others and to set better boundaries in a proactive manner, no longer taking on the responsibilities that belong with others and blaming herself.

"It's been difficult for you to learn to confront others when you need to and you've worked hard at that," I said. "You've experienced the changes, healing, and growth in your own life and with your children. You now know what it's like to be in safe relationships that are respectful and honoring. Since you've been healing, you have less tolerance, as you should, with people who treat you badly and expect there to be no consequences, and for things you've learned are damaging to you. Your body has been triggered and is telling you that hurtful behavior is not okay with you anymore."

She agreed.

"Do you think maybe you've grown past that relationship and you need to redefine it," I asked.

Sometimes relationships are for a season. Sometimes we just grow out of them. And that is a significant part of this case. Her childhood friend chose a life that is neither God-honoring nor God-centered. Laura, on the other hand, lives a life completely centered on the Word of God and has entered into the kind of relationship I am trying to describe in this book. She is all-in with her Savior! She lives in the deep end of the pool! Their lives are on completely different tracks, headed in completely different directions. In spite of all that, Laura has remained faithful to the friendship and prayed for Maggie regularly.

Maggie's choices made years ago may have been the beginnings of increasing distance between them, but the choices each made about the position of God in their lives made the division clear.

The very foundation of our lives is defined by our relationship with God, whether sand or solid rock (Matthew 7:24-27). The separation only widens from there as we walk through this life hand in hand with the Lover of our souls, choosing to exchange the perishable for the imperishable (1 Corinthians 15:54).

In fact, in my own life, as I sought to move toward the deeper end of God's pool, I realized that, psychologically, somehow we have this automatic programming that we choose God and it's just a choice; it's done, like choosing a notebook for a class, blue or red. And, unfortunately, most modern American churches leave you with that impression.

But that is not the case at all! When we choose the Lord, it is not like choosing which salad dressing you want on your salad. It is choosing to open the door (John 10:9; Revelation 3:20) to a whole new reality, the very smallest beginnings of a relationship, a marriage...to which there is no end! It can grow deeper every day for the rest of your life! There is no ceiling here! No matter how much you learn of our Beloved there is always more to learn, to know, to love.

Laura now realized that was exactly the case.

Knowing this, she realized a different aspect of how the choices we make don't just affect us, they affect everyone around us. They affect how we move through this life. And, yes, we must flex, having some pliability in some ways. *But there are also choices that we have nothing to do with, but to which we must adjust our own boundaries.*

That is what Laura needed to do: redefine the boundaries and expectations of the friendship.

She realized that the relationship must be reorganized to a different level of friendship, a friendship circle that is not as close, which requires different boundaries, and different internal expectations and understanding of the new type and level of friendship it is to be.

This healing journey we are discussing here is amazing, changes everything, and never ends until we are with our Lord in the afterlife. This is a way of life for the mature believer.

So, rather than needing correction for what she first thought could have been selfish or intolerant on her part, Laura realized it was a shining example of her own growth and healing.

The kind of wounding that she had been programmed to stuff, feelings she had learned to bury, danger signals she'd been taught to ignore, were no longer silent: now they are being heard loud and clear! The feelings and red flag signals that used to be unconscious, but that exist in her because God put them there to alert her to varying degrees of danger, are now getting through. And they are urging her to make choices, and to set new and better boundaries.

This is evidence that the bondage from trauma and negative life patterns continues to dissolve. It is growth both in the body and in the spirit.

Laura and I discussed the friendship and ways to address the conflict. We found a way for Laura to express in a loving way what she believes to be the impetus for the distance in the friendship, which includes Maggie's choices of plunging head first into a self-centered, big money, thoroughly materialistic culture, and relegating her relationship with the Lord to the outermost perimeters of her heart.

Laura is wholly devoted to Yeshua, walks with Him deeply every day, raises her children in that way, and has learned over the years to recognize Yeshua as the goel (*goel*: Hebrew; *kinsman redeemer)*, the love of her life.

Laura spoke with Maggie. Unfortunately, Maggie did what has become typical for her: she took no responsibility for her own choices and the fact that her choices can impact many people in her life, and chose to blame Laura.

As painful as it was, it both demonstrated to Laura how far she had come in her own healing and confirmed to her the choices she felt she needed to make in redefining the friendship.

As we engage in the process described in this book; as we set our hand to the plow of healing work to get free from past trauma and bondage; as we swim from the vastly more popular shallow end of God's pool where the children keep themselves occupied, to the deep end where there is no bottom visible to the human eye; as we learn to develop healthy boundaries which are both honoring to God and healthy for us and those around us; it is not only the past trauma that heals: *everything* is changed, from the inside out.

God Never Works In Ones

Now that you're moving through this process, as dots connect, you may be seeing the beauty of all of these things.

God never works in ones.

Even when He's working in you, He's always working in other people, other situations, other dimensions. Maybe you've seen shocking God-appointments that could only be orchestrated by the hand of the King of Kings. Everything He allows in our lives, not negative things we have brought upon ourselves but what He allows in our lives, is for a purpose, and that purpose is not limited to this timeline: it impacts all of eternity.

What we have learned, what we have overcome, becomes our most powerful ministry, a calling, a passion. There are people who need your story, to see the fire of God in operation in your life.

This is about the harvest being ripe and God needing workers. We step into a calling we may have never known was for us. But it is the most amazing journey of your life and your journal will record miracles of salvation and supernatural victory.

God's Fingerprints

This is such a faith and relationship game-changer! You begin to see His fingerprints everywhere!

Every time you are praying for strength and in that same moment get an encouraging text from a friend with the same scripture you are reading, that is a love note from your Bridegroom.

Every time someone calls and leaves a message that she was praying for you that morning, at the very moment you were struggling with fear, your Savior just sent you a God-hug to let you know He sees you and is prompting others within the Body of Christ to pray for you.

Every time you are running low on grocery money and you receive a blank envelope that contains a gift card for the grocery store where you shop, it contains the fingerprints of our Goel, our Kinsman Redeemer.

The Joy Of Correction

By this point, I'm sure the Lord has been working on your heart. He is gentle and loving and, if we are in constant communication with Him, if we've learned that He is the love of our lives, His correction is gentle also, always pointing toward *restoration* of relationship. Yes, He can also be fearsome if we are stuck in rebellion as Jonah would tell you. But now we are listening to and seeking His loving instructions. It is evidence that we have learned we can trust Him, that we've learned Who He is, and that we don't deserve His goodness yet He continues to give it to us anyway.

But the danger for mature believers is that these words can lose their meaning.

Restoration.

He desires *restoration* of relationship because sin puts a barrier between you and your Savior that affects the relationship. And that separation can be dangerous, just as a toddler wandering too far away from his father in a park can be dangerous. Your Abba doesn't want anything separating you from Him. And, if you have taken the time to go through this book, you too desire to remove anything that is between you.

Too often our idea of correction came from our own parent who was very flawed; most of my clients deal with this reality. Those patterns get automatically transferred to our idea of our heavenly Father and our idea of His correction, often even when we don't realize it.

You may have subconscious expectations that correction should produce shame and separation. Maybe as a child you were rejected when you exhibited anything less than perfection. So, you tried your best to be perfect...and to hide mistakes when they occurred.

Jesus is not like that. He does correct. He does send conviction of the heart. But it is gentle; He desires you to recognize the mistake, to come to Him, to be cleansed from it, and be reunited with Him. Maybe you haven't even realized a chasm has been growing between you. He is calling you to come home.

"Our motivation," Pastor Mark Biltz said, "should be, not the consequences of our sin, but of what broke God's heart."[90]

So, instead of running when he convicts our hearts, we can truly come to a place where we immediately turn toward Him:

"What? I'm so sorry, I didn't realize I was wandering too far away from Your arms. Thank You, my Lord, for alerting me to the danger! Thank You for loving me so much that You called to me. I repent of the sin and anything that even hurt Your heart. Wash me clean by the blood of the Lamb so I can stand clean before Your throne, so my praise will be received, and my prayers will be heard. Search me and know me, my King, and remove anything that is not pleasing to You. I've learned of Your character, Who You are, and how much You love me. I've learned I can trust You more than I can trust myself or anyone on this earth. Show me, I'm listening. And I joyfully receive Your correction so I can be back in your embrace."

The correction is evidence of His love for us. But in an age where the world has been brainwashed to believe that all of life revolves around what they feel in any given moment, and they seek only what is easy and what brings pleasure, that may be a difficult concept to realize.

> *My son, do not reject the discipline of the LORD or loathe*
> *His reproof, for whom the LORD loves He reproves, even as*
> *a father corrects the son in whom he delights.*
> *Proverbs 3:11-12*
>
> *Blessed is the man whom You chasten, O LORD, and*
> *whom You teach out of Your law.*
> *Psalm 94:12*
>
> *I know, O LORD, that Your judgments are righteous, and*
> *that in faithfulness You have afflicted me. O may Your*
> *lovingkindness comfort me, according to Your word to Your*
> *servant.*
> *Psalm 119:75-76*

My prayer is for you meet the Lover of your soul, your spiritual Bridegroom, your Abba, on an entirely new level.

Correction is a big part of that relationship.

But there truly is joy in His correction.

The Joys IN Battle

As counter-intuitive as it may sound, even though it is at times exhausting, there are many joys *in* the battle.

Once we get the backlog of bondage and attachment dissolved in the Blood of the Lamb, we are set on a new path, walking in power, love, and a sound mind. We can then deal with new battles with skill and agility.

I'm so happy that I don't have to be a victim of the assaults of these creatures! I love seeing these evil beings turn tail and run away at the name of Yeshua, my Savior and King! Every time I see this happen my faith grows deeper and stronger! The dark forces are forever defeated! I am so excited that I get to walk with my Captain as He does the work! I am now confident because when something tries to sneak in, I know exactly what to do and they are not able to get a toe hold ever again! I get to assist others who are suffering with this "lack of knowledge" (Hosea 4:6) and watch them be set free!

Hey, might that be joy??

I'm walking with Him; He is walking in me because my body is His body. When I'm aligned with Him and He's walking in me, I always win in the battle with these entities because El Elyon, the God Most High, always wins! There is no gap or delay in communication. I've learned it is true: He never leaves us alone or forsakes us when we stay with Him!

And, because God uses patterns, just as He does with the feasts, we learn to listen to the shofar blasts that will one day announce His entrance, and we learn about the feast that is the Marriage Supper of the Lamb! We get to rehearse these things so we will be ready!

So to, with learning how to walk in victory with Him. We are rehearsing! We will join Him in the air and watch the army of His Kingdom obliterate the Orcs (*Lord of the Rings* reference) and reverse all the destruction. Life will spring forth once again!

We've talked about how this is not a calling for a few unusual people. It is the calling on every believer.

I hope now you are seeing that *it is intimately connected with our very relationship with Yeshua.* And, if we refuse this calling of spiritual warfare proficiency and walking in victory, we are rejecting that aspect of our Savior!

After seeing all the evil ferociously overtaking our land and people, wouldn't you leap from your sofa and cheer if you got to see the Lion of the Tribe of Judah kick the stuffing out of the Prince of Darkness and his evil army??

That's what we're talking about! This is the joy of the battle! We are rehearsing for that final battle when we will see the ultimate victory! We are to walk in victory and joy *through* the battle not just *after* it's over. It's also connected to faith, faith in what hasn't been completely fulfilled yet.

> *You need not fight this battle. Take up your positions, stand*
> *firm, and see the salvation of the LORD on your behalf,*
> *O Judah and Jerusalem. Do not be afraid or discouraged.*
> *Go out and face them tomorrow, for the LORD is with you.*
> *2 Chronicles 20:17, BSB*

This joy, both in and through the battle, is a vital component of our walk with Jesus. It is part of the very foundation of our relationship with Him. When we walk in victory, when people are being delivered and forever changed by an encounter with the Living God, the spiritually starving are drawn to The bright Light like moths to a flame.

This is the key to transforming lifeless churches and dry, brittle souls longing for living water.

Expel the darkness! Take the territory back with a shout and blowing of the shofar! Declare from the pulpit salvation, sin, and walking in holiness! Train up the warriors! Watch the enemy flee! Watch the walls implode! The unsaved and the pew-sitters that haven't even realized they aren't saved will be awakened from demonic slumber and realize that there is only one God who answers by fire: El Shaddai the Almighty God!

> *After these things I heard something like a loud voice of a*
> *great multitude in heaven, saying, "Hallelujah! Salvation*
> *and glory and power belong to our God; BECAUSE HIS*
> *JUDGMENTS ARE TRUE AND RIGHTEOUS; for He has*
> *judged the great harlot who was corrupting the earth with*
> *her immorality, and HE HAS AVENGED THE BLOOD*
> *OF HIS BOND-SERVANTS ON HER."*
> *Revelation 19:1-2*

The Check List

Here is a summarized check list for daily spiritual covering.

Morning

1. *First Fruits – Thoughts*: your first thoughts as you are awakening should be directed to the Lord in praise.

2. *First Fruits – Speech*: the first words from your mouth should speak praise to the Lord and dedicate your day to Him.

3. *Armor of God*: as your feet hit the ground, be putting on the armor.

Day

Armor On – "Shields up!" Throughout the day, anytime the armor of God even comes to mind, put it on again because it's probably the Holy Spirit alerting you to something approaching.

Night

Dedicate Sleep & Dreams

1. *Set The Boundary* – "Lord, set a boundary around me, my sleep and my dreams, with the *Blood of the Lamb*. I do not receive dreams or communication from any spirit except for the Spirit of the Living God."

2. *Dedicate To The Lord* – "I dedicate my sleep and dreams to You, Lord."

3. *Invitation To The Lord* – "I invite You, Lord, to speak to me during this time."

4. *Armor Of God* – "I put on the whole armor of God..."

Journal

Be faithful and intentional with noting what the Lord is showing you. Note dreams, memories, words, titles, or names that pop into your mind during prayer. Seek the Lord about all the information and ask Him to lead you to freedom from all forms of bondage.

Spend Time With Your Savior

This process cannot succeed if you don't spend time with your Captain. Do not give this up. Direct your thoughts to Him all throughout the day and spend time with Him alone.

Pray Without Ceasing

The goal is to be in prayer and worship all the time, no matter what you're doing. Whatever you do, bring Jesus with you. Always keep your communication connection active.

Worship

This list contains music that I use in my personal worship time with the Lord. Nothing listed here is a paid ad or endorsement.

One of the hallmarks of Messianic worship is that it is very scripture rich or composed entirely of scripture.

All these artists have videos available on YouTube.

Paul Wilbur – The video presentations of his worship events are much more than just music, including Messianic worship dancers. I use the videos almost as often as the CDs in my worship time.

wilburministries.com/

Miqedem – This band is one of my all-time favorites for God-honoring worship. All their songs are literal scripture put to music in a modern style. Incredible writing, arranging, and production are on display with each of their projects. All in Hebrew, a written translation of lyrics into English is available.

Among my favorites are *Adonai Ro'i* (Psalm 23) from *Miqedem Vol.2*, and *Halleluhu* from their first release, *Miqedem*.

miqedem.net/

Joshua Aaron – Utilizing both Hebrew and English, Aaron presents worship in a modern style.

joshua-aaron.com/

Sarah Liberman – Her release, *Lefanecha*, is mostly in Hebrew and beautiful. Be sure to check out the video, *Fire of Your Spirit*.

sarahliberman.com/

Yuval Arts – Worship in Hebrew from Israel in both modern and traditional styles, including stunning ancient songs of repentance, all with lyrics in both Hebrew and English.

yuvalarts.org/worship/

Avinu Malkenu / Our Father, Our King – Lord, have mercy and save us. Believed to have been written between 40A.D. and 145 A.D., this is a song the earliest congregations may have sung. I often use this when interceding for my country.

Adon Haselichot / Lord of Forgiveness – An ancient liturgical song of repentance written between the 11th and 13th centuries.

Their concert play list is available on YouTube.

About the Ministry

Who We Are

Many ministries provide either counseling or deliverance. Myrtle Ministries provides a unique, three pillar approach to inner healing by combining counseling to address trauma, wounding and negative life patterns, with spiritual warfare to address bondage, together with a strong discipleship component.

Through our teaching ministry, we also work to educate believers in effective and powerful spiritual warfare according to the biblical model, which has largely been sanitized from or diluted in many congregations, for both greater individual freedom and in order to be equipped for powerful ministry.

Our Goal

We are called to equip and empower the remnant to be effective in the last days. We can't be effective for kingdom work, nor can we experience the fullness of the relationship with Jesus that is available to us, if we are bound by destructive patterns, trauma, and spiritual oppression. We work to minister the mercy and power of Yeshua Jesus to bring freedom from bondage and to move into deeper relationship with the Savior of our souls, so that we can boldly take back the territory the enemy has stolen.

Inner Healing

We can't move forward in life or in ministry if we are bound by the past. Counseling enables us to address wounds and discover veiled origins of pain, trauma, and negative life patterns.

Spiritual Warfare

As we prayerfully address past trauma and uncover the root sources of pain and negative life patterns, with the power and direction of the Holy Spirit we break any bondage as it is revealed.

Discipleship

Our ministry is based on a strong discipleship model. We walk alongside you as you learn to break bondage and walk in power, love, and a sound mind: for life. It also equips you to be used in ministry to others.

Our Name

"Myrtle", hadas, סְדָה in Hebrew, is a flowering tree native to Israel. The Hebrew letters are:

Hey - "behold; reveal",

Dalet - "pathway to enter", and

Samech - "to support".

We feel this is a beautiful representation of our ministry goals. Myrtle is a symbol of peace and joy, is one of the four plants used to build a sukkah during the Feast of Tabernacles, and the blooms have a sweet fragrance that has been used for millennia to craft perfume. It is also a root form of Queen Esther's Hebrew name, Hadassah, הָסְדָה, which also means *myrtle*.

MyrtleMinistries.com

Acknowledgements

This book could not have been possible without the support and assistance of many people.

To Jeffrey Mardis – Thank you for a gorgeous cover design that perfectly captured the spirit of the book.

To Judi Klug and Darrin Geisinger – Thank you for joining in this journey with me and obeying the voice of the Lord. The Lord used you to bring it all together.

To the donors – Thank you for your generosity. You understand very well the magnitude of the need and have joined with me in this work to bring the Living Water to thirsty souls.

To all my clients who joyfully agreed to share a portion of their stories. Thank you for allowing me to walk the healing journey with you!

To all other friends and intercessors – This type of ministry, in particular, depends upon your prayers. We cannot do the work without you. Thank you on behalf of all the clients who have been forever changed by the work of El Elyon!

Finally, to my mentor, Barbara. I would not be here without your support and patient impartation. Our sisterhood in Yeshua is an amazing and wonderful thing!

Resources

Downloads
    Genogram / Family Tree
        Myrtleministries.com
        Go to: Resources tab>Downloads

Suggested Reading
    The Cosmic Chess Match
        L.A. Marzulli
    The Supernatural Worldview
        Cris Putnam
    Defeating Dark Angels
        Charles H. Kraft
    Deep Wounds, Deep Healing
        Charles H. Kraft
    Rediscovering The Hebrew Roots of our Faith
        John Klein & Adam Spears
    Penetrating the Darkness
        Jack Hayford
    The Pursuit of God
        A.W. Tozer
    The Kingdom of the Cults
        Dr. Walter Martin

What Was I Thinking?
Pastor Caspar McCloud

Uncovering the Mystery of MPD
Dr. James G. Friesen

Victory of the Darkness
Dr. Neil T. Anderson

Resources On The Global Order and Elite

The True Story of the Bilderberg Group
Daniel Estulin

Bloodlines of the Illuminati
Fritz Springmeir

Ritual Abuse
Los Angeles County Commission for Women

Exo-Vaticana
Thomas Horn & Cris Putnam

On The Path of the Immortals
Thomas Horn & Cris Putnam

Petrus Romanus
Thomas Horn & Cris Putnam

Resources On 5G

Deborah Tavares; stopthecrime.net

The Common Sense Show channel on YouTube;
The Latest on 5G, July 15, 2019

The April 2019 CTIA document: *Global Race to 5G – Update*

Dr. Dave Janda, *Operation Freedom*; interview with
Frank Clegg; *The 5G Rollout: The Future or a Better Option:
Insider Insight - Frank Clegg - Part 1*, May 27, 2019

Other Resources

Dr. Michael Lake – Biblical Life TV

https://www.youtube.com/user/biblicallife

Highly Recommended:

Understanding the Kingdom series:

https://www.youtube.com/watch?v=txvoochjWHo

Russ Dizdar – free online training, books for purchase:

www.ShatterTheDarkness.net

http://thirdmillenniumtheology.com/

Rabbi Kirt Schneider – television and video ministry, *Discovering the Jewish Jesus;* Self-Deliverance series:

Available on YouTube and cable

https://discoveringthejewishjesus.com/

End Notes

1. Russ Dizdar; interview on David Heavener TV; 12/1/18; *Warning: Don't Confront a Demon Until You Hear This!*

2. Cris Putnam, *The Supernatural Worldview*, pg 36, 37,38.

3. Ibid, pg. 39

4. Ibid, pg. 40

5. James W. Sire, The Universe Next Door: A Basic Worldview Catalogue, pg. 12

6. https://www.barna.com/research/barna-survey-examines-changes-in-worldview-among-christians-over-the-past-13-years/

7. *The Supernatural Worldview*, pg. 46

8. https://www.barna.com/research/barna-survey-examines-changes-in-worldview-among-christians-over-the-past-13-years/

9. *The Supernatural Worldview*, pg. 46

10. *The Supernatural Worldview,* pg. 51

11. https://www.youtube.com/watch?v=w4EciRd4ckY

12. https://www.biblestudy.org/bibleref/meaning-of-numbers-in-bible/5.html

13. https://bible.org/seriespage/29-workers-vineyard-matthew-201-16

14. https://www.drugabuse.gov/trends-statistics/monitoring-future/monitoring-future-study-trends-in-prevalence-various-drugs

15. https://www.cbsnews.com/news/study-shows-70-percent-of-americans-take-prescription-drugs/

16. https://newsnetwork.mayoclinic.org/discussion/nearly-7-in-10-americans-take-prescription-drugs-mayo-clinic-olmsted-medical-center-find/

17. https://www.drugabuse.gov/related-topics/trends-statistics/overdose-death-rates

18. https://www.naturalnews.com/2019-07-08-addiction-and-od-being-an-american.html

19. https://fightthenewdrug.org/10-porn-stats-that-will-blow-your-mind/

20. Ibid

21. https://fightthenewdrug.org/get-the-facts/

22. https://conquerseries.com/why-68-percent-of-christian-men-watch-porn/

23. https://www.scientificamerican.com/article/fearful-memories-passed-down/

24. https://www.nature.com/articles/nn.3594

25. https://www.scientificamerican.com/article/fearful-memories-passed-down/

26. Exodus 20:5, 34:6-7, Numbers 14:18, Deuteronomy 5:9

27. https://www.ncbi.nlm.nih.gov/pubmed/16084184

28. https://www.sciencedaily.com/releases/2014/10/141001090238.htm

29. https://www.collective-evolution.com/2014/03/18/this-study-will-make-you-think-twice-about-who-you-are-getting-into-bed-with/

30. https://johnramirez.org/

31. https://www.withoneaccord.org/

32. https://www.youtube.com/watch?v=4ZNuO2jITTk

33. https://www.youtube.com/watch?v=pK4_pSETOww

34. https://www.youtube.com/watch?v=A1OvAVPKESA
35. http://www.centerformedicalprogress.org/cmp/investigative-footage/

36. http://shatterthedarkness.net/

37. https://www.amazon.com/Uncovering-Mystery-Mpd-James-Fries
    en/ dp/1579100627/ref=pd_sim_14_1?ie=UTF8&dpID=41etjZHpf
    vL&dpSrc=sims&preST=_AC_UL320_SR214%2C320_&refRID=0
    584FZX2JGPW7CBQ84W9

38. https://www.youtube.com/watch?v=v-VMPrp380w

39. https://reasonsforjesus.com/

40. https://www.youtube.com/watch?v=zlLdg8uWTYw

41. https://thesecondcomingofthenewage.com/

42. https://www.youtube.com/watch?v=VjqGB_DPDjs

43. https://www.dailymail.co.uk/health/article-90598/What-happens-
    body-youre-asleep.html

44. https://www.dailymail.co.uk/health/article-90598/What-happens-
    body-youre-asleep.html

45. https://www.hopkinsmedicine.org/health/healthy-sleep/health-
    risks/the-effects-of-sleep-deprivation

46. https://www.psychologytoday.com/us/blog/dreaming-in-the-
    digital-age/201412/why-sleep-deprivation-is-torture

47. https://www.psychologytoday.com/us/blog/dreaming-in-the-
    digital-age/201412/why-sleep-deprivation-is-torture

48. https://www.dictionary.com/browse/witching-hour

49. https://en.wikipedia.org/wiki/Witching_hour_(supernatural)

50. https://en.wikipedia.org/wiki/Triple_Goddess_(Neopaganism)

51. http://gala.gre.ac.uk/12514/1/2014_-_IJDR_-_Luke_%26_
    Zychowicz.pdf

52. https://www.dailymail.co.uk/health/article-90598/What-happens-body-youre-asleep.html

53. https://www.merriam-webster.com/dictionary/longing

54. https://biblehub.com/topical/l/longing.htm

55. https://www.dictionary.com/browse/intent

56. https://biblehub.com/topical/r/repentance.htm

57. C. McCloud, Linda Lange, *What Was I Thinking*

58. Sarah J. Thiessen, *Splankna*, pg 44

59. Cris Putnam, *The Supernatural Worldview*, pg. 45

60. https://www.dailymail.co.uk/health/article-90598/What-happens-body-youre-asleep.html

61. https://www.youtube.com/watch?v=w4EciRd4ckY

62. And all the inhabitants of The Earth will worship it, those who are not written in The Book of Life of The Lamb slain before the foundation of the world"; Revelation 13:8, Aramaic Bible; "For He was foreknown before the foundation of the world, but has appeared in these last times for the sake of you"; 1 Peter 1:20, NASV.

63. Psalm 51:5

64. Jim Staley; Truth or Traditions; https://www.youtube.com/watch?v=FqomQ4fF7s0

65. http://www.apologeticspress.org/APContent.aspx?category=11&article=886

66. https://www.youtube.com/watch?v=OGMRIxVTotY

67. https://answersingenesis.org/the-word-of-god/3-unity-of-the-bible/

68. Ibid.

69. https://biologos.org/articles/when-was-genesis-written-and-why-does-it-matter/

70. https://www.bible-studys.org/Bible%20Books/Genesis/Book%20of%20Genesis.html

71. http://www.theopenscroll.com/hosting/SatanicCalendar.htm

72. https://www.bibliotecapleyades.net/cienciareal/cienciareal20.htm

73. https://www.biblehub.com/commentaries/mhc/john/1.htm

74. https://biblehub.com/topical/b/beelzebub.htm

75. https://biblehub.com/topical/r/repentance.htm

76. https://biblehub.com/topical/r/repentance.htm

77. https://biblehub.com/commentaries/mhc/leviticus/19.htm

78. https://biblehub.com/topical/h/holiness.htm#web

79. https://biblehub.com/topical/h/holiness.htm#web

80. https://www.heartmath.org/articles-of-the-heart/science-of-the-heart/the-energetic-heart-is-unfolding/

81. https://hebrew4christians.com/Holidays/Fall_Holidays/Elul/Shofar/shofar.html

82. Caspar McCloud, *What Was I Thinking?*

83. https://bible.org/article/doctrine-sin

84. https://www.merriam-webster.com/dictionary/worship

85. https://www.merriam-webster.com/dictionary/praise

86. https://www.youtube.com/watch?v=vosprI9WV3U&list=OLAK5uy_nSCnV4JGo-wDaplqjtks0Idn4WAetWMq0&index=3

87. https://www.youtube.com/watch?v=xcx2O9WXvn8

88. Caspar McCloud, *What Was I Thinking?* pg. 22-24

89. https://www.youtube.com/watch?v=OV0F3cSrtuM

90. Ibid.

CPSIA information can be obtained
at www.ICGtesting.com
Printed in the USA
BVHW030208020321
601484BV00009B/181